Saley Goldberg

Law and The Writer

Law and The Writer

Edited by Kirk Polking
and Leonard S. Meranus

Writer's Digest Books

Bibliography: p.
Includes index.
1. Authors and publishers — United States.
2. Copyright — United States. I. Polking, Kirk. II. Meranus,
Leonard S.
KF3084.L36   346'.73'0482   77-20201
ISBN 0-911654-53-4

Writer's Digest
Div., F&W Publishing Corporation
9933 Alliance Road
Cincinnati, Ohio 45242

Contents

Do freelance writers enjoy the same protection of the law as fulltime journalists? According to the First Amendment, freelancers and staff writers are equally protected — or equally vulnerable, depending on how you look at it.

Student writers and editors do have some protection under the First Amendment. Press freedoms in college and in high school are discussed in this chapter.

The writer should establish a reflex-like routine for watching what he says in a manuscript before it is published. This chapter defines the necessary elements of actionable libel, and ways to avoid slip-ups that could result in a lawsuit.

Sitting alone in one's bedroom typing fiction about the illegitimate origin of the smart aleck next door is all right, if you tear up the paper before anyone reads it. Guidelines for avoiding problems with works of fiction are included herein.

Acknowledgments

Some of the chapters in this book are newly revised from earlier versions in the following publications: "College Student Press Law," published by the ERIC Clearinghouse on Reading and Communication Skills, Urbana, Illinois. "Libel," Copyright 1973 by *Folio* Magazine Publishing Corp., reprinted by permission. "Fiction," Copyright 1971, *Writer's Yearbook*. "Invasion of Privacy," Copyright 1977 Harry M. Johnston III, reprinted from *Folio* Magazine. "Subsidiary Rights," Copyright 1969, *Writer's Yearbook*. "Long Arm Law," Copyright 1969, WRITER'S DIGEST. "Photography," Copyright 1972 *Writer's Yearbook,* and "Elements of Photo Reporting," Copyright 1971, American Photographic Book Publishing Co., Inc. "Federal Taxes," Copyright 1977 WRITER'S DIGEST. "State and Local Government," Copyright 1973, *Writer's Yearbook*. "Social Security," Copyright 1969, WRITER'S DIGEST. "Retirement," Copyright 1973, *Writer's Yearbook*.

Charts, contracts, and rate schedules appear in this book by permission of the original owners as follows: 1977 Theatrical and Television Basic Agreement, Copyright 1977, Writers Guild of America, West, Inc. Public Broadcasting and the use of copyright materials, from *Public Telecommunications Review,* Copyright 1976, National Association of Educational Broadcasters. Feature Writing Agreement, Copyright 1978 Copley News Service. Newscaster's Guide to Legalese, Copyright 1973, Pennsylvania Bar Association. Small Claims Courts provisions from *A Preliminary Report* on an empirical study of 15 small claims courts, by John C. Ruhnka and Steven Weller, National Center for State Courts — Small Claims Project, May 1977.

Preface

There is no substitute for a lawyer when a writer has legal problems. The writer, though, can avoid most legal difficulties by being aware of troublesome areas and having a general understanding of laws relating to them. That is the purpose of this book.

Law and The Writer is designed to present an introduction to major areas of concern — freedom of speech, libel, literary contracts — and alert the writer to laws and regulations affecting his "business" of writing. The Bibliography shows where to look further.

The new Federal Copyright Law is included in its entirety in the Appendix, but specific questions about the law and its effect on writers are answered by Waldo Moore, Chief of the Reference Division of the United States Copyright Office, in Chapter Six.

Since the new Copyright Law protects the author's work for his life plus 50 years, there is now even more reason for the writer to have an estate plan (which might be nothing more than a simple will) clearly providing for future rights to his literary properties and royalties. If the writer wants to prohibit or restrict the use of any of his published or unpublished works, this might also be covered in his estate plan.

Although the Supreme Court's recent ruling permitting lawyers to advertise may eventually help the writer locate a lawyer who specializes in literary law, there are at present only a few references a writer can consult for this information. The *Martindale-Hubbell Law Directory* is the most comprehensive of these publications. The American Bar Association Committee on Specialization hopes soon to develop a program by which state and local bar associations can indicate to the public the nature of a lawyer's practice in a truthful and accessible manner.

What kind of fees can a writer expect to pay an attorney? The answer depends on a number of factors such as prevailing rates in the community, the type of legal problem, the degree of expertise required, and in some cases, the result. Although there are significant exceptions, most lawyers charge hourly rates. Depending on the nature of the legal matter, hourly rates could range from $25 to $30 an hour for a lawyer in a rural community or a young lawyer in a law firm, up to $150 an hour or more for a senior partner in a law firm in a major city. In some situations, such as plaintiff's lawsuits, lawyers will take cases on a contingent fee basis, with the fee based on the amount recovered. Again, depending on the type of case and whether it is settled, goes to trial or is appealed, contingent fees are usually in the range of 25% to 40% of the amount recovered plus court costs and other out-of-pocket expenses. If there is no recovery the lawyer gets no fee, but the client is still responsible for expenses.

When retaining a lawyer, it is advisable to discuss fees with him in advance. Lawyers are accustomed to such inquiries and usually keep written records of their time so they can substantiate their charges.

Future editions of this book will reflect changes in the law as they occur. Freelance writers are invited to share with us any personal experiences touching on any of the chapters so that we can, where possible, share them with other writers through future editions of *Law and The Writer*.

The Editors

1. The Freelance Writer and Freedom of the Press

by William E. Francois

Do freelance writers enjoy the same protection of the law as full-time journalists? The answer depends on which kind of law is being examined. There are these kinds of law: constitutional, common law, case law, statutory law, and regulatory law (the latter resulting from rules and regulations put forth by various regulatory agencies, such as the Federal Communications Commission and Federal Trade Commission). In addition, laws can be sub-divided into federal law, state law and the laws of smaller political entities, such as cities, counties, school districts, etc. If we look at constitutional law, and specifically the protection afforded freelance writers by the First Amendment, generally what we find is that the First Amendment does not make a distinction between freelancers and "professional journalists." They are equally protected or equally vulnerable, depending on one's point of view. The same cannot be said of some state laws. But before turning to state laws, let's look more closely at the First Amendment.

Concerning the protectiveness of this basic law of the land, the critical factor is not *who* — staff writer or freelancer — wrote or said something, but rather *what* was said or printed about *whom*. For example, in 1964, in the case of *New York Times v. Sullivan,* the U.S. Supreme Court unanimously expanded the protection afforded by the First Amendment in order to reduce the likelihood of successful libel actions brought by *public officials* against the news media. Even when probably false statements were published about such officials, a successful suit for damages was no longer inevitable. The Court voted to protect *some* false statements in order to make public debate more robust and uninhibited, and to reduce the threat of large damage awards in libel actions which were having a chilling effect on First Amendment freedoms.

The new First Amendment standard requires that such officials must show "actual malice" on the part of publisher or writer before a lawsuit can succeed, and "actual malice" is defined as knowingly publishing falsehoods, or reckless disregard of the truth. Significantly, it makes no difference who writes the libelous story. If the public official can prove actual malice, he can win a lawsuit against the publisher and writer.

Although the First Amendment standard now includes *public figures,* it does not include *private individuals.* Problems of definition obviously exist. Sometimes it's not easy to distinguish between a public figure and a private individual. First Amendment protection depends on the nature of the content and the type of person identified in that story. There is more protection when writing about public officials and public figures than when delving into the lives of private citizens. The "nature" of the story or article refers to subject matter. The First Amendment protection applies to those stories or articles which are *of public interest,* or *in* the public interest, or *newsworthy.* Some courts, especially those in California and in Florida, have added a qualifier — *legitimate* public interest — to denote the kind of published information that is constitutionally protected in the sense that actual malice must be shown before a lawsuit can be successful. The distinction is between mere public curiosity and information of genuine public concern. Again, definitions are a problem. Not all judges would define the content of a given story or article as being of public interest, or as newsworthy. And where the content is not so defined, considerable First Amendment protection is lost.

For example, if you write a story about alleged corruption in your city or county government, or you examine the care afforded to the elderly, such a story undoubtedly would be considered newsworthy or in the public interest. Articles about *recent* crimes and the perpetrators of those crimes fall into the public interest-newsworthy category. But what about articles which resurrect the past, particularly those that identify the perpetrators of crimes which happened long ago? Might not the state have an interest in the rehabilitation of such persons who, by now, may be living useful, productive lives in society? California and Florida courts have considered such circumstances in deciding whether a magazine article is or is not newsworthy and therefore entitled to the protection of the First Amendment.

Invasion of Privacy

Some invasion of privacy lawsuits also can be defended against on the basis of the newsworthiness test. If an article is newsworthy; if it is not published with actual malice; and if it does not disclose any private facts which might be offensive to a reasonable person, then in all likelihood the First Amendment protects such publication. Generally speaking, the news media are accorded considerable latitude in deciding what is and what is not newsworthy; but the ultimate decision, should a libel or invasion of privacy lawsuit result, rests with the courts.

At this point I should emphasize a cardinal rule; namely, the First Amendment is not a license to trespass, steal, or intrude by electronic or other means into the privacy of another person's home or office. Nor does the First Amendment give the media the right to use a person's name or likeness for commercial purposes without first obtaining that person's approval. Therefore, don't rely on the First Amendment to protect you from an invasion of privacy suit if you use a person's photograph in an advertisement without first obtaining that person's consent, or, if you open another person's mail to obtain information, or eavesdrop on a telephone conversation. Under such circumstances, the First Amendment won't ward off lawsuits.

State "Shield" Laws

Turning to state laws, there is one type of statute which generally does not accord freelancers the protection given to "professional journalists." About half of the states statutorily provide that under certain conditions journalists do not have to disclose confidential sources. In most of these states the term *journalist* does not include a freelance writer. For example, New York's "shield" law states that "no professional journalist . . . shall be adjudged in contempt of any court" for refusing to disclose the source of any news coming into his possession. Arizona's law provides that "any person employed by the news media" may shield confidential sources of news. Most of the state laws allow "professional news persons" to shield confidential sources. But in California, prior to 1975, the courts interpreted the much-amended shield law as protecting newspaper and radio-TV journalists, but not magazine journalists. The law was amended in 1975 to remedy this. Freelancers should let their legislators know that those who write magazine articles and books warrant equal protection whenever shield legislation is being considered.

Very few of the state shield laws provide "absolute" protection; and in some there are so many loopholes in the law that the journalist is virtually unprotected. In fact, the New Mexico Supreme Court struck down the shield law in that state in 1976 because the court believed the law infringed upon the judiciary's function. The law, in the opinion of the court, infringed upon the separation of powers doctrine because the legislature was attempting to tell the courts what they could or could not do by way of compelling witnesses — journalists — to disclose certain information on pain of contempt of court. A similar result has been recorded in California courts.

For a time in the late 1960s and early 1970s, journalists contended that the First Amendment gave them a right to shield confidential sources; but in 1972 the U.S. Supreme Court *seemed* to say that reporters cannot refuse to answer questions put to them by properly constituted investigative bodies, such as grand juries, when criminal matters are being probed. *Seemed* to say this because the Court split five to four and one of the associate justices, Lewis F. Powell Jr., wrote what has been described as an "enigmatic" concurring opinion, thereby leaving considerable uncertainty about the right of journalists to refuse to disclose confidential sources under the First Amendment guarantee of free speech. One of the reasons cited by the majority of the Court in apparently deciding against such right was the difficulty of determining who would qualify for the protection. Would anyone who writes for the media have the constitutional right to refuse to answer questions put to them by a lawfully constituted investigative body? Freelancers? "Underground" journalists?

The Supreme Court observed that Congress could, if it wished, pass a federal shield law and decide the issue statutorily. Congress has not yet chosen to legislate in this area even though many bills have been introduced since the 1972 decision by the Supreme Court.

One of the things you can do is write your congressman urging the inclusion of freelancers in the "reach" of such protective legislation.

Interestingly, freelancers did gain a measure of protection from being subpoenaed to testify before grand juries when the Justice Department amended its guidelines in late 1975. Under guidelines that were issued in 1970, only fulltime staffers of the "establishment" news media probably were protected from harassment by federal attorneys by the requirement that such officials obtain the personal approval of the U.S. attorney general before a subpoena could be issued. Additionally, all other potential sources for the information being sought first had to be exhausted before the newsperson could be summoned to appear before a federal grand jury. But in 1975, the then United States attorney general, Edward Levi, expanded the protection of the guidelines to include anyone "engaged in reporting public affairs." This broadened the Justice Department's regulations to include authors, documentary film producers, and representatives of the nontraditional press. Freelancers clearly are included within these guidelines.

The Freedom of Information Act (FOIA)

Concerning the collection of information, as contrasted with attempts to shield information or the sources of information, the freelancers are on an equal footing with other information-seekers who wish to use the Freedom of Information Act (FOIA) to compel the federal government to disclose.

FOIA went into effect July 4, 1967, providing the public with its first legal right to know what the federal government is doing. Some important changes were made in the law in 1974 to facilitate the flow of information to the public, although there remain nine categories of information which are exempt from disclosure. These categories are: national security-foreign affairs, internal practices of an agency, interagency memoranda, investigatory files, trade or commercial secrets, personnel and medical files, reports on regulation of financial institutions, geological data, and data specifically exempt from disclosure under other laws.

The Federal Bureau of Investigation and Central Intelligence Agency were inundated with FOIA requests in 1976 and 1977 and had to make special staff arrangements to handle them. Records show that the most frequently used exemptions to disclosure were the investigatory files and interagency memoranda categories. And the turndowns sparked considerable litigation. FOIA allows a lawsuit to be filed in U.S. District Courts in an effort to force disclosure, and the courts are given the authority to inspect records *in camera* (privately) to determine if any or all of the information has been wrongfully withheld by the agency.

A freelancer who wishes to use FOIA to pry information from a federal agency must reasonably describe the records or information being sought. The request should be sent to the appropriate agency which has ten working days in which to decide whether to comply with the request. Several agencies, including the FBI and CIA, were granted an extension of time to comply with FOIA requests because of the heavy backlog. In those instances, courts ordered the requests to be handled on a first-in, first-out basis.

A freelancer's quest for information also received additional support from a series of U.S. Supreme Court decisions in 1975 and 1976. The Court, in substance, held that the judiciary or a state could not prevent the media from publishing truthful, accurate information which is a part of public judicial records. In other words, what is on the public court record can be published, notwithstanding a law or judge's order to the contrary. Thus, a freelancer sitting in open court cannot be constitutionally denied the right to publish whatever is on the record of that court.

Free Press vs. Fair Trial

The cases which led to such a declaration involved the identification of a rape victim, contrary to Georgia state law; a judge's order in Nebraska prohibiting publication of certain information in connection with a murder trial, such as the existence of a confession; and a judge's order prohibiting the press from identifying an Oklahoma youth who had been charged in connection with a slaying. In the three cases, the information that was ordered withheld or forbidden by law from being published already had been disclosed in the public records of judicial proceedings.

The conflict between press and judiciary stems from occasional clashes between the First Amendment guarantee of free speech and the Sixth Amendment which requires a "speedy and public trial, by an impartial jury. . . ." Sometimes legislatures and courts, in their efforts to ensure an impartial jury, enact laws or issue orders which are overly protective, and result in prior restraint of the press. As a general rule, such restraint is unconstitutional.

Obscenity and the Writer

Another area of the law that occasionally may be troublesome to writers and/or photographers pertains to obscenity. To begin with, the definitional problem is enormous. The Supreme Court has been struggling for decades to come up with a definition that is tolerable in the light of the First Amendment. Once something has been legally defined as obscene, then it no longer is protected by the First Amendment. In 1973 a majority of the United States Supreme Court changed the test of what constitutes obscenity. The tripartite test laid down in *Miller v. California* is: (1) whether the average person, applying contemporary community standards, would find that the work, taken as a whole, appeals to prurient interest; (2) whether the work depicts or describes, in a patently offensive way, sexual conduct specifically defined by the applicable state law; and (3) whether the work, taken as a whole, lacks serious literary, artistic, political or scientific value.

There has been considerable debate and various legal results, and the Supreme Court is itself split, usually by a six to three or five to four margin, as to how specific the applicable state or federal law must be. Also, there's a troublesome question: who decides what the contemporary community standards are? A majority of the Supreme Court currently holds that local community juries do this, but therein lies a problem. Concededly, what is obscene can vary from community to community.Nonetheless, many convictions on obscenity grounds are being upheld by the United States Supreme Court. And yet the author of several Supreme Court decisions which enunciated obscenity standards prior to the *Miller* case, William Brennan Jr., had this to say in a dissenting opinion in *Miller:*

" . . . [A]fter 15 years of experimentation and debate I am reluctantly forced to the conclusion that none of the available formulas, including the one announced today, can reduce the vagueness to a tolerable level while at the same time striking an acceptable balance between the protections of the First and Fourteenth Amendments, on the one hand, and on the other the asserted state interest in regulating the dissemination of certain sexually oriented materials."

Different Rules for Mass Media?

There are other, equally troubling, legal questions pertaining to the rights enshrined in the First Amendment. For example, can the First Amendment be differentially applied to the mass media? The answer is yes. Radio and TV are more regulatable than is the print medium. There are reasons given for this, including the fact that the public owns the airwaves, licensees are fiduciaries or proxies for the public, and, according to several decisions, TV is the most powerful medium of mass communication and therefore is subject to more governmental regulation.

A parallel question can be raised vis-a-vis the student press and First Amendment guarantees. Do student journalists enjoy the same protection as the "pros"? The answer probably is "yes," if suitable time and place regulations are taken into consideration. As the Supreme Court said in 1969, in *Tinker v. Des Moines Independent School District,* students are possessed of fundamental rights which the state must respect. Among these is freedom of expression.

Basically, therefore, the student, like the freelance writer or part-time photographer, is entitled to the same constitutional protection as the "pros."

2. The Student Press and the First Amendment

by Robert Trager

Press Freedom in College

The Supreme Court has said that freedom of expression must be protected in colleges and universities. Universities are seen as the training ground for democracy, and "to impose any strait-jacket upon the intellectual leaders in our colleges and universities would imperil the future of our nation," according to the Court. This view of American education has flourished in case after case and has become the starting line for extending constitutional guarantees to students on public college campuses.

In *Tinker v. Des Moines Independent Community School District,* the leading case granting constitutional rights to students, the Supreme Court stated, "It can hardly be argued that either students or teachers shed their constitutional right to freedom of speech or expression at the schoolhouse gate." In numerous cases, school officials and administrators have been forbidden to censor expression which they dislike and have been constantly reminded that they are not the "unrestrained masters of what they create," having no power to tell a student what thoughts to communicate. This freedom extends to student publications on public college campuses.

While freedom of the press is stronger on the university campus than in high schools, that freedom is not absolute. Courts have reiterated that college students have freedom of expression, but courts have also drawn boundaries around it. In fact, freedom of the press can give way to several administrative considerations. A student editor at Troy State College in Alabama tried to print an editorial criti-

cal of the governor and state legislators, but was told such criticisms
were not appropriate in a school paper. While a federal court would
not allow administrators to stop him from registering the following
semester as punishment for printing "Censored" in the editorial
space, the court stated that "school officials cannot infringe on their
students' right of free and unrestricted expression . . . where the exercise of such a right does not materially and substantially interfere
with requirements of appropriate discipline in the operation of the
school." Thus, "material and substantial interference" is a qualifica-
tion for freedom of the press on university campuses.

Similarly, a student editor at Fitchburg State College in Massachusetts tried to reprint an article by black activist Eldridge Cleaver in
the school paper. A federal court would not allow the school president to establish a board to review all material before publication,
saying prior restraint generally was not permissible on public college
campuses, but did say that rights of students "may be modified by
regulations reasonably designed to adjust these rights to the needs of
the school environment." The "needs" were defined as the school's
obligation to "maintain the order and discipline necessary for the
success of the educational process."

Even if there is no substantial disruption or threat to the discipline
and order of the campus, school officials may promulgate rules as to
time, place, and manner of distribution of a publication. These cannot be arbitrary rules and may not be confined to the expression of
ideas. Any regulatory action a public university takes against student
publications must be a nondiscriminatory application of reasonable
rules governing conduct, and not affecting otherwise protected content.

Of course, as with off-campus publications, students must legally
answer when they publish libel and obscenity. Although the courts
have consistently defended the press's right to participate in "wide
open and robust debate" on topics of public interest, that right is always tempered by the state's concern for the individual's right to be
free from ridicule. The courts have also consistently held that
obscenity is not protected by the First Amendment. The definition of
"obscenity," however, is still being formulated in the courts.

The courts have been willing to look upon the campus as a unique
place in our society where ideas are born, nurtured, and brought to

maturity. Thus, restricting freedom of expression and imposing restraints not only violate the basic principles of academic and political freedom but also severely hamper the university's educational goals. But allowing students to publish provocative or controversial material may upset certain administrators and community members. One college president has said that a student publication supported by state funds has no right to "reflect discredit and embarrassment upon the university." A federal court said that this reasoning, however, based on poor grammar and spelling and factual mistakes in stories in the university paper, was not sufficient to warrant firing the student editors.

Forms of administrative control are numerous, ranging from disciplinary action against student editors to restriction of funds for the publications. Most of these methods have been found to violate students' First Amendment rights. For instance, administrators must be very careful in cutting funds. One federal court has said, "Censorship cannot be imposed by asserting any form of censorial oversight based on the institution's power of the purse." Recently, a new kind of pressure has developed. Students themselves are beginning to censor campus publications. In many colleges, publication funding comes from mandatory student activity fees which are distributed by the student government. In some cases, student governments have restricted funds for publications for various reasons, including disagreement with content or a desire to have control over content. No court has yet ruled on whether this practice is constitutional.

In order to avoid the possibility that unwanted material will get into a student publication, administrators and schools of journalism may set up an adviser or review board to oversee content. A federal court has said that when such review boards or advisers act as approving or censoring agents, it is clearly a usurpation of the First Amendment. However, if they only advise and review, this apparently is legal.

Two federal courts of appeals have disagreed over whether student newspaper editors have the right to refuse to accept certain "editorial" advertising, that is, advertising not for products or services, but promoting an idea or opinion. In one case, the court ordered the paper to accept anti-Vietnam war advertising; in the other, the court told the editor he did not have to accept an advertisement or announcement for a meeting of the Mississippi Gay Alliance. Courts have expressed little doubt that student editors are entirely at liberty to accept or reject material for the news and editorial columns at their discretion.

Generally, then, courts have held that once a university has established a student publication, it "may not then place limits upon the use of that forum which interfere with protected speech" and which are not justified by an overriding state interest in avoiding material and substantial interference with campus discipline. The same freedoms are extended to non-school sponsored materials which students want to distribute.

Press Freedom in High School

In the last decade, public high school students have achieved considerable freedom of expression. Today, students are generally free to publish and distribute material according to established rules regarding time, place, and manner if it is neither libelous nor obscene (both being matters for court determination) and if it does not "materially and substantially" disrupt school activities.

In 1969, in a case involving the wearing of black arm bands to school to protest the Vietnam war, the Supreme Court of the United States said that school officials do not possess absolute authority over their students. School administrators "cannot infringe their students' right to free and unrestricted expression as guaranteed to them under the First Amendment to the Constitution, where the exercise of such rights . . . [does] not materially and substantially interfere with the requirements of appropriate discipline in the operation of the school," said the Court.

Mere dislike of the content or purpose of the expression is not sufficient grounds for forbidding it or punishing students, said the Court, nor is an "undifferentiated fear" of the consequences of allowing the expression. The burden of proving that the expression would cause material and substantial disruption is on administrators; students do not have to prove the contrary. Courts have interpreted this standard quite liberally. For instance, students in a Houston high school handed out underground newspapers in front of the school gate.

When copies appeared in paper towel dispensers and sewing machines in home economics classrooms, and when a few students were found reading the paper in classes, the students who distributed the paper were suspended. A federal court told administrators that there was no material and substantial disruption and that offending students should be disciplined, not those who exercised their First Amendment rights.

Similarly, students in a Joliet, Illinois high school distributed an underground paper saying a school dean had a "sick mind" and telling students to ignore attendance regulations. Their suspensions were overturned by a federal court which said that no material and substantial disruption did occur or would have occurred, despite the students admitting they intended to cause turmoil.

Courts have long held that obscene material is not protected by the First Amendment. Public school students, therefore, cannot distribute such material with impunity. However, the definition of "obscenity" is still evolving. Also, courts have held that material may be obscene for juveniles while not obscene for adults. Generally, though, courts will not forbid students from distributing material on the basis of obscenity unless the words are clearly meant in a sexual context intended to appeal to the prurient interest in sex. Thus, "four-letter words," thought by some to be obscene, are protected expression if not used in a sexual context.

Like obscene material, expression that contains an actionable libel is not protected by the First Amendment. For high school students, the concern is that some school administrators believe they are able to identify libelous material and will restrain a publication on that basis. Libel law is extremely complex and whether material contains an actionable libel should be a court determination. For instance, a California high school principal stopped distribution of an underground paper because he considered a story saying another principal had lied to be libelous. The California Supreme Court said such a statement was not libelous and ordered the principal to allow distribution.

Similarly, severe criticism, even of school officials, is protected expression unless administrators can prove it would materially and substantially disrupt the educational process. An underground paper in Houston contained a satirical column attributed to "Edmund P.

Senile," obviously meant to be the school principal, which said in part, " . . . the senior class is formin one of them extortion rackets to collect $500 for a 17-foot facsimile of mah posterior to be erected at the front gate so that all students might kiss the baloney stone each day before classes." A federal court considered this to be protected expression.

Courts are in disagreement over allowing prior restraint in public high schools, that is, allowing school administrators to approve all material before it can be distributed on campus (including stories for the school paper, magazine, and/or yearbook). The Court of Appeals for the Seventh Circuit, with jurisdiction over Illinois, Indiana, and Wisconsin, has held that prior restraint is no more permissible in public high schools than it is in the community at large. Generally, this means that, with certain narrowly-drawn exceptions (e.g., revealing information that could endanger national security), distribution of material should be allowed and subsequent punishment can be imposed if appropriate.

Several other Courts of Appeals, however, have held that prior restraint is permissible in public high schools if, (1) there are precise guidelines concerning the review procedures, making certain of a swift review and avenues for appeal in case of an adverse decision, and (2) it is clearly specified what material will not be considered acceptable for distribution. It is not always easy for school districts to formulate such regulations to a court's satisfaction. One Maryland district submitted prior restraint regulations to a federal court five times before they were accepted, and they were then found unacceptable by an appeals court.

The adviser's status regarding prior review is not yet clear. Is the adviser a school official who either cannot subject material to prior restraint (in the Seventh Circuit) or must follow certain narrowly drawn guidelines? No court cases have yet resolved this question, though it may be assumed that an adviser with day-to-day control over a high school student publication would be considered as exercising editorial discretion in reviewing material rather than censorship.

Application of the First Amendment to public high school student publications, then, has generally been held to mean:(1) Students have the freedom to disseminate otherwise protected printed material on high school campuses unless administrators can prove material and substantial disruption of school activities. (2) Expression cannot be suppressed because of disagreement with or dislike for its content. (3) School officials have a responsibility to curtail disruption caused by students opposed to the content of protected student expression, instead of suppressing the expression itself. (4) Provably obscene material is not afforded First Amendment protection and may be prohibited. (5) Libelous material is subject to post-publication punishment. (6) Student publications are subject to reasonable, non-discriminatory regulation of time, place, and manner of distribution. (7) In areas where courts have so ruled, prior restraint of student-distributed material is permitted if there are regulations containing acceptable procedural guidelines and specifying material which cannot be distributed. Prior restraint is not acceptable in Illinois, Indiana and Wisconsin.

3. Guidelines Against Libel

by Michael S. Lasky

You may never have been sued for libel. You may never have even thought of being sued. But it can come from anywhere at anytime from anyone.

As with any law that deals with what is "truth," the subtleties and nuances create particular problems of their own. In libel cases, it is not only the letter of the law with which the writer and editor must be concerned but also *where* the law is written. There are 50 different libel laws — one for each state. Despite this fact, the basic common law tenets of libel law philosophy upon which state laws are based are unwavering and it is a risky business indeed to misunderstand these tenets. The State of New York defines libel as: "A malicious publication which exposes any living person or the memory of any person deceased, to hatred, contempt, ridicule or obloquy, or which causes, or tends to cause any person to be shunned or avoided, or which has a tendency to injure any person, corporation or association of persons, in his or their business or occupation, is a libel." (New York Consolidated Laws, 1909 — no revisions since.)

The Necessary Elements of Actionable Libel

If any of the following three elements is missing, there is no libel.

Defamation — Generally defined as injury to reputation, it must apply to an identifiable person and it must be published.

Identification — Unless the plaintiff can prove that the defamatory meaning actually applies to that individual, there is no libel. A third party must understand that the reference is to the plaintiff whether by nickname, pseudonym or circumstance.

Publication — Printing, posting or circulating are the first steps in publication of a libel; someone reading the message is the second step. Most courts subscribe to what is called the *single publication rule.* This means an entire edition of a newspaper or magazine is treated as a single publication of one copy, rather than every single copy constituting a separate case of libel.

Preventive Journalism?

Most magazine publishers follow a course of preventive rather than corrective efforts in dealing with libel. That is, they prefer to stay out of court rather than to win a lawsuit.

At *New York* Magazine, which prides itself on its crusading journalism, former editor Sheldon Zalaznick pointed out that the magazine meticulously researches articles and that particularly controversial pieces are "lawyered" from start to finish.

"There is no substitute for first rate counsel," he feels. "The magazine's attorney views articles in three ways. After reading the story under scrutiny he will say 'this is libelous' or 'you're home free' or 'this is defensible.' The last is not to say the story might invite a lawsuit but that it could be defended if necessary. This is where the hard to-publish-or-not-to-publish judgments come and where the prospect of a costly court battle looms."

For even if you take your case to court and win, the magazine still has to pay the combat expenses. Libel cases that reach court are usually pyrrhic victories for publications, at best.

A few years back *New York* published a sensational account on the dubious practices of some New York doctors. The physicians' names were removed reluctantly at press time, recalls Zalaznick. "Our lawyer said that while it was defensible, the doctors would feel obliged to sue us just for the record — so that they would have something to tell their patients and the medical association."

Known for its outspoken and provocative writing, ("The 10 Worst Judges in N.Y.," "Radical Chic") *New York* will send its writers to attorneys even before they start writing. A firm grasp of libel law as it may affect the piece the writer is about to tackle can save them in later research, *New York* has found.

Even after the "lawyered" article is written, the editors aided by a host of researchers, will go through the piece flagging what is thought to need further corroboration. "I will literally ask the author to come to the office with his or her notes and files and prove the accuracy of what is said in the article. Occasionally a staff researcher will venture beyond what the writer offers for substantiation.

"In my 'primer' of things to do," says Zalaznick, "I think that first, you get a good lawyer. Without a good lawyer, you are nowhere. An overly cautious lawyer will usually take the viewpoint of the plaintiff instead of the publication. Next you check context and phraseology. Sometimes it is not what you say but how, in the context of the story, you say it. And third in my primer, take special care in editing and checking before the article is sent to the printer."

After a suit occurs, editors are usually the first to see points they realize they should have caught but were somehow missed. Much of the time, however, the editor isn't culpable for libel actions.

As noted libel attorney, Douglas Hamilton, notes, "It's hard to forecast where libel actions are going to grow — on what branches they are going to grow — because most of them come from articles and statements from sources you can't prevent." Sometimes a libel action will emerge from a coincidental event that could not be predicted but which changes the nature of the facts as they appear in a story.

The classic case of a simple birth announcement demonstrates this. A newspaper reported the birth of Mrs. Smith's baby. It was during World War II, however, and Mr. Smith had not been home for several years — even on a furlough. It was therefore physically impossible for the baby to be his child. The woman sued because of the resulting verbal abuse the announcement caused.

One of the best ways to prevent libel in all situations, according to Hamilton, is to get in touch with the "victim" of the article and get his or her side. "It's the best insurance I can think of," attorney Hamilton submits.

The other universal defense against libel is, simply, the truth. It is the writer's sword, but it is also his or her shield.

Determining the truth in the context of a magazine story can be a fine-grained problem. A magazine's prerogative to expand upon the facts and offer to readers interpretation and analysis is usually the place where libel is born.

Harold Hayes, former editor of *Esquire,* explains that this monthly magazine approaches observational and interpretative journalism with a keen eye and a pointed pencil. "You must have evidence to justify your interpretation," Hayes states. "A magazine should be able to document sufficiently whatever interpretation it is going to make . . . if it goes beyond what the evidence suggests, it would be my responsibility to restrict the degree of the author's comment."

The dichotomy between accurate reporting and truth must be emphasized. Accuracy, according to the courts, is not enough. You can accurately report some false charge or fact which is libelous.

It is *how* you treat and present the truth that ascertains whether you have published libel.

Truth Is Not Always A Cure

Because of the very nature of the journalistic profession, it is often difficult to prove that you printed the truth.

The dilemma stems from an entirely different issue now being bandied about in the courts — the question of the privilege of the reporter. Central to these current cases — most of them involving newspaper reporters — is the debate over whether a reporter has the right to keep the sources confidential. These cases are closely connected with libel actions.

To get vital information a writer often must agree to keep his or her sources anonymous. If journalists were to open up their confidential files to legislative investigation, grand juries and courts, the basic First Amendment freedom, it is argued, would be violated, as would the sources.

Thus, truth, as revealed in a story, frequently cannot be used in a defense. But the privilege of reporting, insured by the Constitution, can be.

This right is interpreted by the courts to be held by anyone — not just the press. It supplies immunity from libel damages for objective reports on events of public interest. These range from commonplace news conferences to court proceedings to daily news coverage. The only conditions to this defense are that the article in question be a *report* which is *balanced* (fair) and *accurate* (true).

Ads Can Be Libelous, Too

Just as the editorial copy in a publication must be clean so, too, must the advertising.

The rule stems from an action brought against the *New York Times* in 1960. An advertisement for the Committee to Defend Martin Luther King and the Struggle for Freedom in the South appeared in the *Times* in March, 1960. Five libel suits based on this ad and totaling some $3 million were filed. One of the first cases tried in the Alabama courts was that of L.B. Sullivan, Commissioner of Public affairs for Montgomery.

While not mentioned by name, Sullivan felt that the word "police" referred to him and that the public knew it, because they knew he was in charge of the police.

The case was first decided in favor of the Commissioner for the full $500,000 in damages that he demanded. The *Times* appealed to the Supreme Court who in 1964 decided in favor of the *Times*.

The Court said that the rule would apply only when the libel concerned the official's public conduct and the remarks were not a knowing lie or reckless disregard of the truth.

The *New York Times* rule, as it is now called, "prohibits a public official from recovering damages from a defamatory falsehood relating to his official conduct unless he proves that the statement was made with 'actual malice,' that is, with knowledge that it was false or with reckless disregard of whether it was false or not."

Subsequent cases that reached the Supreme Court have allowed the justices to expand upon the *Times* rule and allow even more leeway for the print media to publish freely.

In 1966, the Court enlarged upon the *Times* rule and said it extended not only to public officials but to all people or events in the *public interest*. The extension was the result of *Time Inc. v. Hill.* This case began back in 1955 when *Life* magazine published a picture story about the opening of a play entitled "The Desperate Hours" based on a novel of the same title. The article claimed that the play was a re-enactment of the experiences of the James Hill family who three years earlier were held captive by three escaped convicts. Hill sued, claiming *Life* invaded his family's privacy. In the lower courts, Hill was awarded $30,000, but when the case reached the Supreme Court, a new interpretation of the law favored Time Inc.

The Court said that if the press was saddled with the "impossible burden of verifying to a certainty the facts associated in an article with a person's name, picture or portrait," it would no longer be free. "Fear of large verdicts in damage suits for innocent or more negligent misstatement, even fear of the expense involved in their defense," it was submitted, "would diminish the power of an effective press."

In 1976, however, the Supreme Court restricted the broad protection given the press against libel suits brought by "public figures." In *Time Inc. v. Firestone,* the Supreme Court limited its definition of public figures, as well as subjected reporters and publishers to libel judgments for misreporting court decisions, even when a news story is "a rational interpretation of an ambiguous document." The Firestone case came to the courts as a result of an inaccurate *Time* Magazine account of the divorce proceedings of Mrs. Firestone. Although a well-known name in Palm Beach society, the courts decided she was not a "public figure" for the purposes of deciding how much constitutional protection could be allowed a publisher in misreporting a court proceeding.

The matter is not yet settled, however, and the question of exactly what constitutes a libelous publication is certain to be fought in the courts for years to come.

What is Malice?

In *Times v. Sullivan,* the Court cautioned that "calculated falsehoods" do not enjoy the constitutional protection afforded to information that contributes to the exposition of ideas.

What is considered reckless disregard of the truth was made clear in 1967 when the high court decided against the *Saturday Evening Post* in its appeal of a $360,000 libel verdict handed down in 1963.

In the March 23, 1963, issue of the now defunct mass biweekly, it was alleged that Wallace Butts, then the University of Georgia's athletic director, gave information about Georgia players and strategy to Paul (Bear) Bryant, a University of Alabama coach.

The libelous story said that an insurance salesman had accidentally been cut into a telephone conversation between Butts and Bryant. The magazine's conclusion was clearly that Butts and Bryant had conspired to fix the outcome of the game.

Editor Clay Blair Jr., claimed the *Post* was following a policy of "sophisticated muckraking." While muckraking might be a praiseworthy venture, it is safe from a claim of libel only when the muck is true.

The jury decided that the *Post's* journalism was not so sophisticated. An inaccurate date, an unattributable quote and other flaws demonstrated the "reckless disregard of the truth."

The Supreme Court conceded that Butts as a public official came under the *Times* rule, but added that the malice of the story did also.

Malice is not considered *fair comment,* another avenue of defense. Used primarily when matters of opinion in columns, reviews, letters to the editor and other comments of a critical nature are in question, *fair comment* hinges on the following criteria:

- The libelous comment must be an opinion — not statement of fact.
- The opinion must be fair.
- There must be no malice.
- The opinion must rest on the facts.

As the *Saturday Evening Post* case proved, hefty awards can be made if libel is found.

Damages

Damages represent a triple threat to the publisher.

Compensatory damages are given for injury to reputation. When libel is found to exist, damage is presumed and the jury must decide the amount of the award. The court may review the jury's award and lower the amount if it is out of proportion to the injury suffered. The plaintiff does not have to even show damages.

The second threat is *special* damages which represent the actual pecuniary loss suffered because of the libel. Here the victim must prove damages precisely.

The third and final danger to the publisher's coffers comes in the guise of *punitive* damages — sometimes called "smut money." These damages are assigned to punish past libel and discourage any future malice. Actual malice must be proven by the plaintiff — the entire burden of proof rests on the victim's shoulders.

Courts usually award punitive damages only when a high degree of fault is found.

Thus, when the *Saturday Evening Post* lost, the jury at first awarded three million dollars in punitive damages. (This was reduced by the judge to $400,000.) As one member of the jury summed up its motives:

"We wanted the public to know that we would not condone that kind of journalism and we wanted it in unmistakable terms to keep the *Post* from doing the same thing to someone else, maybe in a high place."

For this reason alone, newsweeklies such as *Newsweek, Time* and *Business Week* go to great lengths to check and recheck a story before it is published.

A Time Inc. staff attorney notes that all its magazines make reasonable efforts to ascertain the accuracy of what is said *before* publication. While there is no particular order to researching stories, a reporter will submit anything questionable to the legal department before proceeding. Researchers will red-dot any word or phrase that is tenuous. Because of *Times'* deadline, a fair amount of material is summarily forwarded to the lawyers from the editors, writers and researchers. The legal department will return the material in question to researchers or writers for further clarification or corroboration.

At *Business Week,* managing editor Paul Finney explains that "accuracy is more important than interpretation and style. We edit for fairness first."

Libel Insurance

According to the Insurance Information Institute — a public relations arm of the industry — libel insurance and other umbrella coverage for all publication liabilities are available from almost any large insurance company.

The criteria usually used to calculate premiums are based on the particular publication.

Premiums can range, according to industry spokesmen, from a lowly $100 per year for a small noncontroversial trade magazine to several thousand dollars for a large circulation monthly or weekly. It depends on the magazine's circulation, frequency of publication, content, length of publishing history, advertisers and other factors.

"Firms such as Employers Reinsurance Corporation of Kansas City, Missouri offer libel insurance to publishers but rarely to freelance writers. When they do, the coverage applies to a specific book for which the writer has already obtained a contract from the publisher. Employers Re's minimum premium on a libel insurance policy for a book ranges from $500 to $2,500 but those premiums may be increased to recognize unusual libel or copyright infringement exposures. The premium is payable one time only. For accounting purposes, the policy is issued for a one-year period, but the book is actually covered as long as it is not revised or supplemented and until the statute of limitations, which runs from one to three years in various states, has expired."

Who Takes The Blame — Editor or Writer?

Unlike other news magazines, *Business Week* requires that reporters be responsible for the final accuracy test. Even if a story goes through to the editors, it is returned for final OK by the reporter.

"Cutting can lead to distortions and context changes," says Finney. "The original reporter can correct this."

While the reporter is checking the veracity of the story, the editor must always be concerned with whether a story, however true, is defensible.

The editor is the troubleshooter. He or she weighs the risks of publishing the story — and the value of those risks. The editor examines the stature of the sources for reliability and/or prestige. He or she analyses whether a story is defensible enough to still be worth publishing.

But even when these editorial judgments are made correctly, there are still pitfalls for the editor.

Two other problem areas should be noted. First is the creation of a headline, and second, the selection of illustrations or photographs.

Sometimes headlines can be libelous, especially when they vary from what the content of the story suggests. One only has to look as far as some of the provocative catchlines used in movie fan magazines to see libelous discrepancies between what the headlines suggest and what the stories really say.

A headline should get reader attention — not a libel suit. The best way to avoid litigation caused by a head is for the editor to create it on the basis of the concrete facts of the story and not what the story *suggests.*

Pictures should also match the story they illustrate.

Photographs can defame people, whether they were intended for the story or misplaced with another. When a newspaper ran a photo of a woman (who was identified as a bride-to-be) holding a baby in her arms, it lost $500. The bride sued because of the ensuing shame she was subjected to among her friends. The picture was obviously misplaced, but occasionally even ones that are properly set to an article can be dangerous.

The way a photo is cropped or captioned can change the meaning of it. And if an author does not want to actually identify the target of a possibly libelous story, a picture should not show any details which would help identify the person.

Illustrations that make the subject look foolish to others can be libelous also. Yet the editor should not be paranoid in selection. Photos and other artwork are covered under the "fair comment" doctrine and courts broadly interpret libel law when dealing with photos, according to attorneys.

Corrections Won't Keep You Out of Court

Even if a newspaper or magazine publishes a correction of an error brought to its attention, it is not completely off the hook in the courtroom.

Corrections are only a partial defense proving goodwill on the part of the publisher. It helps to show that there was no intended malice.

The word "alleged" does not keep a publication free from liability. It is necessary, then, to be able to prove what happened *did* happen or attribute the reporting of the event to an official source. Editors have found that when possible, submitting the manuscript to the subject for review of inaccuracies — but not revisions in the text itself — may avoid the risk of libel.

Consent of the victim to publish a story is an absolute defense. Refusal to comment when approached by the publication will also help the publication's defense of a libel case.

The single most overriding factor causing defamation lawsuits for publications is, according to lawyer Douglas Hamilton, "editors' carelessness."

While most editors are aware of the dangers of libel, slip-ups can be prevented. If a standard thought process is consciously used by editor and writer alike, chances are that they will prevent libel every time.

The three-pronged approach that could be used is:

- Is the material defamatory to an identifiable individual or group?
- If it *is,* then, is the information privileged?
- If it *is not,* then, is it fundamentally true?

Even though the answer to the last question may be yes, that does not mean the piece should be published. One more question must be asked. Would the target feel obligated to sue to demonstrate denial of the libel? If so, the publisher must weigh the worth of publication versus risk of possible court expenses.

If you can establish some kind of reflex-like routine for watching what you say in your manuscript before publication you will have gone a long way toward keeping the libel wolf away from your door.

4. Fiction Can be Dangerous Too!

by Lipman G. Feld

A *libel* is a false *communication,* damaging a person's reputation through words or by painting, photograph or cartoon. Without the harmful message reaching the mind of another there is no libel. Sitting alone in one's bedroom typing fiction about the illegitimate origin of the smart aleck next door is all right, if you tear up the paper before anyone reads it.

But don't write a novel identifying your pesky neighbor as a · bastard. You may be in for trouble from both the man next door and his parents if he can prove you've used him as a model, even if you changed his name.

The full truth is a full defense, but part truth is not enough. Retraction will not set you free although often it will cut down the damages. You can't avoid liability if the man you defame was previously defamed by someone else. Repetition in libel is actionable.

One author innocently selected the name Artemus Jones as a fictional protagonist for a story about loose affairs. The description hit too close to home. The man Artemus Jones did exist and recovered for defamation. The question is not whose defamation was intended, but who got hurt by the libel (lie). How to avoid this? Check the city directory, if you're using a real town to be sure no one by that name lives there, or better yet, identify your man with a fictional location.

Avoid untruths about the sexual habits, communicable diseases, unethical business or professional practices, and crimes of ordinary citizens.

Quite different from libel or defamation, invasion of the right of privacy, *where truth is no defense,* is the unwarranted publication of a person's private affairs so that he suffers shame, mental distress or humiliation. The exposure may be intended *laudatory* and still get you mixed up with lawyers. The defense is *consent* but consent can be revoked and consent for one purpose may not be consent for another.

A living person's interest in his right to be let alone must be balanced against the social necessity of *fair comment* and *circulation of news.* In your fiction you may truthfully comment upon public figures, such as politicians, high governmental officials, famous writers, actors, criminals and people involved in accidents or fires. But leave ordinary people alone.

Don't fictionize real people; use imaginary ones. Real people keep trying to collect with lawsuits. The decisions are perplexing. Mistaken use of an ordinary person's name in a suit for invasion of privacy might be decided either way.

In New York, John Hersey, who wrote the novel *A Bell for Adano,* touching the life of a military officer, won victory in a suit for invasion of privacy when the officer sued. A mere *word portrayal* not using the same name or physical description of the officer was all right. In 1970 Meyer Levin, who portrayed the Loeb-Leopold murders in his novel *Compulsion,* was protected in the Supreme Court of Illinois, because the murder of Bobby Franks was a matter of public interest. Levin was not required to pay Nathan Leopold the 1.5 million dollars demanded.

On the other hand George Braziller, Inc. got into trouble when an author they published used a man's real name for his pen name. An author's fictional life of Warren Spahn, Milwaukee Brave's pitcher, using the literary techniques of invented dialog, imaginary incidents, manipulated chronology and attributed thoughts and feelings, went too far. Spahn recovered for the commercial exploitation of his name and personality. (In this case, libel was not involved.)

Marjorie Kinnan Rawling's novel, *The Yearling,* and autobiography *Cross Creek* brought her an international reputation as an imaginative interpreter of Florida life. The fictional word picture she reated of Zelma in *Cross Creek,* as an ageless spinster, resembling an angry and efficient canary was favorable, although Zelma (no surname in *Cross Creek)* was described as occasionally profane. The real life Zelma Cason, an ordinary citizen, was adjudged legally entitled to her privacy and could recover a little money after her case ran four or five years in the law courts.

Sports Novels Magazine published a short story "Deuces for the Duke," mentioning the real Solly Krieger or Sol 100 times. Athletic Sol was famous, but the fiction invaded his privacy (again no libel or mistake was involved) because the short story was not of general news interest. Solly could collect because the writer intentionally exploited his sports fame.

5. Invasion Of Privacy

By Harry M. Johnston III

The specter of the systematic accumulation of vast amounts of personal data by public and private agencies of all kinds has generated much fresh interest in the citizen's right of privacy. As this and other new facets of the right of privacy develop, it is important to realize that publishers and the press have long been subject to liability for invasion of several different rights of privacy. The publication in 1890 of an immensely influential article by Louis Brandeis and Samuel Warren articulated the notion that it was necessary to protect an individual against a press perceived by the authors as "overstepping in every direction the obvious bounds of propriety and decency." Against such a press, it was posited, the individual had a right of privacy.

The right of privacy has been described as "the right to be let alone; to live one's life as one chooses, free from assault, intrusion or invasion except as they can be justified by the clear needs of community living under a government of law." Under the classic analysis of the decided cases, there are actually four different rights of privacy which are of interest to writers and publishers. Specifically, the individual may find protection against:

1. Intrusion
2. Misappropriation of his or her name
3. Publicity which places him or her in a false light before the public
4. Publicity which discloses private and embarrassing facts

What follows is a brief exploration of each of these areas of potential liability for writers and publishers.

Intrusion

Perhaps the least complex of the four notions of privacy, this theory says that living individuals are protected against the ac-

quisition of information from or about them which is accomplished through intrusion, i.e., "intrusion whether by physical trespass or not, into spheres from which an ordinary man
. . . could reasonably expect that the (reporter) should be excluded." In a leading case, the surreptitious photographing and
radio recording of an alleged medical quack by reporters posing
as patients to gain admittance to his home-office was found to be
an invasion of privacy. The fact that these actions had been undertaken to gather news did not serve as a defense.

It should be noted that privacy was invaded when the intrusion occurred, and it was not necessary that there be any publication of the information so obtained. In the same way, wire-tap-
ping and electronic eavesdropping, harassment and the
unauthorized taking of another's personal documents have been
alleged to be intrusive invasions of privacy.

Misappropriation

The majority of states — either by common law or by statute
— recognize a cause of action arising from the commercial use of
a person's name or likeness without the person's consent (which
can sometimes, of course, be secured only by payment). Several
states have a statute modeled after that of New York, which
reads in part as follows: "Any person whose name, portrait or
picture is used within this state for advertising purposes or for
the purposes of trade without the written consent first obtained
. . . may maintain an equitable action . . . against the person,
firm or corporation so using his name, portrait or picture, to prevent and restrain the use thereof; and may also sue and recover
damages for any injuries sustained by reason of such
use. . . ." New York rules are not binding in other states, but the
general acceptance of the principles they embody makes consideration of them appropriate.

Read literally, New York's statute would appear to prevent a
daily newspaper from recounting the previous night's events at,
say, a Democratic National Convention — and from depicting
these events through published photographs — without acquiring the prior written consent of every individual whose name or

face appeared in the newspaper's reportage. Of course, such consents are unnecessary and the Democratic Convention example illustrates the *news* exception to the requirements of the statute. Thus, even though it has been contended that the newspaper makes a profit and in this sense can be said to report the news "for purposes of trade," judicial constructions of the New York statute establish beyond doubt that its enactment was not intended to interfere with the legitimate dissemination of news. A person's right of privacy under New York's law, therefore, does not extend to preventing the use of his or her name in publishing the news.

Another broad exception to the statute allows the publication of material on subjects of general interest to the public. These topics — a few examples would be trends in fashion, manners, the arts — are not "hot news" but are nonetheless legitimately of interest to the public, and names and likenesses of individuals connected with them may be used without prior written consent. Photographs of such individuals, unless they bear no relationship whatever to the subject matter or are acquired through some type of intrusion, may, generally speaking, be published under the "general interest" exception without consent and will not give rise to a cause of action for misappropriation. But, if a living person's name or likeness is used without permission in an intentionally fictionalized account of a "news" or "general interest" topic, a misappropriation may have occurred. This was the ruling in *Spahn v. Julius Messner, Inc.* (1966), a case in which Warren Spahn, a well-known baseball player, sued over the publication of an unauthorized biography, alleging that his rights under the New York statute had been invaded. The state's highest court felt that he would have been barred from suing had the biography been factual; however, since the facts of the case indicated that there were significant amounts of intentionally fictionalized material in the book, the baseball player's right of privacy had been invaded.

The principle underlying the news and general interest exceptions to invasion of privacy by misappropriation springs from the First Amendment theory that our system of self-government and ordered liberties is best protected by the widest possible dissemination of speech and ideas. Indeed, New York's courts have shown an awareness that the statute would likely not withstand constitutional attack without the news and general interest exceptions.

The statute does work to prohibit the misappropriation of an individual's name or likeness in pure advertising. Thus, if an automobile manufacturer were to utilize the name of a famous or obscure citizen in an advertising campaign as an endorsement of its newest car, a misappropriation would have occurred in the absence of consent. It has been suggested that this commercial dimension of the misappropriation might be better described as protecting an individual's "right of publicity" than his or her "right of privacy." If so, the individual lacks complete control over his or her right of publicity for, in two cases, magazines have been held not to have violated the New York statute when they used the names and photographs of famous people in advertising promoting their own publications. In the first case, *Booth v. Curtis Publishing Company* (1962), *Holiday* magazine's advertisement reproduced a photograph and description of the actress, Shirley Booth, taken from an article which had appeared earlier in its editorial pages in connection with her attendance at the opening of a new resort hotel. The second case, *Namath v. Time Inc.* (1976), saw *Sports Illustrated* magazine utilize a photograph of Joe Namath in action at the Super Bowl, which had previously been published in the magazine; as well, his name appeared prominently in the text of the advertisement. In neither case had the plaintiffs consented to these uses and in neither case did the court find an invasion of privacy. The reasoning endorsed by New York's highest court was that these uses were not prohibited by the statute since they, like "news uses" and "general interest uses," were merely "incidental" to the dissemination of news. Consequently, so long as the names and likenesses have been previously published editorially and are utilized in advertising only to "illustrate the quality and content" of the publication, no written consent is necessary and no misappropriation has occurred. Naturally, it may well be a question of degree whether a particular use of a name or likeness is "merely incidental"; arguably, if the magazine's advertisement implied an endorsement of the magazine by the individual depicted in it, a misappropriation would occur. In any event, it can be said that publications have a limited privilege under the New York statute to utilize a name and likeness in their own promotional activities without prior consent.

False Light Privacy

This third species of right of privacy states that the publication of nondefamatory but untrue information about an individual, information which places him or her in a "false light" before the public, is an invasion of privacy. It is difficult to pinpoint the precise theoretical basis of this tort; in one sense it can be likened to common law libel since it alleges that an injury occurs through the publication of untrue information; yet, in another sense, it may simply be a misappropriation of an individual's name which, since the account in which it appears is false, is not privileged as being incidental to the system of news dissemination.

The United States Supreme Court held in 1966 that "false light" privacy claims are limited by the freedom of speech and press guarantees of the First Amendment. In this leading case, *Time Inc. v. Hill, Life* magazine had reported the opening of a Broadway production, *The Desperate Hours,* which was an adaptation of a novel based substantially on the true story of a family who had been taken hostage in their home by escaped convicts. The magazine article depicted the family as the historical antecedents of the characters in the play, and it was arguably stated that the play re-enacted the family's experience. Moreover, the article did not clearly identify certain episodes in the drama as fictitious. In these ways, the family alleged, they were portrayed in a "false light" before the public.

The Supreme Court's decision was that damages cannot be awarded for a false light invasion of privacy, arising out of the report of a matter of interest to the public (here, the Broadway opening), unless it can be proved that the untrue material was published "with knowledge of falsity or reckless disregard for the truth." This is, of course, the familiar "actual malice" standard the Court had earlier imposed in libel cases on plaintiffs who are public figures. The same limitations were necessary in false light cases, the Court reasoned, in order to insure that freedoms of expression "have the breathing space that they need to survive."

In a more recent case, *Cantrell v. Forest City Publishing Co.* (1974), the Court's task was to determine, in line with *Hill,* whether the false information at issue had been published with knowledge of falsity or reckless disregard for the truth. In the case, a newspaper carried a follow-up article about a family whose husband and father had perished some months earlier in a widely publicized bridge accident. Among other things, the follow-up article falsely implied that the widow and mother had been present during the reporter's visit to the family home (in fact, only some of the children had been present) and that he had observed her wearing the "same mask of non-expression" she had worn at her husband's funeral. On this basis, the Court upheld a jury verdict that the plaintiff had been portrayed in a false light through knowing or reckless untruth.

Public Disclosure of Private and Embarrassing Facts

"Public disclosure privacy" holds that an individual's privacy may be invaded merely by the publication of facts concerning him or her which are private and embarrassing, albeit truthful. This tort does not depend for its existence on any intrusive gathering of information, as the injury occurs with the publication of the private and embarrassing facts, however acquired. Public disclosure privacy provides a most direct clash with the act of publishing, arraying as it does First Amendment privileges for truthful expression against a right to keep secrets which many people would agree deserves protection.

In 1940, a Federal Court of Appeals decided *Sidis v. F-R Publishing Corp.* The *New Yorker* magazine in 1937 published a biographical sketch of the plaintiff, who had been a celebrated and much publicized child prodigy in 1910. In the ensuing years, the plaintiff had chosen to seek obscurity and to conceal his past identity, and these efforts as well as various eccentricities of the plaintiff were detailed in the 1937 article. Although there was nothing untrue in the article, it was characterized by the court as "a ruthless exposure of a once public character, who has since sought and has now been deprived of the seclusion of private life." Nonetheless, the article was held not to be an invasion of privacy. The plaintiff had once been a public figure and the 1937 article was newsworthy in that it provided answers to the question whether the plaintiff had fulfilled his tremendous promise; hence, there was still a matter of public interest. The court recognized that some revelations might be so intimate and unwarranted as "to outrage the community's notions of decency. But when focused upon public characters, truthful comments upon dress, speech, habits, and the ordinary aspects of personality will usually not transgress this line."

To the opposite effect are two California cases, *Melvin v. Reid* (1931) and *Briscoe v. Reader's Digest* (1971). In the first case, a motion picture accurately portrayed the public testimony of the plaintiff as a witness in a murder trial seven years before. The testimony established that she had been a prostitute but in the intervening years she had reformed and entered respectable society. In *Briscoe,* the defendant accurately reported the plaintiff's commission of a truck hijacking 11 years earlier in an article entitled "The Big Business in Hijacking." After serving his sentence, he, too, rehabilitated himself and concealed the facts of his past from his new associates. Although Briscoe lost his case subsequently at trial, the opinions of the California appellate courts in these cases indicate that the facts as alleged stated causes of action for invasion of privacy. In both cases, it was suggested that crimes committed in the past are certainly matters of public interest; however, the names of the individuals involved may not be when many years have passed and the individuals have reformed. In a sense, such individuals have regained some right of privacy which had earlier been forfeited.

The only United States Supreme Court decision in the area is *Cox Broadcasting v. Cohn,* decided in 1975. The father of a murdered rape victim sued a television station for invasion of his privacy when it broadcast her name, in violation of a state statute prohibiting the revelation of the name of a rape victim, in a report on the sentencing of the rapists. It was held that no invasion of privacy had occurred because the victim's name had been obtained from judicial records that were open to public inspection: "The commission of crime, prosecutions resulting from it, and judicial proceedings arising from the prosecutions . . . are without question events of legitimate concern to the public and consequently fall within the responsibility of the press to report the operations of government."

The most recent public disclosure privacy ruling is *Virgil v. Time Inc.* At issue in this case was the publication of various truthful incidents from the plaintiff's past which were offered as an explanation of his daredevil prowess at body surfing at a particularly dangerous spot in southern California. The alleged private and embarrassing facts — such as extinguishing cigarettes in his mouth to impress women, intentionally injuring himself in order to collect unemployment so as to have time for bodysurfing, eating insects — were revealed to the *Sports Illustrated* reporter by the body surfer but the latter purported to forbid publication of such incidents prior to the publication of the article.

In December of 1976, a federal District Court in southern California held that the plaintiff's suit was without merit and granted summary judgment for the defendant. Recognizing that truthful disclosures are privileged under the First Amendment if they are "newsworthy," the court stated two conditions which must be met in order to lose this constitutional protection. First, the facts must be highly offensive as a matter of community mores, and these were not: "The facts themselves . . . are not sufficiently offensive to reach the very high level of offensiveness necessary . . . to lose newsworthiness protection. . . . The above facts are generally unflattering and perhaps embarrassing, but they are simply not offensive to the degree of morbidity and sensationalism."

Even if the disclosures had shown the requisite offensiveness, the plaintiff was unable to satisfy the second requirement, that the revelation of the facts be for its own sake: "Both parties agree that bodysurfing at the Wedge is a matter of legitimate public interest, and it cannot be doubted that the plaintiff Mike Virgil's unique prowess at the same is also of legitimate public interest. Any reasonable person reading the *Sports Illustrated* article would have to conclude that the personal facts concerning Mike Virgil were included as a legitimate journalistic attempt to explain Virgil's extremely daring and dangerous style of bodysurfing at the Wedge. There is no possibility that a juror could conclude that the personal facts were included for any inherent, morbid, sensational, or curiosity appeal they might have." In finding *Sports Illustrated's* article a legitimate journalistic exercise, the court concluded "that there is a rational and at least arguably close relationship between the facts revealed and the activity to be explained." But, it hastened to add, its opinion "should not be read as in any way endorsing no-holds-barred rummaging by the media through the private lives of persons engaged in activities of public interest under the pretense of elucidating that activity or the person's participation in it."

6. Ten Questions About the New Copyright Law

by Waldo Moore

1. First of all, what is a copyright?

It is the right, accorded by law, to prohibit the unauthorized copying of original works of literature, art, music, and other works of creation. Also it is the right to prohibit certain other acts — such as re-photographing or tracing — that have been likened, by statute or court decisions, to copying. It is the right of the author (that is, the creator of the work) or of someone who has derived his right from the author (such as a movie producer who is adapting an author's novel for the screen). A copyright is a form of personal property which is intangible in nature and therefore separate from the property right in any of the physical objects in which the work may be embodied. For example, you may own a letter sent you by your cousin, but the *ideas and words* in that letter are still the property of the letter writer.

The copyright statutes of the United States are based on a provision of the Constitution which provides that "Congress shall have the Power . . . To promote the Progress of Science and useful Arts, by securing for limited Times to Authors and Inventors the exclusive Right to their respective Writings and Discoveries." And, indeed, there has been such a statute since 1790, when the Second Session of the First Congress passed the first Federal copyright law. The present law was enacted in 1909 and, with amendments thereto, is codified as Title 17 of the United States Code.

2. What are the changes in the new copyright law that has been adopted?

The general revision of the copyright law was enacted as Public Law 94-533 on October 19, 1976. Most provisions of the new law took effect January 1, 1978. Among the highlights of the new law are these:

A. Instead of the present "dual system" of protecting works by common law prior to publication and under the Federal statute after publication, the new law provides for a single national system of statutory coverage for all copyright works, whether they are published or unpublished. For those works already created and under statutory copyright protection as of December 31, 1977, the new law keeps the present first term of 28 years measured from the date of publication, or from the date of registration if registered in the Copyright Office in unpublished form. (Under the old law only certain manuscripts such as plays, TV scripts, songs, and lectures could be copyrighted in unpublished form.) The new law also retains the requirement of renewal in order to have a second term, but it increases the length of the second term to 47 years so that the total protection possible for such works is 75 years.

B. For a work created on or after January 1, 1978, the new law specifies that the copyright will subsist from the creation of the work and will endure "for a term consisting of the life of the author and 50 years after his death." In the case of an anonymous work, a pseudonymous work, or a work made for hire, the copyright will generally last "for a term of 75 years from the year of its first publication, or a term of 100 years from the year of its creation, whichever expires first." (To confirm the date of creation, of course, would require that the author date his unpublished manuscript or a cover title/author page attached to it.)

C. For works created before January 1, 1978 and still under the common law protection on that date, the term will be that described in the preceding paragraph, but in no case "shall the term of copyright in such a work expire before December 31, 2002; and, if the work is published on or before December 31, 2002, the term of copyright shall not expire before December 31, 2027."

D. Another highlight of the new law is the modification of the so-called "manufacturing clause," under which certain works must at the present time be manufactured in this country in order to have full copyright protection here. The new statute will allow 2,000 copies manufactured abroad to be imported during the existence of the copyright (instead of the present limit of 1,500 copies), and will equate manufacture in Canada with manufacture in the United States. If an author first publishes a nondramatic literary work abroad, however, there is no restriction on number of copies which can be imported. And in 1982 the entire manufacturing clause restrictions will be eliminated.

E. Other important provisions of the new Act deal with fair use, sound recordings, United States Government works, and the compulsory licensing of certain uses of copyright works such as Cable TV, juke boxes, etc.

3. *I write novels, short stories, and poems. How will the new law affect me?*

One particular effect that may be of considerable importance to you is that all copyrightable works will be registrable in the Copyright Office in unpublished form. Under the 1909 law the only literary works registrable in unpublished form were dramas, lectures and similar works prepared for oral delivery. Thus most nondramatic literary works were not registrable while unpublished; and this restriction has been the subject of great dissatisfaction. Under the new law, copyright will exist in original works of authorship fixed in any tangible medium of expression, including literary, dramatic, and musical works; pantomimes and choreographic works; pictorial, graphic, and sculptural works; motion pictures and other audiovisual works; and sound recordings. Any work covered by the new statute will be registrable in unpublished or published form.

4. *When I register my literary works in unpublished form, will I have to pay a registration fee for each work, or can I register a collection and pay only one fee?*

A collection of original works of the same nature by the same author that can be the subject of a single copyright claim — such as a collection of newspaper columns that a writer is self-syndicating — is registrable on a single application and fee, if the items are all submitted as a single unit and are so identified. Contact the Register of Copyrights for additional regulations dealing with this subject.

5. *Will publication of a literary work without a copyright notice cause loss of copyright, as it does under the present law?*

Yes. For all practical purposes — unless you had instructed the editor to publish the copyright notice and the editor had failed to do so.

The new law states that whenever a work protected thereunder is published in the United States or elsewhere by authority of the copyright owner, a notice of copyright "shall be placed on all publicly distributed copies of [the] work in which copyright is claimed."

6. *With a term of life plus 50 years and no renewal, how can I retrieve a copyright on a work that I may have signed away?*

The new law eliminates the renewal provision except for works that are already in their first term of statutory protection on January 1, 1978. Instead, for transfer of rights made by an author or certain of the author's heirs after January 1, 1978, the new Act generally permits the author or certain heirs to terminate the transfer after 35 years by serving written notice on the transferee within specified time limits. (See Section 203 of the Copyright Law.)

For works already under statutory copyright protection, a similar right of termination is provided with respect to transfers covering the newly added years extending the present maximum term of the copyright from 56 to 75 years. Within certain time limits (again, see Section 203), an author or specified heirs of the author are generally entitled to file a notice terminating the author's transfers covering any part of the period (usually 19 years) that has now been added to the end of the second term of copyright, in a work already under protection before January 1, 1978.

7. *With a life plus 50 term of copyright, when does a copyright expire on a work by two authors, one of whom dies 20 years before the other?*

With regard to a work which is subject to the life plus 50 term and which is a joint work by two or more authors, the term will consist of "the life of the last surviving author and 50 years after such last surviving author's death." A "joint work" is defined in the new Act as a work prepared by two or more authors "with the intention that their contributions be merged into inseparable or interdependent parts of a unitary whole."

8. *If I sell an article, poem or story to a magazine how can I get the rights back to republish it in a book?*

When the editor of a copyrighted magazine buys first North American serial rights to your work, you are in a sense, granting him an exclusive right to license your work for first-time publication in his magazine, on the condition that it is published in an issue which carries the magazine's proper copyright notice. Since you are granting him a license to only that one-time publication, all other rights in the work remain yours. If the editor wants to buy "all rights," and you want to retain all but one-time publication rights for yourself, your letter to him will have to spell that out clearly.

If you publish a work of yours in an *uncopyrighted* magazine, you would have to make arrangements in advance with the editor, on acceptance of the manuscript, that he will publish your copyright symbol, the date, and your name on the first page of the article, story or poem in his magazine. Then, on publication, send two copies of this page to the Register of Copyrights, Library of Congress, Washington, DC 20559, with a check for $10 and a filled-out Application Form appropriate for a "Contribution to a Periodical" which you would have previously requested from the same office.

9. *Suppose I create and register an anonymous or pseudonymous work. May I or my descendants disclose my identity for the purpose of having the life plus 50 term, instead of the 75/100 year term provided for anonymous and pseudonymous works?*

The law provides that if, before the end of the 75/100 term, the identity of the author of such a work is revealed in the appropriate records of the Copyright Office, the copyright in the work shall endure for the term based on the life of the author; and that any person having an interest in the copyright in such a work may record in the Copyright Office a statement identifying the author of the work.

10. *How do I know how much I can use of copyrighted material without having to ask permission of the owner?*

Under the new law, the factors to be considered in determining fair use include these:

A. Whether the use is for commercial or nonprofit education purposes.

B. The nature of the copyrighted work (for example a teacher's making copies from a magazine designed for student use v. copies from a general interest magazine).

C. The amount used in proportion to the work as a whole.

D. The effect of the use on the market value of the original.

Writers who would like to refer to a complete copy of the new law should see Appendix A to this book. If you wish to receive materials on the new law that the Copyright Office will issue from time to time, they will be glad to put you on the mailing list. Write: The Copyright Office, Library of Congress, Washington DC 20559 with your request and be sure to give your full name, address and Zip Code.

*Editorial Note:*Writers and educators who would like to know the guidelines on photocopying (without copyright infringement) which have been issued by both publishers and librarians, can get copies from the respective professional associations:

Explaining the New Copyright Law, a guide to legitimate photocopying of copyrighted materials, is available for $1 prepaid, to the Association of American Publishers, 1707 L St., NW, Suite 480 Washington DC 20036.

Librarians Guide to the New Copyright Law is available for $2 prepaid to the American Library Association, Order Department, 50 East Huron St., Chicago 60611.

Another publication of interest to some writers is the transcript of the meeting held in Washington in May 1977 by The National Commission on New Technological Uses of Copyrighted Works (CONTU). The meeting was concerned with CONTU committee reports on copyright protection for computer software and automated data bases. Copies of the transcript are available for $5.50, prepaid, from the National Technical Information Service, U.S. Department of Commerce, Springfield, Virginia 22161. NTIS ordering number for the transcript is PB 267 332.

Writers who are concerned with either creating for, or using materials broadcast over public radio or TV, should refer to Section 118 of the new Copyright Law in the Appendix.

Meanwhile the enclosed chart published in *Public Telecommunications Review,* of the National Association of Educational Broadcasters offers some guidelines. (In the chart, "SCA" refers to an industry term for radio subcarrier authorization — a subchannel available to most FM broadcasters. Receivable only through special converters, its most common noncommercial use is the broadcasting of special programming to the visually handicapped. Its most common commercial use is Muzak.)

Public Broadcasting and the Use of Copyrighted Materials: What We Know So Far*

The procedures for implementing the Copyright Act of 1976 are now being established under provisions set forth in the law. What follows is a summary of the statutory language upon which these procedures will be based.

Effective date of law:
Powers of Copyright Royalty Tribunal: Upon nomination and confirmation.
Other provisions: January 1, 1978

"Fair Use" of Copyrighted Works:
Excerpts from copyrighted works can usually be used in public radio and television programs *without* prior clearance or royalty payment. Check full provisions in the law.
In instances where "fair use" does not apply, see below.

Audio-Visual Works: Visual presentations, together with accompanying audio, if any. Examples: motion pictures, television programs, filmstrips.
 1. Prior clearance required.
 2. Royalty payment may be required.

Literary Works:
Dramatic: (Includes dramatic presentations of non-dramatic works.)
 1. Prior clearance required.
 2. Royalty payment may be required.

* This outline was prepared by David Gillmore, director of professional training services for NAEB.

Non-Dramatic:
1. Prior clearance required.
2. Royalty payment may be required. Negotiations are continuing to simplify clearance procedure.

Music Performed on a Program: Non-dramatic musical *compositions* performed on a program. (See also "Sound recordings.")
1. No prior clearance required.
2. Blanket fee to cover public broadcasting currently under negotiation.

Pictorial Works: Photographs; graphics; sculpture.
1. No prior clearance required.
2. Blanket fee to cover public broadcasting currently under negotiation.

Sound Recordings: The audio *performance* of non-dramatic works recorded on discs, tapes, etc.
1. No prior clearance required.
2. No royalty payment required.

Notes: 1. Does *not* apply to audio from audio-visual works.
          2. If music, see *also* "Music" above.

Special Exemptions from Clearance and Royalty Provisions:

Instructional Broadcasts: Non-dramatic literary, pictorial, or musical works may be performed or displayed *without* prior clearance or royalty payment *if:*

1. The program is a regular part of systematic instructional activities of a governmental body or non-profit educational institution.
2. The work is directly related and of material assistance to the teaching content of the program.
3. The primary audience is a group of regularly enrolled students.
4. No more than thirty copies of the program exist at any one time.
5. The program is erased after seven years.

Literary Material for the Handicapped:
The following uses are exempt from prior clearance and royalty payment:

Non-Dramatic Material: Radio (AM, FM, or SCA):
1. Program must be specifically designed for and primarily directed to the visually handicapped.
2. No more than ten copies of the program may exist at any one time.

Television:
1. Program must be specifically designed for and primarily directed to the hearing impaired.
2. No more than ten copies of the program may exist at any one time.

Dramatic Literary Material: Radio (SCA *only*):
1. Program must be specifically designed for and primarily directed to the visually handicapped.
2. The dramatic work must be at least ten years old.
3. The work may be given by same group of performers one time only.
4. The work may be broadcast by a given station one time only.
5. The work may be broadcast on SCA *only*.

7. Your First Book Contract

by Georges Borchardt

At no time is a writer more vulnerable than when he is confronted with his first book contract. At last he is being "recognized." For months, perhaps years, he may have been the only one with faith in his own work; he may, in fact, have been willing to *pay* a publisher to get published. Now, all of a sudden, someone else has faith in him and is willing to pay *him*. Where will he summon the nerve to ask any questions, to bargain with his benefactor? He will need strength, or a literary agent, or both. And the following hints might be of help to him.

Most publishers have their own printed contract forms, on which little is left to be filled out besides the agreed-upon advance and royalty rates. It is this form a writer will be sent by his publisher, with a request that he sign on the last page. Many writers sign the form without reading it, or without understanding it, and they often come to regret it. They should go over each clause of the contract, try to understand what it means, then determine what is *not* in the contract that perhaps should be. Some of the more important points are dealt with here:

The advance. The advance is the amount of money the publisher guarantees he will pay the author. It is sometimes paid in installments, but in the case of a completed manuscript it is usually paid in full on signing the contract. The size of the advance is an indication of the faith a publisher has in a book, and of the nature of his commitment. In some instances the advance is applied to royalties only; more usually it is applied to all earnings by the author under the contract (including the author's share of *subsidiary rights* — see "other rights" below).

The advance should be nonreturnable, except in the case of a commissioned work that the author fails to deliver. But most contracts stipulate that the manuscript must be "satisfactory" to the publisher, leaving the latter free to publish or not publish, as well as free to reclaim the advance he has paid. If such a stipulation is left in the contract, it should at least be amended to read that the author will reimburse the publisher only if he sells his book elsewhere, and only out of the proceeds of his new contract. Otherwise the author might find himself in the awkward position of being asked to refund money he spent long ago, and which he now cannot pay back.

What kind of advances can he expect?

On a juvenile book, it might be as little as $500; but on an adult trade book the advance may be $5,000 to $15,000 and sometimes more. Rock-bottom advances on a novel or nonfiction book, hardcover or paperback still are $1,000 to $2,000.

On commissioned books, the publisher usually pays half the advance on signing the contract, and half on delivery. Since authors need money while writing rather than when they are through, we often have an advance paid in more installments — say, one fourth on signing, one fourth on delivery of half the manuscript and the balance on full delivery.

Royalties. Standard royalties on an adult trade book (as opposed to children's books, or textbooks*) are ten percent of the retail price up to 5,000 copies sold, 12 1/2% from 5,000 copies to 7,500 or 10,000 copies, and 15% thereafter. Royalties on children's books are usually somewhat lower, depending on what kind of illustrations are involved, whether they are supplied by the author, etc. For example, where color illustrations are as important as the text, the royalty (ten to 12 1/2%) would be divided 50/50 between the author and artist. For text with line drawings, eight to ten percent for the author and two percent for the artist would not be unusual. Where illustrations are minimal the publisher may simply pay a flat fee to the artist and the royalty to the author.

It is important to make sure that royalties are based on the retail price, rather than "net receipts." There is nothing essentially wrong

---

*Royalties on textbooks at the college level could range from eight percent to 19% and at the elementary and secondary school level, three to five percent with advances ranging from zero to $1,000 and up.

with basing royalties on "net receipts" (the amount actually received by the publisher from bookstores or jobbers, rather than the amount charged customers by the bookstore) provided the royalty rates are increased sufficiently to make up for the discount granted by the publisher. In other words, a 15% royalty based on net receipts would correspond to a nine percent royalty based on retail price, if we assume the average discount to the bookseller to be 40%.

It is also important to watch the fine print that follows the listing of the agreed-upon rates. All publishers pay lower rates on copies sold by mail order, or copies exported outside of the U.S.; but some also pay lower rates on copies sold at high discounts and their definition of a high discount can vary by several percentage points. Under these special clauses, some publishers sell many more copies at exceptional (lower) rates than they do at the "regular royalty" rates originally negotiated with the author. Contracts of this type are misleading to the extent that they imply the author will be paid higher royalties than he can actually expect to receive.

The "other" rights. In addition to publishing a hardcover edition (and the royalties listed above apply to such editions only), the publisher usually also has the right to publish a paperback edition. There are two kinds of paperback editions: the trade or quality paperbacks, which are sold in bookstores only, and the massmarket paperbacks, which are sold in bookstores and also through a number of other outlets (drugstores, airports, etc.). Trade paperbacks are more expensive, are printed on better paper, and tend to use the same type as hardcover editions. Massmarket paperbacks use inexpensive paper, get more words on the page, and sell for less.

If the publisher publishes his own paperback edition, this will usually be a trade paperback, on which he will normally pay a seven and one-half percent royalty (some contracts may only call for five or six percent, based on the retail [bookstore] price).

The publisher will also have the right to sub-license paperback rights to another publisher, usually (but not always) for a massmarket edition, and will normally share the proceeds 50/50 with the author. We shall deal with this in detail further on.

The publisher has the right to license book-club rights. The traditional division of proceeds is 50/50, where the book club pays an advance and royalties. Some smaller book clubs simply buy copies from the publisher to distribute to their members, and this may call for a different arrangement — possibly ten to 15% of publisher's net receipts to the author.

The author can retain many of the other subsidiary rights, and he will if he is represented by an agent. These rights are the right to publish the book in England and in the British Commonwealth, the right to publish the book in translation, motion picture and television rights, and first serial rights (the right to publish in newspapers and magazines before book publication). However without an agent the author may not know what to do with these rights if he retains them, and the publisher may not let him retain them in the first place. In that event the publisher is entitled to a commission on the sale of each of these rights:

On British rights, where the usual agency commission is 15% the publisher tends to ask for 20%.

On translation rights, where the usual agency commission is 20% the publisher may ask for 25%.

On motion picture and TV rights, as well as first serial rights, where the usual agency commission is ten percent, the publisher will probably also ask for ten percent.

Warning: some publishers have been known to ask for as much as a 50% commission on the sale of these subsidiary rights. In addition, agents who work through sub-agents (in foreign countries, or in Hollywood) share their commission with the sub-agent, thereby not charging the author an extra fee, but publishers often hire sub-agents without absorbing the sub-agent's commission, thereby further reducing the author's share.

Additional warning: your contract should clearly state that all rights not specifically mentioned are reserved by, and are the property of the author.

Massmarket reprint rights. The major source of revenue under most contracts will be from the sale of massmarket editions. Advances paid by reprint houses now range from $1000 to two million dollars; and while the former is far more common than the latter, hardly a month goes by without some million-dollar deal. It may be unrealistic to think in such terms when signing one's first contract, but some knowledge of what is involved might come in handy.

The traditional division of paperback earnings is 50/50, and applies to both the advance and the royalties earned by the paperback edition. Some years ago one publisher — W.W. Norton — introduced a more advantageous (to the author) division in his contract, and at this point the division tends to be a matter up for negotiation. The difference in the income to the author can be very large: if reprint rights in his book are sold for $200,000 his share "normally" would be $100,000, but on the basis of a 60/40 split it would be $120,000, and on the basis of a 2/3 - 1/3 split, $133,334. As of this writing one publisher automatically gives authors better than 50/50; another never gives more than 50/50. The others are usually willing to bargain. The standard massmarket paperback royalty is six percent of the retail price on the first 150,000 copies sold and eight percent thereafter. On a bestselling paperback, royalties go as high as 15%.

The grant. Some publishers buy an author's work outright, against a simple cash payment that represents all the author will earn from his book. For transactions of this sort, which I never recommend, most of what precedes and most of what follows does not apply. In general, however, publishers do not "buy" a book; they are simply acquiring certain rights which are leased to them for a specific amount of time. In other words rights are "licensed" not "sold" to them.

The main right a publisher acquires is the right to publish the book, usually in hardcover, sometimes in paperback form—this should be clearly stated. The contract will also say *where* the publisher may sell his book, *when* his license expires, and *what* rights he acquires besides the right to publish the book (see "other rights" above).

The contract that will be sent to the author by the publisher will in all probability cover the right to publish in all languages, and throughout the world. If the author wishes to retain languages other than English, and the right to license his book separately in England (as he would if he were represented by an agent), then he should limit the grant to the English language, with exclusive publication rights limited to the United States and its possessions, Canada and the Philippines. He can, of course, bargain with the publisher, giving him additional rights in exchange for a higher advance.

The contract will also probably state that the rights granted to the publisher are granted for the duration of the copyright. It is important for the author to make sure that the contract states that should his book go out of print at any time, and should the publisher not reprint it within six months of having received a notice from the author requesting him to do so, all rights granted will revert to the author.

Warning: the publisher's contract may state that the copyright will be registered in the publisher's name, or in the publisher's and the author's name (whichever he chooses). Make sure that this is amended to provide that the copyright will be registered in the author's name, a request that will practically always be granted, and that protects your ownership of any reserved rights.

The warranty clause. The contract will ask you to guarantee certain things to the publisher, some of which should present no problems — that you are the author of your book, that you haven't already licensed it to someone else, and that you have not plagiarized — while others (dealing with libel and invasion of privacy) could drive you into bankruptcy. Most warranty clauses are very sweeping: they make the author responsible for any costs incurred in defending suits, including nuisance suits, and these costs can be enormous. The author should only be liable where there has in fact been a judgment for damages, and if possible the author's liability should be limited to a specific amount. The Author's Guild recommends 30% of income under the contract, but most publishers won't accept a limit. Unfortunately, while publishers can afford insurance to protect them from such lawsuits, such insurance protection may not be available to the authors as the insurance premiums might cost him more than his projected earnings.

The option clause. Your publisher will ask for the right to have a chance at your next book, which in most cases may seem fair. This is not so in all circumstances, however. If a publisher does a terrible job publishing your first book, why should you have to subject your second book to the same fate? Some option clauses state that the publisher may acquire your next book on the same terms as your first; some state that the publisher need not make up his mind until several months after he has published book number one. Both of these stipulations should be avoided. The option to contract for your next book should be on terms to be agreed upon within a stated period of time, and if it is a work of nonfiction the option should be exercised on the basis of a synopsis, within a month of submission. If the publisher and author cannot agree within the stated period of time, the option should expire. Most authors cannot afford to embark on months of research without the knowledge that they will be paid for their work.

The publisher's obligations. The contract submitted to the author will tend to be longer on his obligations than on the publisher's. Having produced his book and handed it over to the publisher, however, the author is certainly entitled to something in exchange. The main thing is, of course, to see his book published. While this seems rather obvious, oddly enough many publisher's contracts do not state when the publisher will publish the book (they may simply state "within a reasonable time"). It is normal to request that the book be published within 12 months of delivery of the final manuscript (publishers now need about nine months from delivery to publication, so this leaves them an additional three months to work out the best schedule for the book). While the contract should state whether the book will be published in hardcover or in paperback form, everything else (price, design, jacket copy, etc.) is usually left to the publisher.

The contract should also state clearly how and when the author gets paid. Most publishers send statements twice a year (but some only report once a year), and make payments three months after the ending of an accounting period. In other words, they pay on March 31 for earnings during the period July 1 to December 31, which means they hold the author's money for anywhere from three to nine months. Some wait even longer. It is advisable to state in the contract that any substantial sums (e.g., over $500) due the author from the licensing of subsidiary rights will be paid to the author within two weeks of receipt by the publisher.

There are a number of other things a contract will cover, such as correcting proofs, receiving free copies of the book, etc., and we cannot deal with all of them here. There are also some special situations — such as the sale of a book to a massmarket publishing house for original paperback publication where some of the above matters will work out differently.

Finally, an author should not expect his contract to solve all the problems that might arise. If he deals with an editor he trusts and the editor remains with the publishing firm from the date of signature of the contract through the life of the book (admittedly a rare occurrence), the author may not have to refer to his contract very often. The choice of a good editor and a good publishing house is at least as important as the contract. But even when the agentless author has made what he thinks is a perfect choice, at some point he may find that in his relationship with a suddenly anonymous publishing entity his contract, if it is a good one, is his only real friend.

Editorial Note: Writers who have published one book within the previous seven years or three articles or stories in national magazines within the previous 18 months may find it helpful to join the Authors' Guild, 234 West 44th St., New York City 10036.

The Guild has helpful information for members on book contracts and other author concerns. Dues are $35 per year.

There are two associations of literary agents: The Society of Authors' Representatives, 101 Park Ave., New York City 10017 (membership list available for a self-addressed, stamped business-size envelope) and the Independent Literary Agents Association, 164 East 93rd St., New York City 10028.

A list of authors' agents with details on types of material they handle, appears in WRITER'S MARKET published by WRITER'S DIGEST.

Sample book contracts are available from the Society of Authors' Representatives, same address as above, for 75c in stamps, plus a self-addressed, stamped envelope. The Science Fiction Writers of America also have sample hardcover and paperback book contracts available at $1 each. Their address is 44 Center Grove Rd., Dover, NH 07801.

8. Subsidiary Rights

Perry H. Knowlton

In book publishing today, the sale of subsidiary rights sometimes means the difference between profit or loss for the publisher and fortune or anonymity for the writer.

The book contract sent the writer after the initial sale stipulates the terms governing publication and sale of the work, and it also defines many of the important areas of subsidiary rights. The territory granted to the publisher determines whether he will be handling foreign rights, and if the publisher is to do so, there will also be a clause governing the division of earnings from those rights. The same thing holds for other subsidiary rights — dramatic, radio, television, motion picture and serial rights.

If the author is represented by an agent, most of these rights are in his hands, and it's his responsibility to see that their potential is exploited in the author's best interests. This doesn't necessarily mean that subsidiary rights are sold to the highest bidder, for the selection of the best British or Italian publisher for any one particular book is more important than a possible difference in advances offered. The same factor enters into the sale of first serial rights, although to a lesser degree.

The agent almost invariably retains for the author first serial rights, all foreign rights and all performing rights (motion picture, television, radio and stage). He traditionally grants to the publisher, with occasional exceptions, the right to handle the licenses to softcover reprinters, book clubs, magazines and newspapers, anthologies and other users after their initial publication of the book. The publisher has, in the past, traditionally expected and received 50% of earnings from these rights. Naturally, publishers claim that they must have this in order to make their usual profit. They would probably like to have a great deal more than 50%. They have, because of the split having been made from a traditional rather than a logical point of view, grown used to the income and find, like so many people who live up to their incomes, that they cannot afford to give it up without a fight. During the past ten years or so, however, agents and authors have been able to arrange for more reasonable division of earnings from reprint licenses and, less often, book club licenses.

Softcover Reprints

The W.W. Norton Co. offers all authors better than the flat 50% on reprints. With one exception, Doubleday, all other publishers will agree to some form of improvement which will be directly proportioned to the degree of their interest in the book or author in question. Doubleday has refused to depart from their 50/50 position. Some houses with wholly-owned reprint subsidiaries like Simon and Schuster (Pocketbooks), Putnam (Berkley), and in reverse, reprinters with hardcover facilities like Dell (now owned by Doubleday), can arrange for the purchase of both hard and softcover rights in the original contract, paying over to the author full 100% royalties on the reprint edition. In making this kind of arrangement, the author denies himself the possibility of competitive bidding which could result in a larger advance guarantee, his share of which could be larger than the royalty eventually accumulating at the 100% rate.

Some bestselling authors with the necessary leverage have been able to separate completely their hardcover rights from their softcover rights. The hardcover publishers, in these instances, are willing to settle for hardcover publication rights. The authors then negotiate the terms of the reprint contracts on their own, getting healthy advances and royalties from each source with no splitting whatsoever.

Over the past few years a great many books have been originated by reprinters. The practice is not new. It started back about 1960, but recently it has become quite common. The reprinter commissions a work and then seeks a hardcover publisher, sometimes through the author's agent, sometimes on his own. The author usually retains between 80% and 90% of both hard- and softcover royalty earnings. For example, if the hardcover royalty on a ten dollar book is ten percent and the paperback royalty on a two dollar book is six percent, the author would earn 80% of one dollar or 80c on each hardcover book sold and 80% of 12c, or nine cents on each paperback sale. The arrangements vary.

More serious, in my opinion, is the other area where fewer sales are being made. For example, the average author of a first novel suffers today because reprinters are being more cautious in their acquisitions. Ten years ago a talented author of a first or second novel could pretty well count on a reprint sale, and equally important, so could his hardcover publisher. Hardcover publishers could usually count on the opportunity at least to cut their losses with a small reprint sale of under a $5,000 guarantee. With diminishing opportunities to do so, the hardcover publisher is less likely to take a chance with a marginal book, so the author or his agent is finding it more difficult to place them.

Serial Rights

In the area of first serial rights, the changes have been more dramatic and apparent. Forty years ago authors like Scott Fitzgerald, Agatha Christie and Sinclair Lewis counted on making more money from first serial sales than from book publication. They depended on book publication for critical success, but the financial expectations from publication of the book were generally secondary to money earned from magazine use. Nowadays, quite obviously, the situation is completely reversed. The author of a book expects relatively little from the disposition of first serial rights. The exception occurs, but the author no longer looks automatically to magazines as a major source of income.

Over the last two decades many major magazine markets disappeared; victims of mismanagement or changing concepts in the advertising business. The remaining magazines, facing decreasing competition in their own categories, are paying less and demanding more in return. They seem more and more to try to buy *all* serial rights rather than the traditional first North American rights, thereby depriving authors of potential income while at the same time paying less that previously.

Movie Rights

There is a great deal of money being spent and being made in the film industry, but we are at a low point in terms of the number of films being produced. In 1976 the total number produced in the United States was about 150. TV has gradually intruded itself so that now it is a more important market for the adaptation of novels than feature film. The advent of the "long form" or, more recently, the "mini-series," has allowed for more generous budgets and much more lavish productions. *Rich Man, Poor Man* and *Roots* would have been impossible in any other form in either medium. And, of course, the film made expressly for TV is more familiar.

One of the factors in the growth of the film on TV has been the increasing acceptance of mature themes and subject matter.

There are two points in the history of a novel (and the occasional work of nonfiction which is suited for a film) which are usually best for pushing toward a sale. The decision as to which point to pick must be made as early as possible. Given a good film possibility, the agent must determine whether to sell it before publication and before much, if anything, is known about it in the industry, or to wait until after the book is out and established. A great many variables bear on the decision, but it comes down to whether the agent and/or author feel they can affect a more advantageous sale before the book is out or after it has been published. Book club interest, usually determined only after the book has reached the galley-proof stage, and therefore too late in some instances to sell film rights, is a factor.

Whether to allow studio story editors to get synopses in the studio files before officially offering the property is another factor to be considered. All major studios have story editors who, in order to earn their keep in their particular jobs, must provide synopses for every potential motion picture property which is published. The earlier and quicker they provide coverage for the studios of these particular properties, the happier and safer they feel. The quality of the synopses suffers as a result, and more often than not the tendency on the reader's part is to label the property with a negative tag since this is a great deal safer than a positive one. Later on when the true value of the book establishes itself, these synopses are in the files, and many an enthusiastic independent has run afoul of those early-bird synopses when he's gone to the major studios for backing. Many an option has been dropped as a result. When I said previously that the galley-proof stage might already be too late to sell film rights, it was because many a story editor's early-bird synopsis has been hurriedly, and usually badly written from a quick reading of galley-proofs illicitly obtained from the printer, publisher or some other source.

Studios, once the source of all good things and the prime movers in the industry, are no longer taking the lead in initiating film projects. The independent producers have virtually taken over the early development of properties, and one incidental effect has been to put increased pressure on agents to show material in the manuscript stage to potentially interested buyers.

Book Clubs

Selection of his book by a book club can mean extra income of a few hundred dollars (in the case of a specialized book and a small book club), to as much as $15,000 to $100,000. Book club royalties range from four and one-half cents per copy to ten percent of the price at which the book club offers the book to its members. Guarantees may be based on expected sales of a few hundred copies to a half a million copies. The Book-Of-The-Month Club minimum guarantee averages $75,000 to the publisher (which is then split with the author), and, of course, for big properties this price is negotiable. Their eventual earnings on each title almost invariably exceed the guarantee. Sometimes as much as twice the guarantee is earned.

At the Literary Guild the minimum guarantee is about $35,000, and this can range up to $100,000. The Junior Literary Guild guarantees on the average about $3,500; the Dollar Book Club guarantees on the average about $30,000. For the Reader's Digest Condensed Book Club, the earnings average from $50,000 to upwards from $100,000. Nonfiction usually earns less, and fiction more.

Commercial rights

As toy makers, T-shirt manufacturers and others search out popular book, movie or TV characters to merchandise, the sale of "commercial rights" increases.

In the purchase, for instance, of *Winnie The Pooh* by the Walt Disney Organization, they insisted on the purchase of commercial rights.

A royalty was provided for, and income from it has been considerable over the years.

Often commercial rights are involved in adult books, both nonfiction and fiction, and agents are in a better position to determine what those rights are worth than the average author.

Foreign Rights

Foreign publication rights are becoming more important now than they have ever been. English language rights in the British Commonwealth have long been a good source of income for American authors, and that market continues pretty much as before. The almost incomprehensible Consent Decree which has been lowered on the English language publishing scene by the United States Justice Department will be making itself felt more and more over the next few years. The Decree established certain restrictions on British and American publishers regarding distribution rights in English-speaking countries. It is difficult to predict its immediate effect on American authors. I would guess that authors' earnings will remain at roughly the same levels but the publication and distribution of books will gradually change.

Translation rights on the continent, however, have been commanding more interest and better contracts. Major improvements in advances are most noticeable in Germany, the Scandinavian countries, and on occasion in Italy. Sales of all kinds of books are up in these countries. France is becoming, more slowly, a more important publishing market, but the book publishers in Paris are almost totally owned by two groups, and a rather over-cautious editorial attitude is an obstacle to growth as it is occurring elsewhere in Europe. Spain, since the passing of Franco's regime, has become a surprisingly lively market for American books. The change is especially apparent because it has been so dramatic. Fees earned by the author on foreign publication rights vary with the book and range from less than $100 to several thousand dollars.

The unagented author will probably grant to his publisher the handling of foreign rights. The publisher, in turn, will probably turn this responsibility over to his agent for foreign rights, although a few handle the problem on their own. A good literary representative will tend the foreign publication rights of his authors with great care these days. There is more involved than the increasing market and growing advances, and more than the author's justified pride in being published all over the world. The shrinking of the world by jet travel and mass satellite communications has made international publication far more important than it was a few short years ago. Publishers of a novelist in Europe, England, and the United States, for instance, find that by near simultaneous publication and by careful trading back and forth of information dealing with a given novel, each publisher gains strength from the others and the novel earns added support by the mere fact of its international publication.

The agent is the man who must be responsible for arranging this kind of cooperative effort, and he must act as the communications pipeline through which all useful information (news of sales, promotion, reviews, etc.) must flow to sub-agents and publishers.

9. Syndication Contracts

by Richard Sherry

In the best of all possible worlds, we like to think that once a contract is signed, it should be put away and never unearthed by either party. The working relationship should serve as the true binder between us.

We have embodied in our Field Syndicate standard contract what we believe to be a fair arrangement. So, let's take a walk through.

First, each party agrees to perform its obvious function. The author will produce the column at stated intervals in an agreed-upon format. The syndicate will sell the column throughout the world.

Here, I should explain that there are basically two ways we at Field syndicate text material. The most common is in column form, such as Erma Bombeck, Ann Landers and Sylvia Porter. But we do have a special service we call "Synergy," which is subscribed to by newspapers on a yearly basis. In its present form — and it is subject to change from year to year — this program includes series on different topics by different writers. The rights for these are generally purchased as a magazine would buy an article, except that we buy all rights to the material — reprint and foreign as well as first publication.

As a matter of practice, however, we will revert the rights to the author, at his request, if he has a market for them and we don't. All this is transacted through an exchange of letters.

The contract I am discussing relates to our most common form of syndication of text, the column. It applies whether the column is once a week or seven times a week, specialized or general.

If the column is of a specialized nature, say, gardening or bridge, it is defined in this first section.

We agree to the title of the column (often left blank because it is a matter of mutual agreement and may change several times between the launching and the time of delivery). The expense of delivery to the syndicate is borne by the author. Cost of production is a shared expense. Production time may vary from several days to several weeks or longer, depending on the timeliness and method of delivery to client newspapers.

Some columns, like the Gallup Poll, are serviced to clients by wire — in this case, the *Chicago Daily News* and *New York Times* hookup — occasionally for release on receipt when it is hard news. Others, like Ann Landers, are mailed with two weeks of releases to a batch, two or three weeks in advance, which means the last dated column is delivered to us as much as six weeks in advance.

The author guarantees the originality of his columns and takes on responsibility for their being free of legal challenge. Whether it be right of privacy, plagiarism or libel, the author indemnifies the syndicate against any action — that is, the author pays liabilities and legal costs arising out of suits. The syndicate has choice of counsel, however.

We do have the right to kill a column that our attorneys tell us is legally questionable and may cause a lawsuit, but we have no obligation to question the legality of our columnists' work. (No more than we have to question their ethics.) Indeed, we may not, in specialized fields, be competent to do so.

We expect our writers to be thorough professionals whose work requires little or no editing. On the other hand, we are ready, willing and able to help an author editorially when he needs it. Particularly before launching, it is in his best interest that we work together closely.

If you don't think close attention is important, you should share my anxiety when a double entendre has slipped through and the threats of cancellation come pouring in from editors.

Financial arrangements with authors under our standard contract are 50/50 after production and promotion costs. There are authors who can command and get more because they have already built a reputation and are being wooed by several syndicates. This is less common than one would think.

More common, but still unusual, is an agreement on the part of the syndicate to share extraordinary costs when a specialized column is expensive to produce because of its very nature.

In one instance we agreed to share phone costs for a column that depended on four WATS lines for incoming calls. It was a special service of the column and this service was essential to the sale. We sold it far and wide, all right. But because the telephone bill ate up all the profits, the special service aspect had to be abandoned.

When prospective contributors learn that production and promotion costs are shared by both the author and syndicate, they have visions of great padded costs eating up their livelihood. Actually, though, these costs never amount to more than a fraction of total revenue.

Even the seven-a-week column, a very rare bird, has low actual production costs. And we want to share promotion costs simply so a contributor will know that he pays, too, when he demands more promotion. We do not charge for editorial time, promotion writing time, or overhead costs. These are absorbed and only printing or photostat, typesetting, unusual labor costs and the like are deducted. These are shared costs and we want to keep them down, too.

The author is free to examine the syndicate's books in regard to the feature, as the contract so states.

The term of our standard agreement is five years with automatic renewal for additional periods of five years. The syndicate can cancel the contract upon adequate notice at the end of each five year period. The author cannot cancel under this provision.

The author can, however, cancel the contract at any time, if, for any six-week period, his share of the net receipts falls below a pre-agreed amount.

Why can't the author cancel after five years the way the syndicate can? Actually he can, if he doesn't go to another syndicate. If he stops writing his column for newspapers, there's nothing we can do about it. But by the same token, the syndicate needs some protection, too.

Suppose, by virtue of our syndication, you become rich and famous. Every syndicate in the country is going to be prostrate at your door. Our deal is 50/50 and along comes another syndicate willing to pay you 90%. Why not? It will cost them nothing to get you where you are. The ten percent they pick up is pure profit with no investment on their part.

We, on the other hand, have probably spent $30,000 to $40,000 the first year on promotion and sales costs — salaries, commissions, travel expenses incurred in selling editors nationwide — which we have absorbed. Our actual profits on the column may not come until the second, the third or even the fourth year of syndication.

Under our standard contract, the syndicate owns the name of the column and the material produced under that name. The author is free to write for anyone else — books, magazine articles, you name it — as long as what he writes is not competitive with his newspaper column. As you can imagine, this can get complicated. If the author writes a book, for example, the book publisher generally will control second serial rights (including newspaper syndication). What both parties may lose sight of is that no material by the author can be syndicated to newspapers which may be in competition with newspapers carrying his column. In fact, it can't be syndicated to newspapers at all without the syndicate's written consent. This is why we feel it is important, whether or not we share in the book deal itself, that we be the syndicate to handle newspaper syndication rights.

We find, for a variety of reasons, that our policy of owning material included in the column is most practical. We have excellent contacts in the book and magazine publishing field, as well as affiliations in those fields. We have a licensing department, geared to make the most of each property. It's really to the author's advantage to "leave the driving to us," unless, of course, he has already made extensive commitments in these fields. Our licensing department has done a wide variety of things from developing the deal with ABC's "Good Morning America" for Erma Bombeck; to licensing a Slow Poke (a dog character) doll for a comic strip called *Granny and Slow Poke*. Book collections of columns are also common.

Some features die with the author; others live on. For older authors, or authors who are already under contract but concerned about their estates, there are definite advantages to ownership by the syndicate. We are happy to make addenda to our standard contracts to make reasonable accommodations in this regard. But probate delays can destroy the value of a property owned by the author.

This brings us to renegotiations or opening up the contract. We feel this is generally not practical. Contracts can be modified by mutual consent as above. Certain provisions can be waived from time to time. Here, again, I want to emphasize the personal working relationship between author and syndicate.

Should you have legal counsel with you when negotiating a contract? Must you consult a lawyer? We have signed many contracts without the authors having legal advice, but we feel just as comfortable with the author having counsel.

In selecting counsel, I would suggest you find a lawyer who is not only familiar with syndicate contracts but who has successfully concluded negotiations on such a contract for someone else.

Points to remember:

We do not pay for travel, research or secretaries, except where such expenses are unusually high due to the nature of the column. The adjustment may be in the percentage or in deductions from revenues.

We retain reprint and foreign rights, because we have a good foreign rights sales department and also so we will have such rights available for books. Our contributors do, of course, share in these revenues as they would in regular domestic newspaper revenues.

Books may be collections of columns. Sometimes the author may be asked to contribute introductory material. Additional payment for such books would be open to negotiation (but unlikely). In some cases we prepare and sell booklets through our columns.

In addition to our regular syndication contracts, we make personal management agreements, whereby we represent the author with tv/radio and lecture bureaus.

Since the foregoing applies to the "standard" contract, what about the terms the "big names" demand?

Such contracts — which are not easily negotiated — are basically marketing decisions. The rule of thumb is a careful analysis of the potential of the author in question. Even here, with a heavy heart, we have waved goodbye to the already rich and famous who were just too rich for our blood.

As my predecessor in this job, the late Robert G. Cowles, used to say, "ours is a nickle and dime business." To which I would add a paraphrase of the famous Chinese proverb, "the journey to a million-dollar column begins with a single three-dollar sale."

Editorial Note: Each syndicate has its own policy on contracts and as Allan Priaulx, executive editor of King Features points out, "Each negotiation with each contributor for each feature seems to have different twists. The differences are dictated by the talent and by the type of feature. We do not have a 'standard contract.' " Lee Salem, managing editor of Universal Press Syndicate reports that unlike Field's standard agreement of five years, "Our contracts are for ten years, with automatic renewal if a certain performance in terms of dollars is satisfied. This is a figure agreed upon prior to the actual signing of the contract. It serves two purposes: 1) It is to protect the syndicate in terms of investment in a particular feature; the other is to guarantee to the creator that the syndicate will perform up to a certain expected and professional level in regard to sales."

Robert J. Cochnar, *vice president and editorial director of the Newspaper Enterprise Association (NEA) adds this comment:*

"Like Field, we don't control our columnists, but when we negotiate a contract, we do present the columnist with our long-established code of ethics and we do expect that he or she will adhere to it.

"While NEA does operate a conventional newspaper syndicate (called Enterprise Features) the base of our newspaper business is the NEA Daily Service, which is not a syndicate at all. This service, an array of newspaper features, columns and comics, is delivered daily to more than 750 newspapers in North America on a franchise basis; thus, the newspaper has the right and option to use any or all materials so provided. This is more or less the system employed by the two national news agencies.

"Obviously, then, we can't offer contract contributors to the Daily Service the standard 50 per cent of the gross revenues, less promotion and production expenses, since the newspaper pays one rate, based on its circulation, for the Daily Service.

"The rate to the author for the feature is negotiated. For the period of the contract (and this varies), the author knows precisely what he or she will receive. All advertising, promotion, sales and production expenses are borne by NEA.

"Subsequent increases in compensation, if any, are based on the success of the feature in the marketplace, as measured by usage.

"We believe there are certain advantages to this arrangement. A conventional syndicate contract shows a rate base of zero. If the feature sells, the author is compensated. But our Service contract provides the talent with immediate compensation. Many of our writers and artists obtain excellent incomes from the NEA features, incomes which are certainly comparable to what they might receive from a syndicate."

Some authors prefer to self-syndicate their own material. They must bear the entire cost of promoting and selling their columns; but similarly they collect 100% of the revenue. One such writer-team is George and Katy Abraham whose "Green Thumb" column is syndicated by them to 130 dailies and weeklies. They've also expanded into the magazine field and write regularly for seven publications. They've been broadcasting on WHAM in Rochester for 29 years and their show is also seen on Channel 13, an ABC-TV affiliate. Writers who'd like to learn more about the techniques of self-syndication will find a chapter on this subject in the book, The Creative Writer *(Writer's Digest Books).*

Although this book, Law and the Writer, *is concerned primarily with the work of authors, some writers are also cartoonists. These persons may be interested in a "Syndicate Survival Kit" which was produced by the Cartoonists Guild, Inc. to advise its members on contractural dealings with newspaper syndicates. The booklet sells for five dollars and is available from the Cartoonists Guild, Inc. at 156 W. 72nd Street, New York City 10023.*

Objections

The Cartoonists Guild does not agree with all of Sherry's comments on the standard form of contract. Here, for example, are some of their objections:

1. "There is no participation in the ownership of the feature on the part of the author. We think the creator should retain ownership of the copyright to his/her feature and assign it to the syndicate for a specified period of time.
2. "Field calls for a 50-50 split with the creator *after* production and promotion costs are deducted. If this percentage split is maintained, the CG believes the creator's share should be deducted from the *gross* receipts, with the syndicate bearing all production and promotion costs. In any case, we believe the creator should negotiate for a more advantageous split.
3. "A five year contract is too long. We call for contracts of one or two years. The Guild also opposes automatic renewals and believes creators should retain the right to re-negotiate at the termination of the current contract period.

4. "Secondary rights should be the subject of special negotiations between the creator and syndicate. We think that a reasonable split when it comes to all spin-off or secondary promotions of the feature is 75% to the creator — 25% to the syndicate.

5. "We strongly believe that a Survivors' Clause or Estate Clause should be negotiated from the outset for inclusion in all contracts with syndicates. (See page 38, item 4, in CG Syndicate Survival Kit for details.)

6. "Legal costs arising out of infringement of privacy, plagiarism or libel suits should be completely borne by the syndicate if it owns the feature, as is the case with the standard Field contract. On the other hand, if the feature is owned by the creator, he/she should be responsible for legal fees and liability.

7. "We think Mr. Sherry's comments about legal counsel for creators in contract negotiations are ill-advised. There is no question that creators should have top professional legal counsel, Otherwise they run the risk of not achieving the best terms and protection possible from the negotiating process."

Sample Syndicate Contract

The following is the contract form used by the Copley News Service with its syndicated feature writers:

FEATURE WRITING AGREEMENT

Copyright 1978, Copley News Service

THIS AGREEMENT is made and entered into as of _____, 1978, by and between COPLEY NEWS SERVICE, a corporation, conducting a newspaper syndicate business under the name of the COPLEY NEWS SERVICE (herein called "CNS") and _____ (herein called "CREATOR").

WITNESSETH:

WHEREAS, _____ is the creator
(Name of CREATOR)
and owner of that certain feature now known as the _____
(herein called the "Feature") and is interested in entering into this
agreement with CNS for the purpose of syndicating the Feature: and
WHEREAS, CNS is engaged in the business of syndicating newspaper features and is interested in syndicating the Feature.

NOW, THEREFORE, in consideration of the covenants and conditions herein set forth, the parties agree as follows:

1. Exclusive Right. CREATOR hereby grants, bargains and sells to CNS the exclusive right and license to syndicate and market the Feature to newspapers and magazines in the United States and throughout the world. CREATOR warrants that he will not make the Feature, or any feature similar thereto, which might in any way conflict with or dilute the rights granted to CNS hereunder, available to any other person, organization or entity during the term of this agreement or any renewal hereof.

2. Marketing. CNS agrees to use its best efforts to syndicate the Feature so long as a demonstrated market exists for the Feature.

3. Format. The Feature shall be in the following format:

_____
(General category description, frequency and length.)
_____
_____
_____

4. Delivery of Feature. CREATOR shall deliver the Feature to CNS in fully finished form to enable CNS to make the best possible arrangements for publication and marketing of the Feature. The original of the Feature shall be delivered to CNS by CREATOR at such reasonable time in advance of publication date as to enable CNS to make timely distribution of the Feature to the publications which have purchased it.

5. First Release. The first release date of the Feature shall be determined by CNS and shall be fixed as soon as CNS can make the necessary preparations and prepare sales promotion material, but in any event shall not be later than _____.

6. Right of Disapproval or Modification. CNS shall have the right to disapprove or modify the Feature, or any portion thereof, submitted by CREATOR, but such right shall not be exercised unreasonably.

7. Compensation. CNS agrees to pay CREATOR fifty percent (50%) of the gross revenue received by CNS from the sale of the Feature to purchasing publications.

8. Statement of Account. CNS shall provide CREATOR a statement of account once during each four-week period subsequent to the first publication date of the Feature, and such statement of account shall be accompanied by payment of any amounts due to CREATOR under the terms of paragraph 7 above. However, where any sales of the Feature are made in foreign countries and payments cannot be made by the buyer to CNS in dollars, the credit in foreign currency given by the buyer in payment for the Feature shall be shared by both parties in accordance with the terms of this agreement.

9. Copyright of Feature. The parties agree that the Feature shall be copyrighted by CNS substantially as follows:

"Copyright 19____ Copley News Service."

CNS agrees, however, that at any time upon demand of CREATOR it will assign its interest in the copyright of the Feature, or any portion thereof, to CREATOR, subject, however, to the rights of CNS under this agreement.

10. Exclusive Rights: Book Contracts. CREATOR hereby grants to CNS the exclusive rights to negotiate contracts for the use of the Feature in book form. Any such contracts shall be submitted to CREATOR by CNS for his approval prior to executing such contracts, but such approval shall not be unreasonably withheld by CREATOR. Upon submission of any such contract by CNS, CREATOR agrees to make a prompt response to CNS. In the event that CNS consummates any contract or contracts for the use of the Feature in book form, CNS agrees to pay CREATOR seventy-five percent (75%) of the gross revenue received by CNS from the sale of any such book based upon the Feature.

11. Television, Radio, Other Rights. The parties agree that CREATOR shall retain all television, radio and other rights not specifically granted to CNS under this agreement. It is, however, understood that

should any contract be consummated for the use of the Feature in any way other than as a book or newspaper feature, whether negotiated by CNS on behalf of CREATOR or by CREATOR himself. CREATOR shall pay to CNS twenty-five percent (25%) of the gross revenue received by CREATOR from any such contract or contracts.

12. Libel and Copyright. CREATOR warrants that any material contained in the Feature as delivered to CNS by CREATOR shall be original, will not infringe the copyrights or trademarks of and will contain no matter which is libelous or otherwise injurious to any other person. If CREATOR uses other copyrighted material, CREATOR shall obtain the necessary authorization and licenses, if any, in advance of use, pay all fees in connection therewith without any reimbursement from CNS and give appropriate credit to the author of the copyrighted material.

13. Independent Contractor. CREATOR is understood to be an independent contractor in connection with the services rendered hereunder and shall render such services as an independent contractor and not as an agent, servant or employee of CNS. CREATOR shall provide his/her own equipment, including typewriter and secretarial services. If CREATOR uses other persons in connection with services rendered hereunder, it is understood that they are the employees of CREATOR, and not of CNS.

14. Workmen's Compensation, Etc. CREATOR hereby acknowledges liability to provide Workmen's Compensation Insurance to all persons employed by him in connection with services rendered hereunder and to pay Social Security and Unemployment Insurance taxes and to make appropriate federal and state tax withholding contributions as required by law.

15. Indemnification. CREATOR hereby agrees to indemnify and hold CNS harmless from and against any and all claims, demands, liabilities, expenses, losses, damages and reasonable attorneys' fees arising from the violation of Paragraphs 12 and 14.

16. Term.

(a) Initial Term. The initial term of this agreement shall commence on the date of this agreement and, unless sooner terminated pursuant to the provisions of 16c, shall terminate on _____.

(b) Automatic Renewal. Subject to the provisions hereinafter set forth, upon the expiration of the initial term hereof, this contract shall be automatically renewed for successive periods of ___ years unless either party notifies the other by registered mail at least six (6) months prior to the end of the contract period then in effect of intention to terminate this agreement, in which event the agreement shall terminate at the end of the contract period then in effect.

(c) Termination. If at any time the average compensation (Paragraph 7 above) paid to CREATOR for any twelve (12) consecutive weeks is less than $___ per week, either party may terminate this agreement by giving at least thirty (30) days written notice of termination to the other party by registered mail.

(d) Commitments After Termination. If this agreement is either terminated or not renewed by either party under the terms hereof, CNS shall not thereafter accept any new commitments for the sales of the Feature, but CREATOR undertakes to supply sufficient material to fulfill all existing commitments for the remainder of the contract period.

17. Miscellaneous. This agreement shall be construed in accordance with the laws of the State of California. This agreement shall constitute the entire agreement between the parties, superseding all previous agreements, negotiations or representations, and shall be modified or amended only by the written agreement of the parties.

IN WITNESS WHEREOF, the parties have executed this agreement as of the day and year above written.

COPLEY NEWS SERVICE   CREATOR

By: _____   _____

10. Other Writers' Contracts

Songwriters

The American Guild of Authors and Composers, 40 W. 57th St., New York City 10019, was formed in 1931 by Edgar Leslie, George Meyer and Billy Rose to obtain better royalty contracts from music publishers. AGAC developed a contract which they felt was fair and the terms of which they attempt to gain from music publishers for their members. For the services of AGAC, the songwriter pays dues of from $25 to $300 per year and five percent commission on his first $20,000 of royalties and 1/2% thereafter with a limit of $1,400. Here are some of the terms in their Uniform Popular Songwriters' Contract:

Uniform Songwriter's Contract

Royalty

The publisher agrees to pay the writer $_____ as an advance against sheet music royalties of no less than 3c a copy (except that when the writer and publisher agree to use the "sliding scale" providing for royalties up to 5c per copy, the minimum for the first 100,000 copies is 2 1/2c per copy). An advance can be deducted only from the earnings of the song on which it was paid (not against any other songs by the writer in the publisher's catalogue) and the advance remains the property of the writer. If the publisher raises his wholesale selling price, then the fixed royalty paid to the writer increases proportionately.

Publication

The publisher agrees to fulfill the following two requirements within one year:
1. Publish and place on sale regular piano copies.
2. Publish and place on sale orchestrations or secure the release of a commercial recording or pay an advance of $250.

The writer is entitled to the return of the song upon written demand, if the publisher does not fulfill the above requirements within one year.

Other income

The publisher agrees to pay the writer no less than 50% of the royalties on recording, transcription and motion picture synchronization rights; and on any foreign sales.

In addition to the American Guild of Authors and Composers which works with authors to collect royalties from music *publishers,* there are three major music licensing organizations which collect royalties from radio and television stations, hotels and nightclubs; and other licensees which *perform* the authors' works.

• The American Society of Composers, Authors and Publishers (ASCAP) 1 Lincoln Plaza, New York City 10023 was founded in 1914 by a group of composers such as Victor Herbert, John Philip Sousa, Irving Berlin and Jerome Kern, to insure compliance with the 1909 Copyright Law.

• Broadcast Music, Inc., (BMI) 40 W. 57th St., New York City 10019 was formed in 1940 by the radio industry when it felt ASCAP's music licensing fees were exorbitant. It signed up writers and composers who were not already members of ASCAP.

• The third, and smallest organization collecting music licensing fees is SESAC, whose initials formerly stood for Standard Editions of Select American Catalogs, but now is simply known by the acronym. SESAC was founded in 1931 by a private organization as a profit-making firm. It's offices are at 10 Columbus Circle, New York City 10019.

Changes Under The New Copyright Law

Under the new Copyright Law songwriters will now be able to collect royalties from juke box operators of eight dollars per calendar year for each coin-operated phonorecord player (e.g. "juke box") to be distributed by a Copyright Royalty Commission to the performing rights societies and copyright owners not affiliated with performing rights societies.

This same Copyright Royalty Commission will also determine royalty rates to be paid by cable-TV operators and public broadcasting stations.

Also under the new law, mechanical royalties on records have been raised to 2-3/4c per copy or 1/2c per minute of playing time or fraction thereof — whichever is more. The previous royalty was 2c.

Under the new Copyright Act, the term of copyright is for the author's life plus 50 years for compositions written after January 1, 1978. The new law also extends the duration of existing United States copyrights to a period of 75 years from the date copyright was originally secured. So songwriters with existing, properly renewed copyrights get an extra 19 years of life for their compositions.

Another facet of the new copyright law allows songwriters, or their widows, children or grandchildren to recapture the copyright on musical compositions which were copyrighted after September 1906 and which are now controlled by a music publisher. In order to reclaim copyrights it is necessary that certain procedures be followed in accordance with the new Copyright Law.

Here is how Ervin Drake, president of the American Guild of Authors and Composers described the new Law for his members:

"By following the established procedures in the revision; *even if you have given away your copyrights in the United States for the initial, renewal and extended terms, those nineteen years revert to you free of any previous grant made to your publisher* in the United States provided you were the author of the work *(as distinguished from an employee-for-hire)* and provided further that if the author is dead — the claim of ownership to the nineteen years is made by the widow(er) and children or grandchildren.

The Bill clearly provides that termination of any prior grant (made to a publisher) may be effected "notwithstanding any agreement to the contrary, including an agreement to make a will or to make any future grant".

The Copyright Office will be establishing formats and procedures as prescribed in the Bill to enable those entitled to be revested with their unencumbered rights."

Songwriters who are members of AGAC can make arrangements through AGAC to refile for their copyrights. Songwriters who are not AGAC members should secure their own copyrights directly, or consult their attorney for this service.

Playwrights

The Minimum Basic Production Contract, as negotiated by the Dramatists Guild with the League of New York Theaters calls for a royalty to the playwright of 5% of the first $5,000 gross, weekly box office receipts; 7 1/2% on the next $2,000 and 10% on receipts over $7,000.

Membership in the Dramatists Guild (234 W. 44th St., New York City 10036) is available in two forms: active members must have had a first class production of one of their plays (such as Broadway or Off-Broadway) and dues are $35 per year. Associate members need only have written one full-length play, and dues are $20 per year. Subscriber membership is open to those persons interested in the theater, who are not playwrights, and dues are $15 per year.

TV and Film

In March, 1977, The Writer's Guild of America (WGA) negotiated a new four-year contract with all the TV and motion picture production companies, including the three networks. The new rate schedules which were established for screenplays are as follows:

WGA 1977 Theatrical and Television Basic Agreement Theatrical Compensation

Employment, Flat Deals	Effective 3/2/77 - 3/1/79		Effective 3/2/79 - 3/1/80		Effective 3/2/80 - 3/1/81	
	Low	High	Low	High	Low	High
A. **Screenplay, Including Treatment**	$11,211	$20,821	$12,220	$22,695	$14,175	$26,326
Installments:						
Delivery of Treatment	4,204	6,406	4,582	6,983	5,315	8,100
Delivery of First Draft Screenplay	5,046	9,610	5,500	10,475	6,380	12,151
Delivery of Final Draft Screenplay	1,961	4.805	2,138	5,237	2,480	6,075
B. **Screenplay, Excluding Treatment**	$ 7,008	$14,414	$ 7,639	$15,711	$ 8,861	$18,225
Installments:						
Delivery of First Draft Screenplay	5,046	9,610	5,500	10,475	6,380	12,151
Delivery of Final Draft Screenplay	1,962	4,804	2,139	5,236	2,481	6,074
C. **Additional Compensation for Story Included in Screenplay**	$ 1,602	$ 3,203	$ 1,746	$ 3,491	$ 2,025	$ 4,050
D. **Story or Treatment**	$ 4,204	$ 6,406	$ 4,582	$ 6,983	$ 5,315	$ 8,100
E. **Original Treatment**	$ 5,806	$ 9,610	$ 6,329	$10,475	$ 7,342	$12,151
F. **First Draft Screenplay, With or Without Option For Final Draft Screenplay**						
First Draft Screenplay	$ 5,046	$ 9,610	$ 5,500	$10,475	$ 6,380	$12,151
Final Draft Screenplay	$ 3,363	$ 6,406	$ 3,666	$ 6,983	$ 4,253	$ 8,100
G. **Rewrite of Screenplay**	$ 4,204	$ 6,406	$ 4,582	$ 6,983	$ 5,315	$ 8,100
H. **Polish of Screenplay**	$ 2,102	$ 3,203	$ 2,291	$ 3,491	$ 2,658	$ 4,050

Low Budget - Photoplay costing less than $1,000,000
High Budget - Photoplay costing $1,000,000 or more

Special minimum terms applicable to low budget photoplays and explanations of discounts, are available in the "Schedule of Minimums" booklet available at 50¢ per copy from Writers Guild of America West, Inc., 8955 Beverly Blvd., Los Angeles 90048.

The new rate schedules for TV programs of 60 minutes or less whose production budget minimums are $52,250 and up, are as follows:

WGA 1977 Theatrical and Television Basic Agreement
Television Compensation

Length of Program: 60 minutes or less (but more than 30 minutes)

High Budget Minimums ($52,250 & over)

	Effective 3/2/77 - 3/1/78	Effective 3/2/78 - 3/1/79	Effective 3/2/79 - 3/1/80	Effective 3/2/80 - 3/1/81
Applicable Minimums				
Story...	$1,901	$2,053	$2,217	$2,417
Teleplay......................................	$3,293	$3,556	$3,840	$4,186
Installments:				
*First Draft: 6% of Agreed Compensation but not less than 90% of minimum				
Final Draft: Balance of Agreed Compensation				
Story & Teleplay.........................	$4,753	$5,133	$5,544	$6,043
Installments:				
*Story: 30% of Agreed Compensation				
First Draft Teleplay: 40% of Agreed Compensation or the difference between the Story Installment and 90% of minimum, whichever is greater				
Final Draft Teleplay: Balance of Agreed Compensation				
** Going Rate (Story & Teleplay).............	$4,770	$5,152	$5,564	$6,065
(Story, Option for Teleplay)...............	$5,194	$5,609	$6,057	$6,603
** Bonus.....................................	$2,650	$2,862	$3,091	$3,369

* On pilots only, the writer is to be paid 10% of the first installment (as an advance against such first installment) upon commencement of services.

If the going rate and bonus are applicable, total compensation for story and teleplay is:

Effective	Story & Teleplay	Story, Option for Teleplay
3/2/77-3/1/78	$7,420	$7,844
3/2/78-3/1/79	$8,014	$8,471
3/2/79-3/1/80	$8,655	$9,148
3/2/80-3/1/81	$9,434	$9,972

** The Going Rate and Bonus are applicable to Stories and/or Teleplays for Network Prime Time.

Detailed explanation of the going rate and bonus for the 60 minute program, as well as complete details on rates for 30 minute, 90 minute and 120 minute programs are also given in the "Schedule of Minimums" booklet. The booklet also covers rates for writers on Comedy-Variety Programs as follows:

WGA 1977 Theatrical and Television Basic Agreement
Television Compensation

Comedy-variety programs

Applicable program minimums Length or Time Bracket	Effective 3/2/77 - 3/1/78	Effective 3/2/78 - 3/1/79	Effective 3/2/79 - 3/1/80	Effective 3/2/80 - 3/1/81
5 minutes	$ 339	366	$ 395	$ 431
10 minutes	675	729	787	858
15 minutes	953	1,029	1,111	1,211
30 minutes	2,067	2,232	2,411	2,628
45 minutes	2,243	2,422	2,616	2,851
60 minutes	2,843	3,070	3,316	3,614
75 minutes	3,310	3,575	3,861	4,208
90 minutes	3,876	4,186	4,521	4,928

The new contract also covers rates for writers if their films or TV programs should subsequently be used on the new video cassettes. They receive a percentage of the gross receipts derived therefrom. The production company must also negotiate new terms and provisions if they employ writers to write for the production of a program or motion picture which is to be used directly for video cassettes or pay TV, et al, as distinguished from an initial release in theaters or on free TV.

Membership in the Writers Guild of America is open to professional writers for films, TV and radio. Initiation fee is $400. Dues are ten dollars per quarter, which is applied against one percent of gross annual earnings. A list of agents who work with Writers Guild members is available for $1 from the WGA at 8955 Beverly Blvd., Los Angeles 90048.

11. The "Long Arm" Law

By William Donaldson

If you ever have the experience of selling your manuscripts to a buyer who refuses to pay for what he has bought, the so-called "long arm" statutes adopted by many states may provide legal remedy.

The concept of the long arm laws originated in the form of state statutes relative to nonresident motorists. Those laws provided that if a nonresident of a state became involved in an automobile accident with a resident, the resident could start suit against him in the courts of the resident's state. The nonresident was thus prevented from evading responsibility by the simple expedient of high-tailing it for his home state before the dust settled from the accident.

The long arm statutes now carry the philosophy of the nonresident motorist laws a step further by providing that a nonresident who transacts business in a state may be subject to the jurisdiction of the courts of that state. What acts constitute doing business within a state is a subject of continuing controversy in the courts, but nevertheless the long arm statutes may make it possible to sue the out-of-state scoundrel. Service of process is usually made through the mails.

My own experience is a case in point. On November 30, 1963, I signed a contract with one of the larger New York syndicates, the gist of which was that I would supply a short weekly legal feature to be sold by the syndicate to newspapers. Shortly after I sent the material I was advised that placement had been made with four papers and that it was hoped more orders would be obtained.

As my contract obligated the buyer to "render statements covering sales for each month not less than thirty or more than forty days after billings for each month," I looked forward to an accounting and a penny or two. When none came after several months of dead silence, I wrote a somewhat timid letter of inquiry. No answer. Again I wrote — 1967 — four years! Thoroughly disgusted, I requested the return of my material so that I could try to place it elsewhere. As usual, no answer.

As I live in Michigan, one of the states which has a long arm law, I mailed the legal papers necessary to force the buyer to appear before a Michigan court to answer my demand for an accounting. *Within a matter of days,* I received a letter from a New York firm of attorneys representing the syndicate. The letter stated that their client had been able to sell my feature to but a few papers with the result that gross sales came to only $831.50. As expenses allegedly incurred by the buyer were $94.75, net sales were $736.75 of which I was entitled to one half, or $368.38. The attorneys were kind enough to offer me the opportunity of coming to New York at my expense to check the accuracy of their client's records. Instead, after further correspondence, we made a compromise settlement in the amount of $500.

I'll never know, of course, how much I really had coming to me. It's a fair presumption that it was more than $500, otherwise this shady buyer would never have paid even that much. I do know that without the "long arm of the law" I could not have collected the postage I spent writing for an accounting.

So don't give up if a distant buyer prefers to ignore you rather than pay you. Check with a local attorney to see if your state has a long arm law. If so, it may be long enough to reach the purchaser's reluctant pocketbook.

How much legal assistance it will take to effectively *open* that buyer's pocketbook, will vary depending on the circumstances in each case. But it's worth looking into.

12. Small Claims Courts in the 50 States

Freelance writers who live near a publisher with whom they have a legal dispute — for nonpayment, or withholding of valuable illustrations illegally, etc. — may be able to take advantage of the Small Claims Courts in their area. As you can see from the following chart, states vary in the limit of the claim, whether the writer can appear without a lawyer, and the kinds of cases that can be handled. Consult a local attorney regarding your specific problem and the choices open to you.

Key Statutory Variations of Small Claims Courts by State

From "A Preliminary Report on an Empirical Study of Fifteen Small Claims Courts," by John C. Ruhnka and Steven Weller, National Center for State Courts — Small Claims Project, May 1977.

State	Type of Court	Small Claims Court Procedure (Latest Amendment)	Claim Limit	Informal Small Claims Procedure?	Assignees Permitted?	Lawyers Permitted?	In-Court Arbitration?	Small Claims Appeals	Other Small Claims Court Provisions
Alabama	Small Claims Division of District Court	Statute 1/16/77	$500	Yes	Yes	Yes	No	de novo/Circuit Court bond required	Equitable relief & defense permitted; no jury trial
Alaska	Small Claims Procedure in District Court	Statute 1959	$1000	Yes	Yes	Yes	No	Plaintiff or Defendant if over $50; on record	No libel or slander; either side may request jury trial; Court may order new trial or appeal at its discretion

State	Court	Authority	Limit					Appeal	Notes
Arizona	Justice Courts	Statute	$999.99	No	Yes	Yes	No	Plaintiff or Defendant if over $20; de novo to Superior Court bond required;	No Small Claims system yet; Superior Court rules apply; jury trial for either side
Arkansas	Municipal & Justice Courts	Rule 1973	$300 ($100 if personal)	Yes	Yes	Yes	No	Plaintiff or Defendant to Circuit Court; bond required	Small Claims Division of Boone County Circuit Court established by local rule 1973; $500 claim limit, no assignees, no lawyers, no jury trials, Plaintiff or Defendant may appeal to Supreme Court
California	Small Claims part of Municipal or Justice Courts	Statute 1976	$750	Yes	No	No	No	Defendant only, de novo; bond required	No corporation or Plaintiff/shareholder can be represented by attorney unless all officers are attorneys; no jury trials; Defendant waives appeal if requests affirmative relief
Colorado	Small Claims Division of County Court	Statute 1976	$500	Yes	No	No	No	Plaintiff or Defendant; to County Court; on record	No libel or slander, Federal, injunctive relief or replevin; Small Claims action transferred to County Court if Defendant requests attorney; filing limit 5 cases/-Plaintiff/year
Connecticut	Small Claims Procedure in Court of Common Pleas	Statute 1976	$750	Yes	Yes	Yes	No	None	No libel or slander; Plaintiff waives jury, Defendant can request transfer to regular civil court for jury trial; lawyer-referees will be used for Small Claims trials in some courts beginning 1977.
Delaware	Justice of the Peace Courts	Statute	$1,500	Yes	Yes	Yes	No	Plaintiff or Defendant, de novo;	No Small Claims system yet; Plaintiff waives jury; Defendant can transfer to Court of Common Pleas for jury trial
District of Columbia	Small Claims Division/Superior Court	Federal Statute 1963	$750	Yes	Yes	Yes	Yes*	Plaintiff or Defendant, at discretion of Superior Court No bond	* Either side may request law student to assist in settlement negotiations; excess counterclaim does not result in transfer; request for jury results in transfer; judge can use installment payment of judgments; one evening session/week
Florida	Small Claims Division/County Court	Rule 1973	$2,500 (attorney required if over $1,500)	Yes	Yes	Yes	No	Plaintiff or Defendant,	All defaults must be proved; jury trial available in Small Claims Court for both sides

State	Court	Statute/Rule	Amount					Appeal	Comments
Georgia	Justice of the Peace Courts (Small Claims Division in County Court in 45 out of 159 counties)	Small Claims by Rule 1952	$200 in Justice of the Peace Court; $300 in Small Claims Court	Yes in Small Claims No in Justice of the Peace	Yes*	Yes	No	Justice of the Peace both sides de novo; Small Claims both sides to Appellate Division of County Court	*Cannot use Small Claims for commercial transaction claims (OK in Justice of the Peace Court); jury trial available for either side
Hawaii	Small Claims Division of District Court	Statute 1970	$300	Yes	Yes	Yes*	No	None	*Attorneys not permitted at trial in security deposit cases; court clerks can help litigants file papers; either side can transfer for jury trial
Idaho	Small Claims Division of Magistrate Division of District Courts	Statute 1976	$500	Yes	No	No	No	Yes; bond required	No jury trial in Small Claims Court
Illinois	Small Claims Division/Circuit Court	Statute 1968	$1,000	Yes	Yes	Yes	No	Plaintiff or Defendant on record	Jury trial for either side in Small Claims, for Defendant only in Pro-Se Court
	Cook County Pro-Se Court	1973	$300	Yes	No*	No	No		*Pro-Se Court also bars partnerships, corporations & associations as Plaintiff
Indiana	Small Claims docket Superior Circuit & County Court, Small Claims Court in Marion County	Statute 1976	$3,000	Yes	Yes	Yes	No	Limit to Questions of law, to Court/appellate bond required	Plaintiff waives jury, Defendant may transfer to jury. Court rules requires one evening session/week
Iowa	Small Claims procedure in District Court	Statute 1973	$1,000	Yes	Yes	Yes	No	On record (judge's notes); bond required	No jury either side; clerks assist litigants; judge can arrange installment payments
Kansas	Small Claims procedure in County Courts	Statute 1973	$300	Yes	No	No	No	Trial de novo; no bond required	Filing limit 5 claims in same Court/year; no jury either side; no transfer because of excessive counter-claim
Kentucky	Justice of the Peace Court, Small Claims Division District Court	Statute 1978	$500	No	Yes	Yes	No	Trial de novo; bond required	
	Jefferson County Court	Rule 1974	$500	Yes	No	Yes	No		Consumer Court permits consumer plaintiff's only; no jury trial in consumer courts; pre-trial mediation required in consumer court
Louisiana	Justice of the Peace & District Courts New Orleans City Courts	Statute	$300 / $25 for City Court	No	Yes	Yes	No	Trial de novo; bond	No Small Claims system yet, under consideration for 1978

Maine	Small Claims procedure/District Courts	Statute 1954	$800	Yes	Yes	Yes	No	Trial de novo; bond required	No jury trial either side
Maryland	Informal procedings District Court	Rule 1976	$500	Yes	Yes	Yes	No	Trial de novo; bond required	No formal pleadings permitted for the informal procedure
Massachusetts	Small Claims procedure District Court & Boston Municipal Court	Statute 1960	$400	Yes	Yes	Yes*	No	Defendant only de novo; bond required	* Unless both sides have attorneys, limited to information only; no libel or slander; no jury trial in Small Claims Court
Michigan	Small Clamis Division/District Court	Statute 1968	$300	Yes	No	No*	No	None	* Attorneys permitted in Detroit Small Claims Court; no jury; either side may transfer to District Court for jury trial
Minnesota	Conciliation Court in Municipal & County Court	Statute 1975	$1,000 $500 in Minneapolis/St. Paul	Yes	Yes	No*	No	De novo both sides; bond required	* Attorneys permitted in Minneapolis/St. Paul; participation at trial can be limited by judge; no jury trial in Small Claims
Mississippi	Justice of the Peace Court	Statute	$500	Yes	Yes	Yes	No	De novo, both sides; bond required	Not a Small Claims system; jury trial available for both sides
Missouri	Small Claims docket/Magistrate Courts	Statute 1976	$500	Yes	No	Yes	No	De novo; bond required	Filing limit 4 claims in 12 month period; no jury trial
Montana	Small Claims part in District Court (local option)	Statute 1975	$1,500	Yes	No	Yes*	Yes*	De novo; no bond required	Small Claims option not adopted in District yet; * no party may use attorney at trial unless both sides have attorneys; Plaintiff waives jury; excess counterclaim does not result in transfer
Nebraska	Small Claims Division Municipal or County Courts	Statute 1972	$500	Yes	No	No	No	De novo; bond required	Filing limit 2 claims/week, 10/year; equitable relief available to disaffirm avoid or rescind contracts; no jury, but Defendant may transfer for jury
Nevada	Small Claims procedure/Justice Courts	Statute	$300	Yes	Yes	Yes	No	Both sides de novo; bond required	No garnishment or attachment on Small Claims judgments; Court clerks can assist in drafting claims; no jury in Small Claims
New Hampshire	Small Claims procedure District Courts & Municipal Courts	Statute	$500	Yes	Yes	Yes	No	Limited Questions of law; no bond required	No libel or slander in Small Claim; no jury trials

State	Court	Statute/Rule	Amount					Appeal	Remarks
New Jersey	Small Claims Division District Court or County Court	Statute	$500	Yes	No	Yes	No	Both sides de novo	No jury in Small Claims, Defendant can transfer for jury trial
New Mexico	Magistrate Courts, Small Claims Courts in Albuquerque	Statute	$2,000	No	Yes	Yes	No	Limited Questions of	Only one Small Claims Court in state; Plaintiff
		Statute	$2,000	Yes	Yes	Yes	No	law both sides de novo	waives jury, Defendant may transfer for jury
New York	Small Claims Division New York City Civil Court, District County & City Courts	Statute 1975	$1,000	Yes	No	Yes	No*	Limited substantial injustice	* Corporations & insurers also barred; arbitration option in New York City Small Claims Courts; no appeal from arbitration; paralegal assistance in New York City Small Claims Court
North Carolina	Small Claims procedure District Court	Statute 1968	$500	No	Yes	Yes	No	Both sides de novo; bond required	Simplified pleadings, but regular District Court procedures rules; Plaintiff waives jury, Defendant may transfer
North Dakota	Small Claims procedure County Courts, Justice Court	Statute 1971	$200/Justice Court, $500 County Court	Yes	No	Yes	No	None	Small Claims can cancel contract for fraud, misrepresentation; Plaintiff waives jury, Defendant may transfer; no garnishment or attachment
Ohio	Small Claims Division County & Municipal Courts	Statute 1967	$300	Yes	No	Yes	No*	Both sides on record; bond required	Individual Courts may establish voluntary conciliation by rule; filing limit 6 claims/month; Small Claims may use attorney-referee; Plaintiff waives jury, Defendant may transfer
Oklahoma	Small Claims procedure District Court	Statute 1976	$600	Yes	No	Yes	No	Both sides on record; bond required	Court Clerks may assist litigants; no libel or slander in Small Claims; jury trial for either side
Oregon	Small Claims Department District & Justice Courts	Statute 1971	$500	Yes	Yes	No*	No	None from Justice Court; Defendant only from District Court; bond required	* Attorneys may appear only by consent of judge; Plaintiff waives jury, Defendant can transfer for jury
Pennsylvania	Justice of the Peace	Statute	$1,000	No	Yes	Yes	No	Both sides de novo	No state-wide Small Claims Court until 1977
	Philadelphia Small Claims Courts	Rule 1969	$1,000	Yes	Yes	Yes	No	Both sides de novo	Plaintiff waives jury, Defendant can transfer for jury
Rhode Island	Small Claims procedure District Court	Statute	$300	Yes	Yes	Yes	No	Defendant only, on record	No jury trial in Small Claims

State	Court	Statute	Amount					Appeal	Notes
South Carolina	Magistrate Court	Statute	$200 - $3,000	Yes	Yes	Yes	No	Both sides de novo	No state-wide Small Claims Court; jury trial available for either side
South Dakota	Small Claims procedure Magistrate Courts	Statute 1975	$500 No L&T	No*	Yes	Yes	No	None	Regular civil rules, some judges use informal procedure; Plaintiff waives jury, Defendant can transfer; Court clerk can screen claims and give advice
Tennessee	Justice of the Peace or General Sessions	Statute	$3,000	No	Yes	Yes	No	Both sides de novo; bond required	No Small Claims procedure, some judges use informal rules; no jury
Texas	Small Claims part Justice of the Peace Court	Statute 1953	$150 $200 if wages	Yes	No*	Yes	No	De novo if over $20	* No assignees, collection agencies or person or entity lending money at interest as primary or secondary business; jury available in Small Claims
Utah	Small Claims Department City & Justice of the Peace Courts	Statute 1951	$200	Yes	No	Yes	No	Defendant only de novo; bond required	Court clerks can assist in preparation of claims; no jury trial in Small Claims
Vermont	Small Claims procedure District Court	Statute	$250 No L&T	Yes	Yes	Yes	No	Both sides on record; no bond	Plaintiff waives jury, Defendant can request jury
Virginia	General District Court	Statute	$5,000	Yes	Yes	Yes	No	Both sides de novo if over $20; bond	No Small Claims procedure; no jury trial, Defendant can transfer for jury if over $500
Washington	Small Claims Department District Court & Justice Courts	Statute	$300	Yes	No*	No	No	Defendant only, if exceeds $100; bond required	* Assignees permitted in Justice Courts only; Attorney permitted at trial only by consent of judge; no jury in Small Claims
West Virginia	Magistrate Courts	Statute 1976	$1,500	No	Yes	Yes	No	Both sides de novo; bond required	No Small Claims procedure; removal to Circuit Court for jury trial
Wisconsin	Small Claims procedure County Court	Statute	$500	Yes	Yes	Yes	No	De novo	Jury trial for either side
Wyoming	Small Claims procedure Justice of the Peace & County Court	Statute	$200	Yes	Yes	Yes	No	Both sides on record bond required	Court clerks can assist litigants; jury trial available for either side

13. Pornography, the Supreme Court and the Writer

by Herald Price Fahringer

On June 21, 1973, five members of the United States Supreme Court suddenly overturned the whole body of law governing obscenity prosecutions. The majority concluded that the community standards used to judge a work should be "local," rather than national and that no expert advice was needed to prove a book or film's obscene character. The requirement that a work be "utterly without redeeming social value" was renounced; rather, it must now have "serious literary, artistic, political, or scientific value" to escape censure. In writing this most chilling chapter in First Amendment history, the court again rejected the right of consenting adults to privately read or see what they pleased.

Specifically, in *Miller* v. *California,* 413 U.S. 15 (1973), the court drastically changed the formula for measuring obscenity by declaring:

> "The basic guidelines for the trier of fact must be (a) whether 'the average person, applying contemporary standards, would find that the work, taken as a whole, appeals to the prurient interest . . . (b) whether the work depicts or describes, in a patently offensive way, sexual conduct specifically defined by the applicable state law, and (c) whether the work, taken as a whole, lacks serious literary, artistic, political, or scientific value.' "

Since each branch of this test is important, separate discussion of the various elements is required.

Average Person

The "average person," as used in the Supreme Court's formula, is defined as a normal adult person. The "average person" is to be arrived at by blending together a cross section of the entire community, including persons of all religions, nationalities, creeds, ages, levels of educational attainment and economic status. The material charged with being obscene is to be judged by its impact on the average person, not by its effect on persons who are easily influenced or sensitive. The jury is not to consider the effect of the book upon children or adolescents under the age of 18 years.

Contemporary Community Standards

Historically, the Supreme Court had held, since a national constitution was being interpreted, that a national standard of community toleration of sexual material should be applied to a challenged book. Otherwise, a book found legal in New York City could be judged illegal in Fargo,,North Dakota, because of the obvious differences in community standards. However, in the *Miller* case, the court decreed that local communities are authorized to apply their own standards in assessing the obscenity of a given publication. In most jurisdictions, the boundaries of the community are fixed by county lines. In some places a statewide community governs. For instance, California and New York apply a statewide standard. In evaluating contemporary community standards, the jury is permitted to draw on its own knowledge of the community from which it comes. The phrase "contemporary community standards" has been interpreted to mean the average conscience of the time and the present critical point in the compromise between candor and shame at which the community may have arrived. Significantly, in applying this test, the jury is not to consider its own personal standards of what is good or bad. In other words, if a juror believes his own personal views are stricter than those generally held in the community, he or she is not to be guided by what he would prefer the community standards to be. Prosecutors throughout the country have already begun to exploit this new advantage given them by the United States Supreme Court. They have successfully forced the distributors of *Deep Throat* to defend their film in Memphis, Tennessee, the heart of the Bible belt. Al Goldstein and James Buckley, publishers of *Screw Magazine,* were required to stand trial in Wichita, Kansas. And finally, Larry Flynt, publisher of *Hustler Magazine,* the most recent victim of these tactics, was required to defend his magazine in Cincinnati, Ohio, although his magazine is published in Columbus. Under this new rule, publishers and writers are much more vulnerable to prosecution in foreign jurisdictions and will inevitably have instilled in them an understandable fear that is bound to inhibit many worthwhile stories. Under the influence of this new principle, book publishers will be tempted to sanitize their books so that they suit the tastes of the most pedestrian community.

Prurient Interest

Material appealing to the prurient interest is that which beckons to a shameful, morbid, degrading, unhealthy, or unwholesome interest in sex. A prurient interest in sex does *not* involve a normal or healthy interest in that subject. In judging the book, the jury may not consider its effect upon the perverted or other persons in the community who possess abnormal sexual appetites. The only exception to this basic rule is where it can be shown that a given book was designed for and disseminated to a well-defined deviant sexual group.

"Taken as a Whole"

In evaluating the impact of a publication upon the average person, the jury must consider whether the predominant or controlling theme of the book, when viewed as a whole, and not part by part, appeals to the prurient interest. The material, when taken as a whole, means that the jury is to view the publication in its entirety. It is to be judged, as a whole, on the basis of its total effect and not on the basis of isolated passages or parts. One explicit scene in a film, or passage in a book, or picture in a magazine cannot condemn the entire publication.

"Specifically Defined by the Applicable State Law"

The Supreme Court, in a bold but potentially dangerous experiment, concluded in the *Miller* case, that the subject of obscenity must be calibrated by precise statutes which particularly describe the form of sexual depiction sought to be suppressed by the state. In the wake of the *Miller* case, obscenity statutes across the country, that were general in nature, were capsized. Many states, after *Miller,* began rebuilding their obscenity laws by including, within the borders of those statutes, the various forms of sexual conduct sought to be disallowed. However, it is of little help to either an author or publisher to examine these statutes, since most of them include every conceivable kind of sexual venture. The new requirement that an obscenity statute specify every form of proscribed sexual portrayal endangers the other two branches of the court's equation which requires that the material appeal to the average person's prurient interests and that it be patently offensive. For example, a state statute forbidding the depiction of cunnilingus, by implication, decrees that the portrayal of this form of sexual activity violates contemporary community standards and appeals to a person's prurient interests. Thus, a statute which rigidly forbids a particular form of sexual description impairs the sensitive testing procedures designed to make more flexible the judging process, and is bound to generate even more litigation in this troublesome field.

"Lack of Serious Literary, Artistic Political, or Scientific Value"

In 1966, the Supreme Court fortified the test of obscenity by welding onto it the requirement that a book must be "utterly without redeeming social value" before it could be denounced. Perhaps these five words, more than any others in the English language, contributed to the expansion of what the American public could read. Innumerable books throughout the country escaped prosecution because prosecutors were fearful that they could not prove the publication was "utterly without redeeming social value." This branch of the obscenity test has now been drastically weakened with the new measuring device that requires a book have "serious literary, artistic, political, or scientific value" to avoid condemnation. Conspicuously missing from this litany is entertainment or amusement value. Furthermore, this term "serious" can be effectively manipulated by prosecutors claiming, for instance, that a sex manual is not a bonafide instruction book, but merely a vehicle to convey to the public pictures of men and women engaged in sexual acts.

The prosecution has the burden of proving that a given publication "lacks serious literary, artistic, political, or scientific value." There has been very little judicial delineation of what constitutes serious literary, artistic, scientific, or political value.

The Written Word

Of particular interest to authors and publishers should be the vulnerability of unillustrated books that contain nothing more than the written word. On June 12, 1967, the Supreme Court, acting under the able leadership of Chief Justice Earl Warren, overturned convictions involving 35 paperback novels on the ground that they were not obscene as a matter of law. This remarkable action left publishers and authors with the impression that the printed word was constitutionally protected. Under this important judgment, lawyers were led to believe that any story about people and places, no matter how frankly it described their sexual experiences, had some redeeming social value and thus, was immune from criminal prosecution.

However, in *Kaplan* v. *California,* 413 U.S. 115 (1973), decided at the same time the *Miller* decision was rendered, this thesis was specifically rejected by the subsequent Burger Supreme Court. Murray Kaplan was convicted of selling an unillustrated paperback novel suggestively entitled *Sweet 69.* Since the book contained no pictures, the petitioner urged that the written word could not, under any circumstances, be considered legally obscene. The court disagreed, deciding that this historic form of expression enjoyed no absolute protections.

The consequences of the *Kaplan* case can be terrifying. It holds that the most skillful or artistic writers hold no special franchise to the First Amendment's freedom of expression. The difficulty with the Supreme Court's ruling in the Kaplan case is that it disregards the fact that whether we approve or disapprove of these novels, they reflect the tenor of our times. Moreover, it fails to recognize that marginal works must be protected if the objectives of the First Amendment are to be fulfilled. The *Kaplan* case may well lead to the exile of a large mass of literature that the American public should have access to if they so desire.

Proof of Obscenity

Perhaps the most disappointing procedural aspect of the court's recent obscenity decisions was the holding that the prosecution need not produce any proof bearing on the issue of obscenity. In an unbroken series of cases extending over a long stretch of the United State's Supreme Court's history it has been a requirement in every criminal prosecution that evidence must be offered to prove beyond a reasonable doubt each and every element of the crime charged. In the simplest bookmaking case, the government must come forward with evidence, expert or otherwise, to show that the slips of paper seized are the contraband proscribed by the statute. This well-settled rule of law had been applied in obscenity prosecutions in an overwhelming majority of the cases decided. For that matter, the courts have traditionally held that since pornography prosecutions always involve First Amendment considerations, even more stringent procedural safeguards are required. Nevertheless, this entire line of cases requiring proof of obscenity was obliterated by the Supreme Court's decision in the Miller case. The consequences of this rule have been staggering. Failure to provide any proof on the essential elements of obscenity is an open invitation for jurors to confuse personal distaste with prurient appeal. It also encourages jurors to become puritanical and to suppress materials without any objective basis. It is unrealistic to assume that 12 people in any community will know whether a given work appeals to a person's prurient interest or exceeds the state's contemporary standards. And in a great many cases, jurors must have some guidance concerning whether a publication has serious "literary, artistic, political, or scientific value." The elimination of the need for any proof on the issue of obscenity is bound to launch juries on a rampage of legal sorcery that, in the words of one of our appellate courts, may put the Salem Witch Trials to shame.

Conclusion

The prevalence in our society today of x-rated movies, peep shows, girlie magazines, and "dirty" books, is distressing to many. However, this phenomenon apparently proves that a nation gets the kind of art and entertainment it wants and is willing to pay for. Tastelessness can never be the basis of condemning publications. If the law suppressed that which sizeable minorities in our society dislike, our cultural store would be sparsely stocked.

Under a democratic system it is imperative that all new and unconventional ideas, no matter how offensive, be read in order that we may discover the few that are of value. History has taught us that the main restraining force on official misconduct is a free and independent press which, of course, includes magazines like *Hustler,* newspapers like *Screw,* and even the most tawdry paperback novels. Although the uncovering of political espionage affects a wider range of public interest, the social commentaries evident in *Deep Throat* and *The Love Machine* are also of value. Consequently, those who may be said to dwell on the dark side of the First Amendment, selling so called dirty books, or writing dirty stories, must be protected if first rate publications are to remain safe. There are no simple solutions to these complex legal and social problems, but one thing is certain: if the breaks in the seams of the First Amendment are not stitched up soon, that great freedom, so essential to a democracy, may be irredeemably lost. We must all — publishers, authors, lawyers, and government officials — devote ourselves unsparingly to the task of restoring the First Amendment to its original place in our hierarchy of constitutional values.

Editorial Note: If you are a freelancer intending to work in the field of erotic literature, this chapter shows you some of the problems you may face. While most of the recent litigation in this area has been against publishers and distributors rather than the authors, they could be challenged too, in the future.

As the attitudes of the public and the courts about constitutional rights and censorship seesaw back and forth, the law changes to reflect it. We'll report those changes as they occur, in the pages of Writer's Digest *and in future editions of this book.*

14. Photography, the Law and the Writer

by Richard H. Logan III

After the press photographer has been taking photographs for some time, he will probably take a picture that someone wishes to use in an advertisement. If it is a picture of a store front, building, or some other object with no recognizable human beings shown, there is ordinarily no legal problem. The photographer can sell or give the picture to the client who wants to use it in an ad and no one is likely to be involved in a legal suit. Even a recognizable photograph of a store proprietor or some member of his family appearing in the ad of the store carries with it the implication that the owner had consented to the publication of the photograph.

Model Releases

If the subject of the picture is another person, however, even a model or a good friend of the photographer, he should obtain a written model release before using any picture for other than ordinary news purposes. State laws vary, but it is always safer to get a signed model release than to rely on oral consent. Even the written consent of a minor to the use of his picture is not adequate, for the signature of his parent or guardian is necessary to make the model release valid. In most states, a minor is any person under the age of 18. A few states still retain 21 as the age of majority, and two states use the age of 19.

The more exact the language and the broader the release, the greater the legal protection given to the photographer. But even a written model release does not prevent the photographer from being sued if the picture has been altered or used in some way embarrassing to the subject for which he has not given his legal consent. It is also important to remember that the release must be voluntary on the part of the signer and not obtained by coercion or fraud.

From experience, I have found it best to obtain a model release at the time the picture is taken. In my release, I usually mention a consideration, which may be a sum of money, the gift of a finished photograph, or something else of value. I also include the date and state that the person signing the release gives his consent for the various advertising and publication uses, including the electronic media. A photographer can usually buy model release blanks from firms advertising in photography journals, or he may have his own forms printed or typed.

Right of Privacy

The model release comes under the right of privacy. There have been legal cases involving the right of privacy in which the photograph in question was not published but was only seen by a third person. Public figures, generally speaking, have little or no right of privacy, and the person who takes a picture of an actor, famous scientist, or politician has the right to reproduce it in publications for informative purposes. It cannot, however, be used for advertising under any circumstances without the subject's permission.

The majority of lawsuits brought against photographers involve the right of privacy. As with most legal rulings, what constitutes an offense in this area depends upon the laws of a particular state and the intent of the photographer. In New York, a photographer can display samples of his work in his studio but must remove any picture for which he does not have consent if the subject of the picture objects. Other states may or may not allow such display, and for this reason, it is best for the photographer to be familiar with the laws of his own state on this point.

If a picture is taken in pursuit of news and published in a newspaper or magazine, the courts have usually held that the same picture may be used without the subject's consent in an ad to increase circulation of the publication or in some similar way. The picture cannot be used in connection with a product, however, or any other item not related to the original legitimate news in the publication. The same rule usually applies to the use of a news picture in a book if the picture is of an informative nature or if it is of a public figure who, in a sense, has more or less surrendered the greater part of his right of privacy in becoming a public personage.

There are also questions of decency to consider in the taking of photographs. If the photographer is in doubt about a picture, it is best for him to ask his editor or some equally well-informed person, such as the newspaper's attorney.

Libel and Truth

In the Roaring Twenties, from 1924 to 1932, the New York *Evening Graphic* became famous as a perpetrator of sensational journalism and clever photomontage reproductions called *composographs*. In a circulation war with other New York newspapers, the *Graphic* used these photographs as a means of attracting a great number of readers. The composographs were made by superimposing models onto real photographs or by cutting out people's heads and placing them on the bodies of models posed in such a way as to illustrate news stories in the paper.

Even though there were no photographic wire services at the time of Lindbergh's safe arrival in Paris, the *Graphic* came out with a "scoop" in the form of a composograph showing Charles Lindbergh in Paris after the first non-stop solo crossing of the Atlantic. Many people knew the picture was not true, but they bought the paper anyway. The captions stated that the pictures were composographs. Such pictures would not be published today because of a change in newspaper ethics and in the laws of libel and privacy.

Because truth is one of the defenses in libel cases and photographs are considered to be actual representations of scenes, it would appear that libel suits from "true" photographs would never develop. This is not necessarily so, although such suits are uncommon. Libel suits have been won where the photograph subjected a person to ridicule or was otherwise degrading to him. Photographs may not always tell the truth because of the perspective that certain lenses create. The distortion may make the subject appear grotesque or even obscene.

Libel cases may also derive from the captions on photographs, from improper use of photographs, or even from cases of mistaken identity. Many libel suits involving photographs come not from the caption but from the use of the photograph with an article that may imply that the subject is dishonest when he is not or in some other way debases the subject's character.

Generally speaking, news pictures reporting current happenings or illustrating other news items of public interest need not have the permission of the subject in order to be used. Persons who attend public events may have their picture taken as part of the audience, even though they may not desire that this be done. One person in such a situation cannot be singled out, however, unless he is newsworthy. Here, the fine line drawn between what is newsworthy and what is not may be difficult to determine at times. The photographer is usually safe in taking such a picture if it is customary to do so at certain types of events, such as a New Year's Eve celebration, a fashion show, or a political rally.

Obscenity

Determining the difference between an obscene and an artistic picture in photographing nudes is somewhat difficult, particularly in the light of many court decisions which have obscured the meaning of obscenity. In the more recent court cases there are at least four factors which must be dealt with: (1) whether the viewers are adults or children; (2) whether the photography is in the form of movies or stills; (3) whether the photographic material is considered hard-core pornography, rather than artistic; and (4) whether the use of the United States Postal Service is involved.

Because of a number of liberal court interpretations of the First and Fourteenth Amendments of the United States Constitution dealing with free speech and a free press, there is very little left under federal and most state laws which can be considered "obscene," except in some cases of sexual activity being pictured. What is permissible in motion pictures may not be permissible in single still photos, or a series of still photos depicting the same material that appeared in the motion picture. Children often come under more restrictive laws than do adults.

Determining just what is hard-core pornography will vary from one legal decision to another, and even though the photographs are offensive, distasteful, puerile or lewd, they may not be considered legally obscene. The line of demarcation can be very close in a court decision, even depending upon the publisher's intent and his advertising. The term "hard-core pornography" itself raises doubts, because it is legally imprecise in nature. State laws on obscenity and hard-core pornography will vary, even within the federal court interpretation.

The United States Postal Service has changed substantially (as a result of certain legal decisions) its former policy on "questionable photographs," although the present policies are not as liberal as might be expected. Even though the showing of pubic hair, or those photos which were thought to incite immoral thoughts or deeds are no longer necessarily on the prohibition list, those items which do fall within hard-core pornography or depict sexual activity may be prohibited. There have always been exceptions to post office policies when photographic material is for medical or similar purposes. If you are in doubt, consult your local postmaster or other postal authority for the latest information.

Copyrighting Photographs

If a photographer wishes to prevent unauthorized use of a picture, he should register his claim for a copyright with the Register of Copyrights, Library of Congress, Washington, D.C. The cost of each copyright is $10, and two copies of each photograph must be sent for deposit with the application. Application forms may be obtained from that office.

Because copyrighting each photograph is expensive, some photographers have placed a number of individual photographs on a piece of photographic paper and registered the whole group for one fee. In the case of photographs being published in the editorial sections of a magazine, the publisher may copyright the magazine and thus protect the photograph, providing the photographer has retained the right to resell the picture. Every time the picture is published, the words "Copyright by" . . . and the owner's name should appear either on the published picture or just below it, unless the whole publication is copyrighted. The copyright symbol, ©, accompanied by the copyright owner's name, is frequently used. The date need not appear on photographs.

If publication of the picture is permitted without the copyright notice either on it or with it, the owner loses his copyright protection.

In general, for photographs published after January 1, 1978, the copyright is good for the life of the photographer plus 50 years. The photographer need not apply immediately for a copyright; it may be obtained within three months after first publication. The notice of copyright must appear with all photographs whether the copyright has been obtained or not, however, if the photographer wishes to protect himself.

One publishing firm I know published a children's book for an author with the copyright notice inadvertently omitted. The author later wanted to protect herself by copyright but could not do so because the book had been published first without the notice of copyright. Under the law there may be some means of recovery when a copyright notice has been omitted or printed in error. See Chapter Four of the Law in the Appendix.

Insurance

Because camera equipment is quite expensive and subject to theft, breakage, falling off a pier into the water, and many other hazards, the cheapest insurance a photographer can get is insurance on his equipment. The policy with the greatest coverage is called a *floater policy,* which covers almost anything that can happen to the photographer's equipment outside of mechanical repairs or deterioration from normal use. I have found some insurance agents unfamiliar with this type policy, so it is advisable to be sure that the agent understands your insurance needs.

A second type of policy covers fire, theft, and storm damage but not breakage from accidental dropping and is included in the insurance of either a person's place of business or household effects. Different companies have different types of policies, and it is necessary to make comparisons among various coverage plans offered before making a decision. Premiums for floater policies usually run about $2 per $100 valuation, with the premium for household policies usually less. If the photographer has only a small amount of photo equipment, it would perhaps be better to insure it under the latter type of policy. If he has a considerable amount of equipment, however, carries it with him frequently, and uses it in earning either all or part of his income, the floater policy is perhaps more advantageous for him because of the wide protection it affords. Generally speaking, there is a minimum of about a $250 valuation, or a $5 premium per year on a floater policy.

The photographer should also protect himself from financial loss due to suits or out-of-court settlements with subjects injured from a fall or similar accidents while working with the photographer or while the subject is on the photographer's property.

All sorts of freak accidents occur, injuring and sometimes killing persons. One such accident killed a high school cheerleader in the fall of 1966 while she was posing with six other cheerleaders on a crossbar of the goalpost. It was the last picture of a shooting session, and the students were perched on the crossbar about ten feet above the ground, when the bar broke and one of the goalposts fell on the girl, fatally injuring her.

Normally, a photographer working for a company will be protected by the company's personal liability insurance, but a self-employed photographer will need protection for himself. Even though the photographer may not in any way be at fault in an accident, lawsuits are costly and no one knows how a jury will decide until the verdict is announced. Personal liability insurance coverage should be discussed with several agents and the cost and protection compared for the various policies.

The photographer who hires others and has employees who may handle money or financial transactions should consider bonding those employees through an insurance company. Most large companies follow this procedure, because it is impossible to determine who is honest or dishonest until the person embezzles or otherwise misappropriates the funds or property of the firm.

The most trusted person in the firm often turns to embezzling, because of the very trust in which he is held. It has been found in bank embezzlements that the guilty party is often the trusted "little old lady" who has been an employee for many years and is well thought of in the community. Her male counterpart may be the accountant or financial officer who is a church member and an apparently outstanding citizen of the community, until it is discovered that he has "borrowed" company funds to place bets on horse races or to invest in highly speculative securities. He always had every intention of paying back the funds, of course, but was unable to do so because of his losses. Remember that many small businesses have been bankrupted by an employee's dishonest actions. Bonding insurance is reasonable in cost and is sold by a great number of insurance companies.

Military and Civilian Restrictions

Many newsworthy pictures are obtained through the cooperation of police, fire, and military authorities. The photographer covering such beats will soon learn what pictures he can take and how to get along with civilian and military authorities without becoming meddlesome. In large cities, press photographers carry special passes from local officials that allow them to go into places where there are fires, accidents, or other tragedies closed to the general public.

There have been occasions when even the police have destroyed a photographer's exposed film or his camera or roughed him up personally in some way. These cases are rare, and usually the photographer from a publication or press organization receives favorable treatment from civic and military authorities.

Military authorities have more restrictions on taking pictures, and sometimes it is difficult to get pictures of a crash of a military plane, an explosion on a military base, or some other restricted area. Often the military will release only pictures that their own photographers have taken and will not allow newsmen to take pictures on their own.

Various agencies of the federal government have a "managed news" policy and will not allow certain types of pictures to be taken or statements quoted from government officials. This policy varies, sometimes being quite lenient and other times, quite strict.

When an accident involves two of the city's fire trucks or a policeman wrecks a car while under the influence of alcohol, a photographer will usually find it extremely difficult to get pictures of the event. The agency in question may pass it off as "taking all measures to protect the city and the public at large" or some similar ruse.

Whether pictures can be taken in a courtroom depends largely on the judge and the custom of that particular court. The American Bar Association in 1937 adopted a rule known as "Canon 35," which stated that the association felt that taking pictures while the court was in session or during recesses detracted from the dignity of the court and otherwise created misconceptions in the mind of the public and that any type of photography in the courtroom should be prohibited. The National Press Photographers' Association fought hard to have this rule changed, using as a basis for argument the fact that cameras with fast lenses and high-speed film could take pictures in the courtroom without distracting or interfering with court proceedings.

An amendment in 1952 provided that certain proceedings could be photographed. Actually, the *Canons of Judicial Ethics* are not laws but guidelines for the nation's judges and attorneys. Some states strongly enforce this rule, and a violation can lead to a contempt citation with a possible fine or jail sentence for the photographer.

Pre-Trial Publicity

In June, 1966, the United States Supreme Court ruled that Dr. Samuel Sheppard, Cleveland, Ohio, had not had a fair trial when convicted of his wife's murder in 1954. The decision of the court was based on the widespread coverage by radio, tv, and newspapers of Dr.Sheppard's arrest and trial, holding that because of the nature and the intensity of this coverage, Dr. Sheppard was entitled to a new trial.

A number of other cases have developed in the same area, all having to do with pre-trial news coverage. Because of such cases, news media are finding it increasingly difficult to hold interviews, take photographs, and write news stories on important criminal cases.

Regulations and Licensing

A photographer employed by a publication does not need an occupation license. When he goes into business for himself, he will be governed by the laws and ordinances governing businesses of the community in which he lives and/or works. There are certain restrictions covering sanitation, commercial zoning, sales tax licenses, occupation licenses, and other areas which a professional photographer must observe. It is wise to inquire what regulations affect photographers before establishing a part-time or fulltime business. Some cities permit darkrooms in residential areas but not studios. Others may permit home studios but restrict advertising and displays or even have regulations on customer parking. These restrictions will vary from area to area. By joining one of the professional photographer's associations, the photographer can often learn more quickly about new legal and ethical problems. Of course, he also has the opportunity to attend clinics and conferences and to meet other persons active in his field.

Ethics in Photography

Ethics is one important aspect of photography that the beginner might never consider. An ethical violation might not be brought before a court of law, although lawsuits can arise from such infringements, but both the photographer's business and personal reputation can be damaged by an inadvertent action on his part if he is unaware of ethical complications that may arise. Photography has its own special pitfalls, and they are not always easy to predict or judge with mere common sense and good instincts.

The photographer seldom, if ever needs to come into direct physical contact with a subject, and it is best to refrain from touching the person in any way, especially in taking studio pictures or portraits. Although a young child may be lifted or moved about slightly, young people and adults should be directed either by voice or by gesture or both, without actual physical contact being necessary.

The photographer wishing to avoid the wrong reputation should use discretion when alone in the studio with a subject. For example, when I once owned a portrait studio in a small city, a young lady telephoned to ask if I took drape shots. I replied that I did but had no one in the studio and that she should bring her mother, sister, or a girlfriend to help her with the drape. I prefer to have a woman assistant to smooth the wrinkles from a dress, straighten sleeves, put hair in place, or otherwise arrange a subject's clothes and help with posing. Even though the photographer may innocently touch someone, the subject may receive the wrong impression due to the reputation that fiction has given photographers.

The photographer should never give the picture of a subject to anyone else without the subject's express permission, even though the picture may have been used for a news story and permission may have been obtained when the picture was taken. A boy may come in and ask for a photograph of a pretty girl, claiming to be her boyfriend. The girl may not want him to have her picture, and although giving him the picture without her consent might not bring about a lawsuit, it could very well damage the photographer's public image permanently.

Photographers need to build their reputation on sound ethical and business practices. False advertising, shoddy work, or other unethical tactics have no place in the professional photographer's life. The Professional Photographers of America, Inc., and other similar organizations have adopted codes of ethics, and it is a good idea for the beginning photographer to familiarize himself with these codes as a guide to his professional conduct.

Good Taste

Gruesome pictures of tragedies are taken from time to time. For example, a Buddhist nun is photographed after setting herself on fire, the burning funeral pyre of a great leader such as Mahatma Gandhi is shown, or grisly pictures of accident victims are made.Newspaper readers often criticize the publication of pictures that they think are in poor taste or are unpleasant to view.

Much of the decision as to whether to publish such a picture in the paper rests upon the shoulders of the editor. Photographers working with newspapers or wire services will know what to take and what to omit from experience and from guidelines set down by the organization's policy. Although there may be some legal questions involved in such pictures, usually the publication of gory or distasteful photos comes under the category of ethics rather than of legality. Such pictures do serve as warnings to others and definitely fall into the newsworthy class; however, some papers thrive on sensationalism and carry the publication of such pictures much too far. The paper should keep in mind the dignity of the victims of the tragedy, as well as the feelings of the audience the publication reaches. Whether to publish a picture of a tragedy is often a difficult decision for the photo editor to make.

Pricing

Two of the greatest problems I have found with beginning photographers is that they tend to price their work too cheaply and to attempt freelance assignments for which they are not qualified.

The photographer should charge enough money to absorb the costs not only of his materials but also of his time, car expenses, depreciation on equipment, and other overhead expenses, such as insurance and taxes. Even the beginning photographer should charge two or three times as much for an 8 x 10 photograph as the customer would pay to have his own negative enlarged to an 8 x 10 size at the drugstore.

The beginning photographer should charge less, in most cases, for his work than a professional because he lacks skill. He should not, however, try to take business away from a professional by pricing his work ridiculously low. Doing so not only reflects on the photographer's character but hurts the entire photographic profession as well.

I have had unethical and mostly inexperienced photographers solicit some of my better accounts by offering to make photographs for about one-fourth my regular prices. Many times the account would tell me about such photographers, remarking that the other photographer was not even considered because the account manager knew that good photographs could not be obtained at the price quoted.

Once, when I had my own industrial photography business in Denver, I was asked to quote a price for taking a number of 8 x 10 photographs of the interior of a very famous bar. I went to the establishment and talked to the owner, and we came to an agreement of $10 for each 8 x 10 glossy photograph, a price somewhat lower than I normally charged. When I went back to make a definite appointment to take the pictures, the owner told me he had changed his mind because an airman from one of the nearby bases had offered to do the job for 35c per 8 x 10 photograph. As a result, neither of us got the job. The owner felt that I must be overcharging him at $10 a picture, and he did not hire the airman because he did not believe he could do the work properly.

The Summing Up — Legal Points

Whether a photograph is to be used for news or advertising often determines if written consent of any recognizable subject appearing in it is needed. Photographs should not be used for advertising or similar purposes without the written consent of the subject being photographed. This written consent is called a *model release.*

The best time to obtain a model release is before or at the time the picture is taken. Such releases should be signed by parents or guardians if the subject involved is a minor. Public figures generally have little right of privacy and their photos may be reproduced in publications for informative purposes; they cannot be used for advertising, however, without the subject's permission. State laws on this subject differ, which makes it difficult to stipulate one set of rules that fit all conditions.

Another legal factor to be considered in taking photographs is libel. Truth is one defense for libel, but ridicule of a person or a poorly worded or erroneous caption may result in a libel suit. Generally speaking, news pictures used to report current happenings or to illustrate other items of public interest need not have the permission of the subject in order to be used. Sometimes the fine line between what is newsworthy and what is not may be difficult to draw.

Nudity and obscenity are two areas that have been the subject of many court cases. Laws vary from state to state, and even the very purpose for which the photograph is intended may decide whether such photographs are lawful or unlawful. Nude pictures in good taste are often published in magazines or displayed in art exhibits.

One way in which a photographer can prevent unauthorized use of his picture is to obtain a copyright from the Register of Copyrights, Library of Congress, Washington, D.C. Copyrights obtained after January 1, 1978 are for the life of the photographer plus 50 years. Any work that is copyrighted should include a notice of copyright in order to protect the photographer legally.

Because camera equipment is expensive, it should be adequately insured. The floater policy provides the greatest coverage. Other types of insurance a photographer should consider are household insurance, property damage, personal liability, and if the photographer is employing others, insurance against loss of funds by embezzlement.

Certain types of news events, especially those involving military accidents, police personnel, and government officials may be difficult for the photographer to cover because of restrictions made by the authorities in charge. He may also be prohibited from taking pictures in courtrooms or even outside the courtroom, because the factor of pretrial publicity is involved.

A photographer working for a publication does not need an occupation license; if he is doing some types of commercial work, however, he may be required to meet certain licensing and zoning laws of the municipality in which he lives.

Ethical Aspects

Certain precautions should be taken by photographers in order to maintain a good reputation. Even touching a subject may sometimes lead the subject to draw the wrong conclusions. It is always advisable for the male photographer to have another woman present when doing any type of cheesecake, portraiture, or similar type of photography where it may be necessary to rearrange any part of the costume, put the hair in place, and so on.

Even giving a picture to someone other than its subject can give rise to ethical and even legal problems.

Whether to publish gruesome pictures of a tragedy often depends on the decision of the editor rather than the photographer. Publication of such pictures is a matter of taste and not bound by any specific rules. The question is most often decided by the newsworthiness of the picture.

The photographer doing outside work for others should charge enough to cover his materials and time and to net him a profit. He should not attempt to undercut prices of professional photographers, since this is unethical as well as unsound business policy.

A Sample Model's Release

For value received, the receipt and adequacy of which are hereby acknowledged, I hereby give (name of firm or publication) the absolute right and permission to copyright and/or publish, and/or resell photographic portraits or pictures of me, or in which I may be included in whole or in part, for art, advertising, trade or any other lawful purpose whatsoever.

I hereby waive any right that I may have to inspect and/or approve the finished product or the advertising copy that may be used in connection therewith, or the use to which it may be applied.

I hereby release, discharge and agree to save (name of firm or publication) harmless from any liability by virtue of any blurring, distortion, alteration, optical illusion or use in composite form, whether intentional or otherwise, that may occur or be produced in the making of said pictures, or in any processing tending towards the completion of the finished product.

Date_____ Model_____

                              Address_____

                              _____

Witness_____

15. Federal Taxes and the Writer

by Patricia Ann Fox

The Tax Reform Act of 1976 made the most significant changes in the tax laws in almost 30 years, and Congress is already considering new changes. But if I can master enough tax-know-how under the present law to save money with my writing, so can you.

You must get your Internal Revenue Service Form 1040 completed and into the mail by April 15. Don't wait until April 14 to worry about it; keep records all year. When you tally up, let the figures tell the story, and take solace in the deductions.

What You'll Need

Receipts. For each pack of paper, typewriter ribbon, book, magazine or magazine subscription you buy in carrying out your profession as a writer, get a receipt and keep it.

Records. Pay bills by check and buy a ledger. (It's deductible.) No matter how tedious it may be at first, enter each expense accurately, systematically, and religiously. If you keep records hit and miss, the IRS will hit you hard and you'll miss a considerable saving on taxes.

What's Deductible

You may deduct all writing supplies, including paper, carbons, pens, ribbons, envelopes, copying costs, and postage. Repairs and maintenance of writing equipment, including typewriter, tape recorder, and camera are also deductible.

Courses and conferences you attended to enhance your professional knowledge can be deducted, too. It's important to realize, though, that you can't deduct courses you take to *become* a writer. The IRS rule is that courses must be "refresher" or professionally improving in nature to count. Besides deducting the costs of these, also deduct mileage (at 15c a mile) — or actual car expenses, whichever profits you most; cost of tickets for public transportation; cost of hotel/motel rooms; and cost of meals.

Also deduct dues for membership in writers' organizations and courses taken as research on subjects you're writing about. To establish that a course is for research, it would help if you had documentation from the potential publisher of your writings — such as a favorable response to a query. Even if the magazine does not publish what you've written, the response will show the research was done in good faith.

Home office expenses may be deducted. There's been an important change in this category, though. Many of us have been using a portion of a dining or living room to write in, and deducting a percentage for expenses, but this is no longer allowed. To take a home office deduction, you must have a portion of your dwelling set aside *solely* for writing on a *regular basis*. This same rule applies to a separate structure on your property.

For example, you may not use a portion of your garage for writing and a portion for parking your car. If your car goes in, your home office expense is out.

If you are using a room solely for writing, you will be able to deduct a portion for your rent and utilities.

Example: If you rent a five-room apartment for $200 a month and use one room exclusively for writing, you are entitled to deduct one-fifth of the rent, which comes to $40 a month, or $480 a year. Add to this one-fifth of your heating bill and one-fifth of your electric bill and watch the deductions mount up. Keep a list, too, of long-distance phone bills arising from your writing.

Note: There is a limit to home office expenses. You may not exceed in deductible expenses the amount of your gross income from writing. If you made $1,000 last year from writing, you can't deduct any more than that in home office expenses — no matter what your total expenses were.

In taking home office expenses, you must use the designated room as your principal place of business. (If you're only a part-time freelancer, you may have difficulties. IRS has yet to rule on this.)

If you own your home and use one room for writing, you can deduct the allocated expenses of operating that room. Among these allowable expenses are interest on mortgage, real estate taxes, repairs or additions to the home, cost of utilities, home insurance premiums, and depreciation on the room.

Example: If you own a seven-room house, one room used for writing, one-seventh of the total cost of the house can be depreciated, as well as one-seventh of the above mentioned expenses. Again, this must be your principal place of business, used solely for writing, and the deduction may not exceed your amount of gross income from writing.

Deductions for an addition to your home will require you to do more figuring than if you simply calculate for the cost of the unadded-to home.

Example: Let's say you have a ten room home which cost $50,000 and has a life expectancy of 50 years. One of these rooms is solely for your writing. Your yearly deduction would be $100. (One-tenth of the house cost = $5,000. Fifty years into this — $100.)

Now, if you add a $5,000 addition to your $50,000 home, the basis for calculation goes up to $55,000 — and your yearly allowable deduction increases to $110. If the addition cost $5,000 but has only a life expectancy of 25 years (shoddy materials, maybe) the total yearly deduction just for the addition would be $200. Your one-tenth share would be $20. You could deduct, then, $100 (depreciation on the original structure), plus $20 (depreciation on addition), or $120.

The only problem is finding a house so conducive to round-figure calculations.

Mileage

Take 15c a mile for the first 15,000 miles you travel on writing-related missions and ten cents a mile for miles traveled over 15,000. Or you may take the actual cost of operating your car — gas, oil, tires, maintenance and depreciation. (Instructions on figuring depreciation appear later in this chapter.) If you use your car 100% for writing, the total cost of operating it is deductible. If you use it only half-time for writing, then half the expenses are deductible.

Compare mileage deduction to cost deduction, and use the one that gives you the bigger break.

What May Be Depreciated:

You can count depreciation on your typewriter, desk, chair, lamps, tape recorder, files, camera equipment or anything else related to your writing which costs a considerable amount of money and has a useful life of more than one year. The easiest, most common method of depreciation for the writer is the straight line method.

In straight line, you take the depreciable basis (original cost of the asset minus the "salvage value"), divide by the number of useful years, and come up with the yearly depreciation deduction. The salvage value is what you could normally sell the item for after its estimated life of usefulness to you is over.

Example: Electric typewriter, purchased January, 1978 for $350. Estimated life, five years. Salvage value at end of five years, $50. Depreciation allowable for each year is $60. That's what you get when you divide the cost ($350), less salvage value ($50), by the estimated number of useful years (5).

Assets purchased later in the year are usually calculated only for the months you had them.

Example: Electric typewriter purchased in May, 1978 for $350. Estimated life, five years. Salvage value at end of five years, $50. Depreciation allowable for the year is $40. Since the asset was yours for only eight months, your depreciation was calculated by dividing 12 (months) into the yearly deduction of $60. This gives you five dollars a month. This five dollars multiplied by eight months gives you $40 in depreciation.

If salvage value is less than ten percent of your depreciable basis, you can disregard it for computation. However, you can't depreciate below salvage value.

Investment Tax Credit

The IRS allows an additional deduction for business equipment purchased during the year for which you're filing the return. This deduction, called an "investment tax credit," (ITC) comes off your tax liability and is allowed for newly purchased furniture, equipment, and other depreciable assets, except for real estate.

The amount of the credit is ten percent of the cost if the asset's useful life is seven years or more. If the useful life is three to five years, only one-third of the cost is eligible for ITC. Example: Desk bought for $100 — useful life, three to five years. Take one-third of the cost, $33 (forget the cents) and divide by the ten percent eligible for ITC. This equals a credit of $3.30.

If the asset's useful life is five to seven years, the investment tax credit is calculated on two-thirds of the cost. Thus, your $100 desk, if expected to live longer, has an ITC of $6.60.

Once the predicted useful life of an item goes to or beyond seven years, ten percent of the total cost may be deducted. Your $100 desk under this circumstance would yield a ten dollar deduction.

You get the entire investment tax credit on eligible items no matter what time during the year they were purchased.

Social Security Tax

If, after deductions, you earn $400 or more, you are required to pay a Social Security tax of 8.1% of your first $15,300 in earnings. And you must fill out and submit a Schedule SE (for "self-employment").

Tax Forms You Should Know

Many of us file Form 1040 joint return with spouse. As writers, we also file a Schedule C - Profit (or Loss) from Business or Profession, a Schedule SE for Social Security, a Form 3468 — Computation of Investment Credit, and often Schedules A and B (for itemized deductions, dividends and interest income).

Read these forms carefully; a careful reading will show how to provide the information asked for and the advantages for doing so.

When you keep accurate records throughout the year, save receipts and pay by check, preparing for your April 15 deadline won't be so bad.

Ends and Odds

Rejection slips. Keep them.

When the subject of rejection slips comes up at writers' conferences, the instructors generally frown and tell you to throw them away. Be done with them, they advise.

Not me. I advise you to pile the slips in a folder, carton, or spare room - somewhere you won't have to look at them, but where they are accessible should you be the featured guest at a tax audit. What better way to establish you're a working writer than to hit the IRS agent (not physically) with an avalanche of rejection slips or communiques from the publishers?

Encouraging letters? Hold onto them, too, for heaven's sake. And have your *ledger, receipts,* and *cancelled* checks ready. Audits, like toothaches, sometimes happen to the best of us.

Because of new 1976 rules on home office expenses, numerous accountants tell me that taking those expenses will invariably mean a tax audit. So I cannot stress too often that you must have a room just for writing and be able to prove that it is your principal place of business.

One final note: The examples used here are for guides only. Different requirements are made of people in different circumstances. For any long-term writing projects, such as novels or histories, which take more than a year to complete, consult Revenue Ruling 73-395. And remember that the laws keep changing, so be sure you have the latest IRS forms and instruction booklets.

16. State and Local Taxes And The Writer

by Forrest M. Mims

Many writers are not aware of the responsibilities of the freelancer to state and local laws governing operation of a profit-making business. While some regulatory laws are entirely reasonable, overzealous enforcement officials can create a difficult situation for the well-intentioned, but unknowing, freelancer.

I learned about state and local laws and taxes the hard way — through a form letter and threatening phone call from the New Mexico Bureau of Revenue. I was unpleasantly surprised to find that in my state:

1) A freelance writer, whether full or part time, operates a business and must register as such with the Bureau of Revenue.
2) A business must file monthly reports of all earnings for the previous 30 days.
3) A nonexempt business must pay the State of New Mexico a tax of four percent of its gross receipts.

The law provides certain exemptions and deductions for certain businesses and transactions. Failure to comply with the established reporting and payment procedures without intent to defraud means a ten percent penalty and six percent interest on all taxes due plus a minimum fee of five dollars for each month gross receipts are not reported. An attempt to defraud the State results in much stiffer fines and penalties.

Needless to say, these revelations ruined a few good writing days, particularly after a rude employee at the local office of the Bureau of Revenue threatened to obtain a court injunction against further operation of my writing business within the State of New Mexico unless I immediately registered and paid all back taxes, penalties, and interest. In two years of freelancing I had kept careful records of sales and expenses and made all the quarterly income tax and social security payments the United States Internal Revenue Service requires of self-employed persons. So I was very embarrassed to find myself labeled a tax evader.

A few days after the warning call I went downtown to register as a business. A week later a package arrived containing tax reporting forms, instructions, payment envelopes, and a registration certificate bearing the legend: "Display in a Conspicuous Place." From the instructions I learned of a requirement to obtain an occupation license from the city in which my business operates, pay the city an annual occupation tax of one dollar per every $1,000 of gross receipts, and visit the local zoning board to certify my operation qualifies as a legitimate and legal home operated business.

Having registered with city and State, I visited the law library of the University of New Mexico and found that since my articles are sold to out of state buyers they are interstate commerce and their proceeds can then be deducted from gross receipts in calculating tax due. That meant the most I would owe the State was tax and penalty on two $15 newspaper articles sold locally.

My initial protests to the Bureau of Revenue were of no avail. I was not selling a *product,* the Bureau maintained, but a *service,* and since the service was performed within the State of New Mexico interstate commerce was not even involved. A second trip to the law library revealed New Mexico law does indeed declare certain services performed for out of state buyers subject to the gross receipts tax. But the same law clearly provides: "Receipts from transactions in interstate commerce may be deducted from gross receipts to the extent that the imposition of the gross receipts tax would be unlawful under the United States Constitution." With this quote for ammunition and about ten dollars for long distance calls, I finally got a Bureau of Revenue official to verbally concede that my out of state sales were deductible from gross receipts.

But, he added, I would have to *prove* the sales were to out of state buyers. This calls for a complicated procedure wherein the seller (me) forwards a yellow colored form entitled "Application for Authority to Issue Nontaxable Transaction Certificates" from the State of New Mexico. Each time the seller makes a sale, the buyer must send copies of the certificates to the seller and the State, and, under penalty of law, maintain a copy in his records.

The entire procedure is as confusing as it is asinine. On a recent trip to New York I asked several editors what they would do with any State forms I sent in and the unanimous reply was they would toss them in the circular file. The proof procedure is particularly ludicrous in view of the fact it's simple to demonstrate out of state sales with a copy of individual books and magazines.

But the State of New Mexico takes this matter very seriously and my experience is fair warning to freelancers to check with their own local and state governments regarding regulations covering the writer's "business." The lesson here for other freelancers is to always be willing to comply with reasonable business registration and reporting requirements. But vigorously protest laws which unfairly harass writers and jeopardize their relationship with editors. Write local newspapers, elected officials, and university journalism departments. And keep *WRITER'S DIGEST* and national writer's associations informed.

Editorial Note: Writers are also cautioned to consult their local county clerk or city mayor's office to learn if there are any local ordinances covering the "business" of freelance writing. Some communities, for example, require an author who is using a pen name to file a report that he is doing business under a fictitious name.

Others have no such regulations and a freelance writer who wishes to use a pen name need only notify his postmaster that he will be receiving mail in his "business" name; and his bank that he will be receiving checks in that name.

Some states levy income taxes on freelance income; some states collect personal property or intangible taxes on author's royalties. For details on your state, contact the appropriate office below:

Attorney General
State of Alabama
State Administrative Building
Montgomery, Alabama 36130

Attorney General
American Samoa
P.O. Box 7
Pago Pago, American Samoa 96799

Attorney Genreal
State of Alaska
Pouch K, State Capitol
Juneau, Alaska 99811

Attorney General
State of Arizona
200 State Capitol Bldg.
Phoenix, Arizona 85007

Attorney General
State of Arkansas
Justice Building
Little Rock, Arkansas 72201

Attorney General
State of California
800 Tishman Bldg.
3580 Wilshire Blvd. (1)
Los Angeles, California 90010

Attorney General
State of Colorado
1525 Sherman St., 3rd Floor
Denver, Colorado 80203

Attorney General
State of Connecticut
Capitol Annex, 30 Trinity Street
Hartford, Connecticut 06115

Attorney General
State of Delaware
Wilmington Tower
Wilmington, Delaware 19801

Attorney General
State of Florida
State Capitol
Tallahassee, Florida 32304

Attorney General
State of Georgia
132 State Judicial Building
Atlanta, Georgia 30334

Attorney General
Guam
P.O. Box DA
Agana, Guam 96910

Attorney General
State of Hawaii
State Capitol
Honolulu, Hawaii 96813

Attorney General
State of Idaho
State Capitol
Boise, Idaho 83720

Attorney General
State of Illinois
500 South Second (2)
Springfield, Illinois 62701

Attorney General
State of Indiana
219 State House
Indianapolis, Indiana 46204

Attorney General
State of Iowa
State Capitol
Des Moines, Iowa 50319

Attorney General
State of Kansas
State House
Topeka, Kansas 66612

Attorney General
State of Kentucky
State Capitol
Frankfort, Kentucky 40601

Attorney General
State of Louisiana
234 Loyola Bldg., 7th Floor
New Orleans, Louisiana 70112

Attorney General
State of Maine
State House
Augusta, Maine 04330

Attorney General
State of Maryland
One South Calvert Street
Baltimore, Maryland 21202

Attorney General
State of Massachusetts
One Ashburton Place
Boston, Massachusetts 02108

Attorney General
State of Michigan
Law Building
Lansing, Michigan 48913

Attorney General
State of Minnesota
102 State Capitol
St. Paul, Minnesota 55155

Attorney General
State of Mississippi
Carroll Gartin Justice Building
P.O. Box 220
Jackson, Mississippi 39205

Attorney General
State of Missouri
Supreme Court Building
Jefferson City, Missouri 6510

Attorney General
State of Montana
State Capitol
Helena, Montana 59601

Attorney General
State of Nebraska
State Capitol
Lincoln, Nebraska 68509

Attorney General
State of Nevada
Supreme Court Building
Carson City, Nevada 89701

Attorney General
State of New Hampshire
208 State House Annex
Concord, New Hampshire 03301

Attorney General
State of New Jersey
State House Annex, 2nd Floor
Trenton, New Jersey 08625

Attorney General
State of New Mexico
Bataan Bldg., P.O. Box 1508
Santa Fe, New Mexico 87501

Attorney General
State of New York
No. 2, World Trade Center
New York, New York 10047

Attorney General
State of North Carolina
Justice Building, P.O. Box 629
Raleigh, North Carolina 27602

Attorney General
State of North Dakota
State Capitol
Bismarck, North Dakota 58505

Attorney General
State of Ohio
State Office Tower, 30 E. Broad St.
Columbus, Ohio 43215

Attorney General
State of Oklahoma
112 State Capitol
Oklahoma City, Oklahoma 73105

Attorney General
State of Oregon
100 State Office Building
Salem, Oregon 97310

Attorney General
State of Pennsylvania
Capitol Annex, Room No. 1
Harrisburg, Pennsylvania 17120

Attorney General
Puerto Rico
Dept. of Justice, P.O. Box 192
San Juan, Puerto Rico 00902

Attorney General
State of Rhode Island
Providence County Courthouse
Providence, Rhode Island 02903

Attorney General
State of South Carolina
Hampton Office Building
Columbia, South Carolina 29211

Attorney General
State of South Dakota
State Capitol
Pierre, South Dakota 57501

Attorney General
State of Tennessee
450 James Robertson Parkway
Nashville, Tennessee 37219

Attorney General
State of Texas
Capitol Station, P.O. Box 12548
Austin, Texas 78711

Attorney General
State of Utah
236 State Capitol
Salt Lake City, Utah 84114

Attorney General
State of Vermont
Pavilion Office Building
Montpelier, Vermont 05602

Attorney General
State of Virginia
Supreme Court — Library Building
Richmond, Virginia 23219

Attorney General
Virgin Islands
P.O. Box 280
St. Thomas, Virgin Islands 00801

Attorney General
State of Washington
Temple of Justice
Olympia, Washington 98504

Attorney General
State of West Virginia
State Capitol
Charleston, West Virginia 25305

Attorney General
State of Wisconsin
Dept. of Justice, State Capitol
Madison, Wisconsin 53702

Attorney General
State of Wyoming
123 State Capitol
Cheyenne, Wyoming 82001

17. Social Security and the Writer

by Louise Boggess

The freelance writer receives more than his money's worth from social security.

In 1951 Congress required self-employed writers — writers selling their literary work for profit — who earned a net of $400 or more a year to make social security contributions. Writers making such contributions must be writing continually; a one-time venture of short duration into freelance writing does not necessarily constitute a profession, even though the writer may be receiving royalties.

If you have actual net earnings of less than $400 from your writing and related activities but gross earnings of $600 or more, you may wish to consider figuring your net earnings under the optional method so you can get social security. You can use this method only if your actual net earnings amounted to $400 or more in at least two of the previous three years. You cannot use this method more than five times however, and it can only be used if net earnings are less than two-thirds of the gross income. Do not use this method to report an optional amount less than the actual net earnings.

Consider these refinements: When your gross income comes between $600 and $2,400, you may report either two-thirds of the gross income or your actual net earnings if $400 or more. If gross income reaches $2,400 or more and actual net earnings not more than $1,600, you may report either $1,600 or your actual net earnings. In case net earnings exceeded $1,600, you must report your actual net earnings. In this way you build up the amount you receive when you retire.

If you write only one book, or sell only an article or two as a sideline and never revise the book or produce more, your continued writing activities may not qualify you as a self-employed writer. While a majority of writers unquestionably qualify as self-employed.

many borderline cases do exist. Social security decides borderline cases on an individual basis.

Contributions

Your contributions to social security enable you to partially prepare for the day when varying circumstances reduce your income. You may think the salaried employee has the advantage over the self-employed writer because the employer pays half the contribution, but actually you receive favorable treatment too. You contribute 8.10% of your net earnings up to $16,500. On the other hand, an employee pays 6.05%. Remember you pay only on your net earning, and the employee pays on his full salary up to $16,500.

Of this 8.10% contribution, the Federal hospital insurance fund (Medicare) receives 1.10% and the social insurance funds 7.0%.

Qualifying Income

Social security favors the writer in determining qualifying income; you may also count net income from activities related to your writing. Many writers supplement their income by making personal appearances on tv or radio, lecturing, or doing manuscript criticisms. As long as the income flows from your writing production or related activities, you count this as part of your net earnings.

Instructing a class in writing may or may not come under self-employed income. You may count fees from instructing if you organize the writing class and pay the operating costs. When you offer a class through a college, however, you normally become an employee of the college. Some colleges now employ part-time instructors on an independent consultant or operator basis, however. Such earnings would come under self-employment income.

If you work full or part-time as an employee and write on the side, the law requires that you count your salary as an employee first and your net self-employment second toward the $16,500 limit. Suppose you earn $11,300 as an employee and a net of $6000 writing. You pay on the $11,300 first as an employee and then $5,200 of your net writing income. The other $800 from writing does not qualify for contributions toward your social security.

Insured Status

Although you make contributions on qualifying income, you cannot receive any social security benefits until you have attained an insured status. You acquire this insured status by contributing during a certain number of quarters. As a writer, you get a break on earning these quarters.

Ordinarily to receive credit for quarters the employee must earn $50 within the calendar quarters: January 1 to March 31, April 1 to June 30, July 1 to September 30, and October 1 to December 31. If you earn a net of $400 or more as a self-employed writer any time during the year, you receive credit in all four quarters.

When you earn credit for at least one and one-half years of work within three years before death, you become currently insured and your survivors may collect payments. As a self-employed writer, you more than qualify with two years of net earnings at $400 or more within this three-year period. But your currently insured status can expire if you stop writing for too long a period.

You become *fully insured* for life when your credits consist of 40 quarters of coverage or ten years of net earnings of $400 or more. You need not earn these quarters consecutively. Currently insured status entitles you to survivor benefits only.

Retirement Benefits

Most people think of social security in terms of retirement income. At age 65 (62 for reduced payments) you may qualify for monthly retirement benefits. A wife or dependent husband receives a pension equal to 50% of the retiree's check upon reaching the required retirement age, and under recent rulings from the Supreme Court, the husband of a woman writer can receive a benefit in retirement from her earnings. For example, some men work in civil service and do not get social security credit. By the wife being a writer, they are now entitled to 50% of their wives' retirement pay.

Suppose you have dependent minor children when you retire. ("Child" also includes adopted or stepchildren.) Your child under 18 years receives a check for 50% of your retirement pay. By attending college or an approved school fulltime, the payments continue until he reaches age 22. The mother under 65 who has dependent minor or disabled children in her care may also receive a benefit payment.

Payment

Social security electronically computes your benefit payments, but you may want to estimate your monthly payments yourself. The usual computation formula for retirement pay takes the year of your birth plus the number 62. Subtract 1951 from the sum of these two numbers and the resulting number is the number of years for which you will list earnings. You list each year even though you may have earned nothing, and you may eliminate any five years with little or no earnings. Total the earnings for the remaining years and divide the sum by the number of years.

Divide this average yearly wage by 12 for the monthly figure, then check this figure on the table following this article to estimate your cash payment. No matter how little you have earned, you will receive the minimum of $114.30 a month at age 65.

The retirement payment remains the same for the employee unless he goes back to work or Congress increases all social security benefits by law. The self-employed writer who has retired continues to make social security contributions as long as he earns a net of $400 or more a year. Periodically social security reviews your earnings record, and your monthly payment may increase.

The Earnings Test

The earnings test limits how much you can earn without having your retirement payments reduced. When an employee retires, he cannot earn more than $3,000 a year or $250 in a single month without having some of his payments reduced unless he has reached the age of 72. Social security judges a self-employed writer as retired, provided that he does not perform "substantial services" and not on the amount of earnings. You may retire as an employee, but then turn to writing. If so, you should change your status from *employee* to *self-employed* at the social security office.

Under substantial services, time becomes one of the determining factors. Generally, social security makes the decision on an individual basis since the law does not state how much time constitutes substantial services. Usually less than 45 hours a month does not constitute substantial services. To determine these hours of work, you must count researching, actual writing, and any other time spent in related literary production.

You may work as much as 45 hours a month provided you can submit evidence to establish you have not performed substantial services. On the other hand, suppose you have developed exceptional ability, and your writing commands a high price although you work as little as 20 hours a month. Social security may decide you perform substantial services and reduce your monthly check accordingly. Consequently high earnings do not necessarily constitute substantial services nor do low ones exempt you.

In determining substantial services, social security also considers the kind of work you do and how your present hours compare to those in the past at full production. You should keep a record of the amount of hours you spend in full production for several years before you retire, so social security can more accurately determine whether you are performing substantial services.

If an employee earns more than $3,000 or $250 in one month, social security reduces the payment one dollar for each two dollars. A retired writer may earn up to $10,000 or more and not perform substantial services. Should social security decide the retired writer did perform substantial services, he pays the reduction on the net earnings — not the gross as does the retired employee. After age 72 the earnings test does not apply.

The self-employed writer gets another consideration in regard to royalties. If you do not retire until you are 65, royalties from any previous literary sale do not count toward substantial services. For example, you may have sold a book before you retired. After your retirement it sold to the movies and TV. Since the copyright predated your retirement, these sales from subsidiary rights do not constitute substantial services for the earnings test.

Earnings Record

The prudent writer checks his social security record every three years, and social security provides a special double postal card for this purpose. You can make corrections other than clerical errors only within three years, three months, and 15 days following the calender year in which you earned the money.

If you find errors in your earnings record, contact the local social security office. Usually you verify your earnings with your Internal Revenue miscellaneous forms or other such proof of your income.

Other Insurance Programs

Too many people think of social security only as old age retirement, but actually you earn protection in three other social insurance programs: medicare, disability, and survivors. Since social security primarily protects the family from loss of income, the married person receives more extensive protection or returns than the single one.

Medicare. Medicare constitutes an important protection for the older person. At 65 you and your spouse become eligible for hospital insurance if you qualify for social security retirement pay during your working years. Medicare provides 90 days of inpatient care in any participating hospital in each benefit period. For the first 60 days, medicare pays for all covered services except for the first $124. For the 61st through the 90th day, it pays for all covered services except $31 a day. Everyone has a reserve of 60 additional inpatient days. For further benefits check with your social security office.

For a payment of $7.70 each a month you and your spouse can also receive medical insurance that helps pay physician's services, outpatient services, and other medical expenses. In this insurance you pay the first $60 (the annual deductible) in reasonable charges for expenses, and medical insurance will pay 80% of the reasonable charges for services for that year. Again, check with your local social security office for more details.

Disability. Disability insurance offers the writer under 65 the greatest protection. In case of certain illnesses or injuries that last a year or more, you may qualify for disability payments which continue until you can engage in "substantial gainful employment."

The earnings of a self-employed writer receive less consideration in determining ability to engage in substantial gainful activity. You may perform sufficient work but other factors reduce the amount of income. Suppose you work long hours, but do not sell much of what you write. The length of time you worked regardless of the income may show you can engage in substantial gainful employment.

To determine the amount of your disability payment, social security averages your earnings during the previous working years as for retirement computation. You draw this amount until you can return to work. In addition your dependent spouse, minor or disabled children receive payments.

The law has always recognized a child's dependency on the father, but it now accords this same dependent status of the child on the mother. This recognition becomes an important factor in disability insurance for women. Suppose you are a housewife who sells enough of your writing to pay social security. If you become disabled, you and your minor or disabled children can draw disability payments. The local social security office can provide you with more details.

To qualify for disability, you must meet the following requirements:

Before age 24 you need work credit for one and one-half years in the three-year period ending when the disability began.

From age 24 to 30 years you need credit for working half the time between 21 and the time you became disabled; for 31 years or older, you need at least five years of work out of ten ending when you became disabled and if you have fully insured status. If you are a disabled person who qualified for disability benefits two consecutive years or more, you will get hospital insurance automatically.

Survivors. A surviving widow or dependent widower receives 82 1/2% of the deceased's payments at age 62 (100% at age 65). A physically or mentally disabled widow or dependent widower may draw reduced payments between ages 50 and 62.

A widow with a dependent minor child under 18 or a disabled child over 18 in her care qualifies for mother's insurance payments. A surviving dependent minor or disabled child receives 75% of the deceased's pension or disability.

A person who contributed one-half or more to the support of parent or parents may make them eligible for survivor's payments. Social security computes the earnings according to the same process as retirement, listing the earnings years between age 21 and time of death. One dependent parent receives 82 1/2% of this amount but two parents are paid 75% each. A worker's grandchildren become eligible for survivor payments if the natural parents are disabled or dead, provided the grandchildren live with and are supported by the grandparent.

None of these benefits come to you unless you make application for them at the appropriate time; you could lose money by delaying application. The local social security office can provide this information and any other which pertains to you individually as a writer. Remember, the government does not give you these social security benefits — you *pay* for them during your productive years.

Examples of monthly social security payments (effective June 1977)

Average yearly earnings after 1950 covered by social security

Benefits can be paid to a:	$923 or less	$3,000	$4,000	$5,000	$6,000	$8,000*	$10,000*
Retired worker at 65	114.30	236.40	278.10	322.50	364.50	453.10	502.00
Worker under 65 and disabled	114.30	236.40	278.10	322.50	364.50	453.10	502.00
Retired worker at 62	91.50	189.20	222.50	258.00	291.60	362.50	401.60
Wife or husband at 65	57.20	118.20	139.10	161.30	182.30	226.60	251.00
Wife or husband at 62	42.90	88.70	104.40	121.00	136.80	170.00	188.30
Wife under 65 and one child in her care	57.20	125.00	197.20	272.60	304.20	339.80	376.60
Widow or widower at 65 if worker never received reduced benefits	114.30	236.40	278.10	322.50	364.50	453.10	502.00
Widow or widower at 60 if sole survivor	81.80	169.10	198.90	230.60	260.70	324.00	359.00
Widow or widower at 50 and disabled if sole survivor	57.30	118.30	139.20	161.30	182.40	226.60	251.10
Widow or widower with one child in care	171.50	354.60	417.20	483.80	546.80	679.80	753.00
Maximum family payment	171.50	361.40	475.30	595.10	668.60	792.90	878.50

*Maximum earnings covered by social security were lower in past years and must be included in figuring your average earnings. This average determines your payment amount. Because of this, amounts shown in the last two columns generally won't be payable until future years. The maximum retirement benefit generally payable to a worker who is 65 in 1977 is 437.10.

18. Retirement Funds for the Writer

by Grace W. Weinstein

With but ten days remaining to the calendar year I decided it might be wise to put a portion of my freelance earnings into a Keogh self-funded retirement plan. All the advertisements — you've seen them too — make it seem an easy procedure: take up to fifteen per cent off the top of your net earnings, put it in a retirement fund and don't pay taxes on either principal or interest until after retirement when, presumably, your tax bracket will be lower.

It is easy to execute a Keogh Plan, I found, but not so easy to select one. The almost bewildering variety of funding approaches available necessitates careful evaluation of each plan in light of your individual objectives, philosophy and needs. Herewith are the fruits of my research, to help you select the right plan for you.

The "Self-Employed Individuals Tax Retirement Act," usually called the Keogh Act after its most prominent sponsor, New York Representative Eugene Keogh, was initially enacted in 1962. It is designed to permit the self-employed individual whose business is based on personal service — doctors, architects, hairdressers and, of course, writers — to defer paying tax on a specific portion of income set aside in a retirement fund, much the way corporate employers provide retirement pensions for their employees. It has become increasingly popular in recent years, with liberalizations of the law — and the possible tax benefits — in 1966, 1974 and again in 1976.

In brief, the Keogh Plan provides that you, as your own employer (an "owner-employee"), may set aside in an Internal Revenue Service-approved fund, up to 15% of your net earned income each year, to a maximum of $7,500. Alternatively, under a more complex and little-known provision of the 1974 law, you can establish a "defined-benefit" plan under which you stipulate the amount of monthly pension you want to receive, subject to a formula based on current age and income, and contribute whatever amounts are necessary to provide that income. Since the IRS has not yet issued its regulations on defined benefit plans and since few writers, unfortunately, are in a position to contribute more than $7,500 to a retirement plan, we will stick to a description of the more common "defined-contribution" plan where contributions are limited to 15% of your net earned income each year or $7,500.

If you're not doing so well one year, you may still make a minimum contribution: 100% of earned income or $750, whichever is less. If, on the other hand, you are doing well enough to hire a secretary or a researcher for more than 20 hours a week(or 1,000 hours in a twelve-month period), you must include that employee in your plan as well, with contributions based on the same formula as your own. Since most writers go it alone, however, we won't go into the ramifications covering employees.

How It Works

Writer John Doe, for example, who holds down a fulltime job in advertising but freelances on the side, had $3,600 in net income from his freelancing in his last tax year, after deductions for business expenses — stationery, postage, and transportation to interviews. (Under the 1976 Tax Reform Act expenses for an office at home cannot be deducted unless that office is the individual's principal place of business and is used exclusively for business — not also as an extra bedroom or family den. *Writer's Digest* and the Author's League argue that a moonlighting freelance writer's office *is* his principal place of business, but the IRS has not yet ruled on his particular question.)

Although he has a pension plan at his fulltime job, John is particularly eager to build up retirement benefits for himself. Fifteen per cent of $3,600 is $540 but, under the new law, John can and does make a minimum contribution of $750. (While some freelancers feel it is not worth bothering with a retirement plan unless income is substantial, I disagree. If you can put away even a hundred dollars each year without paying taxes on it and then accrue non-taxable interest on that sum, it adds up over the years. And if you keep at it, your income from writing is bound to increase, so why not start small?)

Robert Roe, who is working as a freelancer fulltime, had a net income of $8,500 last year. He took 15% of the $8,500 net and invested $1,275 toward his retirement. Book author Sally Smith, who had a good year and earned $52,000 after deductions, is permitted to invest only the maximum of $7,500.

Whatever the amount, up to the maximum stipulated by the law, your total contribution is tax-deductible. This means, in essence, double benefits since taxes are deferred until after retirement on both the principal and the interest, an advantage over any other possible form of investment. You may begin to withdraw the funds after you reach 59 1/2; you must begin distribution by age 70 1/2. You can keep on working after 70 1/2, and making contributions to your fund, but the IRS insists that you begin to draw on your retirement income at that point.

If your income should continue to grow as you move into your 70s you would not, of course, have the tax benefit that accrues to someone who falls into a much lower tax bracket upon retirement. It may still be worthwhile, however, since you can minimize the tax bite by electing disbursement of the fund over a period of years, either in cash payments or in the form of an annuity. That decision can be deferred until you know what your retirement status will be.

In the meantime contributions can vary from year to year, as your income varies, and can be made whether you are self-employed fulltime or part-time. If you are employed but your employer has no pension plan, you may open an Individual Retirement Account.

The Individual Retirement Account (IRA)

As Keogh Plans are designed for the self-employed, IRAs are designed for people who are employed by companies with no retirement benefits. With an IRA you may contribute a tax-deductible sum of 15% of your earned income, to a maximum of $1,500 a year. Under the Tax Reform Act of 1976 you may, if you have a non working spouse, contribute a maximum of 15% or $1,750, with $875 in each of two IRAs or in subaccounts under a single IRA. Keogh and IRA provisions are similar, but not identical; this article deals primarily with Keogh Plans.

When you calculate your income tax each year you also calculate the amount you can deposit in your retirement fund. Advance contributions may be made on an estimated basis, as long as you come out even at the end; excess contributions will no longer disqualify the plan, but they are subject to a six percent excise tax. New legislation makes life a little easier: instead of having to calculate net income precisely before the end of the year, never quite knowing whether an anticipated check will actually arrive on time, you now have until the date you file your tax return for the tax year. Your Keogh contributions for 1978, in other words, may be made right up to April 15, 1979, with the allowable deduction taken on your 1978 return. Of course, the earlier you make your contribution (or part of your contribution), the sooner it will start to earn tax-sheltered interest.

One nice point: if there should be a year when you have no income from writing — either because you decided to take a paying job or because you were just plain unlucky — you need make no contributions; your prior contributions continue to earn interest and your plan remains in force.

Where the Money Can Go

Now that you know the basic plan, what are your options? Keogh Plan savings can be invested in an almost infinite variety of ways; you must select the one which will best meet your personal objectives. Is security paramount? Or are you willing to take some risks with their chance of greater gain?

You must name a trustee which, unless all funds are invested in some form of insurance, must be a bank or savings institution. (The only requirement when purchasing insurance or annuity contracts as a retirement plan, is that the insurance company have a master plan already approved by Internal Revenue. You then become part of their plan. No trustee is needed.)

But banks can invest your funds, at your direction, in the stock market, real estate, corporate or municipal bonds, mutual funds, life insurance or annuities, a savings account — or various combinations thereof. You might choose a split fund approach and invest part of your principal in an annuity policy, for instance, with the rest in a mutual fund.

Citibank, in New York, has a plan wherein the fund is invested in a combination of stocks and bonds; the participant selects the ratio of stocks to bonds and the bank makes the actual investment. The individual's money is merged with that of many others in a large investment fund so that even a relatively small contribution can be applied in this manner. The investment ratio in this and other split fund plans can be altered from time to time, as you wish or your changing needs dictate.

The American Council of Life Insurance points out that the tax shelter provisions of Keogh favor funding instruments that accrue substantial gains. If you are in your 30s, say, and can afford to look at the long-term prospects of the stock market, you might want to chance speculative investment of your retirement funds, protecting yourself by putting a portion of the money into insurance.

Truly adventurous individuals may elect to manage their stock market transactions themselves. Merrill Lynch, the nation's largest brokerage house, has an IRS-approved program under which an owner-employee directs investment of his own funds, although there is a bank as a trustee. This is not necessarily a good idea, however, unless you have both investment expertise and the time to take from your writing to devote to the stock market.

At the opposite end of the investment spectrum are two more conservative approaches: the bank savings account and United States Retirement Plan Bonds. Both offer stability in lieu of possible gains. The interest rate on government retirement bonds (not to be confused with United States Government Savings Bonds) is now 6%; most savings accounts now earn 5.25%, and time deposit accounts offer guaranteed interest rates of 5.75 to 7.75% for periods of one to six years. Since you can't withdraw the funds before age 59 1/2 anyway, a six-year deposit may make sense.

There are no management fees with government retirement bonds or with most savings accounts, as there may be under more complex investment methods. If you elect a stock plan, of course, brokerage commissions must be paid. And if you put your funds toward an annuity there may be substantial administrative costs in the early years.

Whatever funding medium you select, your trustee should have a master or prototype plan which has been approved by the IRS. You can write your own, but the legal ramifications are complex. You should, in any event, be able to find an approved plan to meet your needs. With an approved plan, all you need do is execute a trust agreement, naming your beneficiary, to get your plan under way. Then, at tax time, you must file IRS forms to substantiate your deductible contributions.

A possible disadvantage to Keogh Plan investment is that your funds are virtually frozen until you reach 59 1/2, unless you become permanently disabled and unable to work. Even if you give up freelancing altogether and take a job, terminating your plan, your funds will remain untouchable; of course they will continue to accrue tax-sheltered interest. The opposite side of this coin is that your funds are protected; they cannot be attached by a creditor or an irate spouse.

If you have sufficient working capital and anticipated income so that you should not need the funds before that magic age, retirement planning does offer many advantages. Some prudent souls do manage to put aside money for retirement without a formal plan but most financial authorities agree that the tax shelter provisions of Keogh (and IRA as well) allow money to accumulate at a more impressive rate — as well as being a form of mandatory savings.

Whether you earn $5,000 or $50,000 from your freelancing, a Keogh Plan may be just what you need. Evaluate your overall objectives and your anticipated — or hoped-for — increases in writing income, then talk over your financial situation with a trusted financial adviser, accountant, lawyer, insurance agent or stockbroker. Booklets spelling out details of Keogh and IRA plans are available from many banks, savings and loan associations and other financial institutions. When you've selected the best plan, go ahead . . . you'll be glad you did at retirement age!

The New (1978) Copyright Law

Public Law 94-553
94th Congress

An Act

Oct. 19, 1976
[S. 22]

For the general revision of the Copyright Law, title 17 of the United States Code, and for other purposes.

Title 17, USC,
Copyrights.

Be it enacted by the Senate and House of Representatives of the United States of America in Congress assembled,

TITLE I—GENERAL REVISION OF COPYRIGHT LAW

SEC. 101. Title 17 of the United States Code, entitled "Copyrights", is hereby amended in its entirety to read as follows:

TITLE 17—COPYRIGHTS

Chapter 1.—SUBJECT MATTER AND SCOPE OF COPYRIGHT

111. Limitations on exclusive rights: Secondary transmissions.
112. Limitations on exclusive rights: Ephemeral recordings.
113. Scope of exclusive rights in pictorial, graphic, and sculptural works.
114. Scope of exclusive rights in sound recordings.
115. Scope of exclusive rights in nondramatic musical works: Compulsory license for making and distributing phonorecords.
116. Scope of exclusive rights in nondramatic musical works: Public performances by means of coin-operated phonorecord players.
117. Scope of exclusive rights: Use in conjunction with computers and similar information systems.
118. Scope of exclusive rights: Use of certain works in connection with noncommercial broadcasting.

§ 101. Definitions

17 USC 101.

As used in this title, the following terms and their variant forms mean the following:

An "anonymous work" is a work on the copies or phonorecords of which no natural person is identified as author.

"Audiovisual works" are works that consist of a series of related images which are intrinsically intended to be shown by the use of machines or devices such as projectors, viewers, or electronic equipment, together with accompanying sounds, if any, regardless of the nature of the material objects, such as films or tapes, in which the works are embodied.

The "best edition" of a work is the edition, published in the United States at any time before the date of deposit, that the Library of Congress determines to be most suitable for its purposes.

A person's "children" are that person's immediate offspring, whether legitimate or not, and any children legally adopted by that person.

A "collective work" is a work, such as a periodical issue, anthology, or encyclopedia, in which a number of contributions, constituting separate and independent works in themselves, are assembled into a collective whole.

A "compilation" is a work formed by the collection and assembling of preexisting materials or of data that are selected, coordinated, or arranged in such a way that the resulting work as a whole constitutes an original work of authorship. The term "compilation" includes collective works.

"Copies" are material objects, other than phonorecords, in which a work is fixed by any method now known or later developed, and from which the work can be perceived, reproduced, or otherwise communicated, either directly or with the aid of a machine or device. The term "copies" includes the material object, other than a phonorecord, in which the work is first fixed.

"Copyright owner", with respect to any one of the exclusive rights comprised in a copyright, refers to the owner of that particular right.

A work is "created" when it is fixed in a copy or phonorecord for the first time; where a work is prepared over a period of time, the portion of it that has been fixed at any particular time constitutes the work as of that time, and where the work has been prepared in different versions, each version constitutes a separate work.

A "derivative work" is a work based upon one or more preexisting works, such as a translation, musical arrangement, dramatization, fictionalization, motion picture version, sound recording, art reproduction, abridgment, condensation, or any other form in which a work may be recast, transformed, or adapted. A work consisting of editorial revisions, annotations, elaborations, or other modifications which, as a whole, represent an original work of authorship, is a "derivative work".

A "device", "machine", or "process" is one now known or later developed.

To "display" a work means to show a copy of it, either directly or by means of a film, slide, television image, or any other device or process or, in the case of a motion picture or other audiovisual work, to show individual images nonsequentially.

A work is "fixed" in a tangible medium of expression when its embodiment in a copy or phonorecord, by or under the authority of the author, is sufficiently permanent or stable to permit it to be perceived, reproduced, or otherwise communicated for a period of more than transitory duration. A work consisting of sounds, images, or both, that are being transmitted, is "fixed" for purposes of this title if a fixation of the work is being made simultaneously with its transmission.

The terms "including" and "such as" are illustrative and not limitative.

A "joint work" is a work prepared by two or more authors with the intention that their contributions be merged into inseparable or interdependent parts of a unitary whole.

"Literary works" are works, other than audiovisual works, expressed in words, numbers, or other verbal or numerical symbols or indicia, regardless of the nature of the material objects, such as books, periodicals, manuscripts, phonorecords, film, tapes, disks, or cards, in which they are embodied.

"Motion pictures" are audiovisual works consisting of a series of related images which, when shown in succession, impart an impression of motion, together with accompanying sounds, if any.

To "perform" a work means to recite, render, play, dance, or act it, either directly or by means of any device or process or, in the case of a motion picture or other audiovisual work, to show its images in any sequence or to make the sounds accompanying it audible.

"Phonorecords" are material objects in which sounds, other than those accompanying a motion picture or other audiovisual work, are fixed by any method now known or later developed, and from which the sounds can be perceived, reproduced, or otherwise communicated, either directly or with the aid of a machine or device. The term "phonorecords" includes the material object in which the sounds are first fixed.

"Pictorial, graphic, and sculptural works" include two-dimensional and three-dimensional works of fine, graphic, and applied art, photographs, prints and art reproductions, maps, globes, charts, technical drawings, diagrams, and models. Such works shall include works of artistic craftsmanship insofar as their form but not their mechanical or utilitarian aspects are concerned; the design of a useful article, as defined in this section, shall be considered a pictorial, graphic, or sculptural work only if, and only to the extent that, such design incorporates pictorial, graphic, or sculptural features that can be identified separately from, and are capable of existing independently of, the utilitarian aspects of the article.

A "pseudonymous work" is a work on the copies or phonorecords of which the author is identified under a fictitious name.

"Publication" is the distribution of copies or phonorecords of a work to the public by sale or other transfer of ownership, or by rental, lease, or lending. The offering to distribute copies or phonorecords to a group of persons for purposes of further distribution, public performance, or public display, constitutes publication. A public performance or display of a work does not of itself constitute publication.

To perform or display a work "publicly" means—
    (1) to perform or display it at a place open to the public or at any place where a substantial number of persons outside of a normal circle of a family and its social acquaintances is gathered; or
    (2) to transmit or otherwise communicate a performance or display of the work to a place specified by clause (1) or to the public, by means of any device or processs, whether the members of the public capable of receiving the performance or display receive it in the same place or in separate places and at the same time or at different times.

"Sound recordings" are works that result from the fixation of a series of musical, spoken, or other sounds, but not including the sounds accompanying a motion picture or other audiovisual work, regardless of the nature of the material objects, such as disks, tapes, or other phonorecords, in which they are embodied.

"State" includes the District of Columbia and the Commonwealth of Puerto Rico, and any territories to which this title is made applicable by an Act of Congress.

A "transfer of copyright ownership" is an assignment, mortgage, exclusive license, or any other conveyance, alienation, or hypothecation of a copyright or of any of the exclusive rights comprised in a copyright, whether or not it is limited in time or place of effect, but not including a nonexclusive license.

A "transmission program" is a body of material that, as an aggregate, has been produced for the sole purpose of transmission to the public in sequence and as a unit.

To "transmit" a performance or display is to communicate it by any device or process whereby images or sounds are received beyond the place from which they are sent.

The "United States", when used in a geographical sense, comprises the several States, the District of Columbia and the Commonwealth of Puerto Rico, and the organized territories under the jurisdiction of the United States Government.

A "useful article" is an article having an intrinsic utilitarian function that is not merely to portray the appearance of the article or to convey information. An article that is normally a part of a useful article is considered a "useful article".

The author's "widow" or "widower" is the author's surviving spouse under the law of the author's domicile at the time of his or her death, whether or not the spouse has later remarried.

A "work of the United States Government" is a work prepared by an officer or employee of the United States Government as part of that person's official duties.

A "work made for hire" is—

  (1) a work prepared by an employee within the scope of his or her employment: or

  (2) a work specially ordered or commissioned for use as a contribution to a collective work, as a part of a motion picture or other audiovisual work, as a translation, as a supplementary work, as a compilation, as an instructional text, as a test, as answer material for a test, or as an atlas, if the parties expressly agree in a written instrument signed by them that the work shall be considered a work made for hire. For the purpose of the foregoing sentence. a "supplementary work" is a work prepared for publication as a secondary adjunct to a work by another author for the purpose of introducing, concluding, illustrating, explaining, revising, commenting upon, or assisting in the use of the other work, such as forewords. afterwords, pictorial illustrations, maps, charts, tables, editorial notes, musical arrangements, answer material for tests, bibliographies. appendixes, and indexes, and an "instructional text" is a literary, pictorial, or graphic work prepared for publication and with the purpose of use in systematic instructional activities.

17 USC 102. § 102. Subject matter of copyright: In general

  (a) Copyright protection subsists, in accordance with this title, in original works of authorship fixed in any tangible medium of expression, now known or later developed, from which they can be perceived, reproduced, or otherwise communicated, either directly or with the aid of a machine or device. Works of authorship include the following categories:

Works of authorship.

(1) literary works;
(2) musical works, including any accompanying words;
(3) dramatic works, including any accompanying music;
(4) pantomimes and choreographic works;
(5) pictorial, graphic, and sculptural works;
(6) motion pictures and other audiovisual works; and
(7) sound recordings.

(b) In no case does copyright protection for an original work of authorship extend to any idea, procedure, process, system, method of operation, concept, principle, or discovery, regardless of the form in which it is described, explained, illustrated, or embodied in such work.

§ 103. **Subject matter of copyright: Compilations and derivative works**

17 USC 103.

(a) The subject matter of copyright as specified by section 102 includes compilations and derivative works, but protection for a work employing preexisting material in which copyright subsists does not extend to any part of the work in which such material has been used unlawfully.

(b) The copyright in a compilation or derivative work extends only to the material contributed by the author of such work, as distinguished from the preexisting material employed in the work, and does not imply any exclusive right in the preexisting material. The copyright in such work is independent of, and does not affect or enlarge the scope, duration, ownership, or subsistence of, any copyright protection in the preexisting material.

§ 104. **Subject matter of copyright: National origin**

17 USC 104.

(a) UNPUBLISHED WORKS.—The works specified by sections 102 and 103, while unpublished, are subject to protection under this title without regard to the nationality or domicile of the author.

(b) PUBLISHED WORKS.—The works specified by sections 102 and 103, when published, are subject to protection under this title if—

(1) on the date of first publication, one or more of the authors is a national or domiciliary of the United States, or is a national, domiciliary, or sovereign authority of a foreign nation that is a party to a copyright treaty to which the United States is also a party, or is a stateless person, wherever that person may be domiciled; or

(2) the work is first published in the United States or in a foreign nation that, on the date of first publication, is a party to the Universal Copyright Convention; or

(3) the work is first published by the United Nations or any

of its specialized agencies, or by the Organization of American States; or

(4) the work comes within the scope of a Presidential proclamation. Whenever the President finds that a particular foreign nation extends, to works by authors who are nationals or domiciliaries of the United States or to works that are first published in the United States, copyright protection on substantially the same basis as that on which the foreign nation extends protection to works of its own nationals and domiciliaries and works first published in that nation, the President may by proclamation extend protection under this title to works of which one or more of the authors is, on the date of first publication, a national, domiciliary, or sovereign authority of that nation, or which was first published in that nation. The President may revise, suspend, or revoke any such proclamation or impose any conditions or limitations on protection under a proclamation.

17 USC 105. **§ 105. Subject matter of copyright: United States Government works**

Copyright protection under this title is not available for any work of the United States Government, but the United States Government is not precluded from receiving and holding copyrights transferred to it by assignment, bequest, or otherwise.

17 USC 106. **§ 106. Exclusive rights in copyrighted works**

Subject to sections 107 through 118, the owner of copyright under this title has the exclusive rights to do and to authorize any of the following:

(1) to reproduce the copyrighted work in copies or phonorecords;

(2) to prepare derivative works based upon the copyrighted work;

(3) to distribute copies or phonorecords of the copyrighted work to the public by sale or other transfer of ownership, or by rental, lease, or lending;

(4) in the case of literary, musical, dramatic, and choreographic works, pantomimes, and motion pictures and other audiovisual works, to perform the copyrighted work publicly; and

(5) in the case of literary, musical, dramatic, and choreographic works, pantomimes, and pictorial, graphic, or sculptural works, including the individual images of a motion picture or other audiovisual work, to display the copyrighted work publicly.

17 USC 107. **§ 107. Limitations on exclusive rights: Fair use**

Notwithstanding the provisions of section 106, the fair use of a copyrighted work, including such use by reproduction in copies or phonorecords or by any other means specified by that section, for purposes such as criticism, comment, news reporting, teaching

(including multiple copies for classroom use), scholarship, or research, is not an infringement of copyright. In determining whether the use made of a work in any particular case is a fair use the factors to be considered shall include—
>   (1) the purpose and character of the use, including whether such use is of a commercial nature or is for nonprofit educational purposes;
>   (2) the nature of the copyrighted work;
>   (3) the amount and substantiality of the portion used in relation to the copyrighted work as a whole; and
>   (4) the effect of the use upon the potential market for or value of the copyrighted work.

§ 108. Limitations on exclusive rights: Reproduction by libraries and archives

17 USC 108.

(a) Notwithstanding the provisions of section 106, it is not an infringement of copyright for a library or archives, or any of its employees acting within the scope of their employment, to reproduce no more than one copy or phonorecord of a work, or to distribute such copy or phonorecord, under the conditions specified by this section, if—
>   (1) the reproduction or distribution is made without any purpose of direct or indirect commercial advantage;
>   (2) the collections of the library or archives are (i) open to the public, or (ii) available not only to researchers affiliated with the library or archives or with the institution of which it is a part, but also to other persons doing research in a specialized field; and
>   (3) the reproduction or distribution of the work includes a notice of copyright.

(b) The rights of reproduction and distribution under this section apply to a copy or phonorecord of an unpublished work duplicated in facsimile form solely for purposes of preservation and security or for deposit for research use in another library or archives of the type described by clause (2) of subsection (a), if the copy or phonorecord reproduced is currently in the collections of the library or archives.

(c) The right of reproduction under this section applies to a copy or phonorecord of a published work duplicated in facsimile form solely for the purpose of replacement of a copy or phonorecord that is damaged, deteriorating, lost, or stolen, if the library or archives has, after a reasonable effort, determined that an unused replacement cannot be obtained at a fair price.

(d) The rights of reproduction and distribution under this section apply to a copy, made from the collection of a library or archives where the user makes his or her request or from that of another library or archives, of no more than one article or other contribution to a copyrighted collection or periodical issue, or to a copy or phonorecord

of a small part of any other copyrighted work, if—
    (1) the copy or phonorecord becomes the property of the user, and the library or archives has had no notice that the copy or phonorecord would be used for any purpose other than private study, scholarship, or research; and
    (2) the library or archives displays prominently, at the place where orders are accepted, and includes on its order form, a warning of copyright in accordance with requirements that the Register of Copyrights shall prescribe by regulation.
  (e) The rights of reproduction and distribution under this section apply to the entire work, or to a substantial part of it, made from the collection of a library or archives where the user makes his or her request or from that of another library or archives, if the library or archives has first determined, on the basis of a reasonable investigation, that a copy or phonorecord of the copyrighted work cannot be obtained at a pair price, if—
    (1) the copy or phonorecord becomes the property of the user, and the library or archives has had no notice that the copy or phonorecord would be used for any purpose other than private study, scholarship, or research; and
    (2) the library or archives displays prominently, at the place where orders are accepted, and includes on its order form, a warning of copyright in accordance with requirements that the Register of Copyrights shall prescribe by regulation.
  (f) Nothing in this section—
    (1) shall be construed to impose liability for copyright infringement upon a library or archives or its employees for the unsupervised use of reproducing equipment located on its premises: *Provided*, That such equipment displays a notice that the making of a copy may be subject to the copyright law;
    (2) excuses a person who uses such reproducing equipment or who requests a copy or phonorecord under subsection (d) from liability for copyright infringement for any such act, or for any later use of such copy or phonorecord, if it exceeds fair use as provided by section 107;
    (3) shall be construed to limit the reproduction and distribution by lending of a limited number of copies and excerpts by a library or archives of an audiovisual news program, subject to clauses (1), (2), and (3) of subsection (a); or
    (4) in any way affects the right of fair use as provided by section 107, or any contractual obligations assumed at any time by the library or archives when it obtained a copy or phonorecord of a work in its collections.
  (g) The rights of reproduction and distribution under this section extend to the isolated and unrelated reproduction or distribution of a single copy or phonorecord of the same material on separate occasions, but do not extend to cases where the library or archives, or its employee—

(1) is aware or has substantial reason to believe that it is engaging in the related or concerted reproduction or distribution of multiple copies or phonorecords of the same material, whether made on one occasion or over a period of time, and whether intended for aggregate use by one or more individuals or for separate use by the individual members of a group; or

(2) engages in the systematic reproduction or distribution of single or multiple copies or phonorecords of material described in subsection (d) : *Provided*, That nothing in this clause prevents a library or archives from participating in interlibrary arrangements that do not have, as their purpose or effect, that the library or archives receiving such copies or phonorecords for distribution does so in such aggregate quantities as to substitute for a subscription to or purchase of such work.

(h) The rights of reproduction and distribution under this section do not apply to a musical work, a pictorial, graphic or sculptural work, cr a motion picture or other audiovisual work other than an audiovisual work dealing with news, except that no such limitation shall apply with respect to rights granted by subsections (b) and (c), or with respect to pictorial or graphic works published as illustrations, diagrams, or similar adjuncts to works of which copies are reproduced or distributed in accordance with subsections (d) and (e).

(i) Five years from the effective date of this Act, and at five-year intervals thereafter, the Register of Copyrights, after consulting with representatives of authors, book and periodical publishers, and other owners of copyrighted materials, and with representatives of library users and librarians, shall submit to the Congress a report setting forth the extent to which this section has achieved the intended statutory balancing of the rights of creators, and the needs of users. The report should also describe any problems that may have arisen, and present legislative or other recommendations, if warranted. **Report to Congress.**

§ 109. Limitations on exclusive rights: Effect of transfer of particular copy or phonorecord 17 USC 109.

(a) Notwithstanding the provisions of section 106(3), the owner of a particular copy or phonorecord lawfully made under this title, or any person authorized by such owner, is entitled, without the authority of the copyright owner; to sell or otherwise dispose of the possession of that copy or phonorecord. **Disposal.**

(b) Notwithstanding the provisions of section 106(5), the owner of a particular copy lawfully made under this title, or any person authorized by such owner, is entitled, without the authority of the copyright owner, to display that copy publicly, either directly or by the projection of no more than one image at a time, to viewers present at the place where the copy is located. **Public display.**

(c) The privileges prescribed by subsections (a) and (b) do not, unless authorized by the copyright owner, extend to any person who has acquired possession of the copy or phonorecord from the copyright owner, by rental, lease, loan, or otherwise, without acquiring ownership of it.

17 USC 110. **§ 110.** **Limitations on exclusive rights: Exemption of certain performances and displays**

Notwithstanding the provisions of section 106, the following are not infringements of copyright:

(1) performance or display of a work by instructors or pupils in the course of face-to-face teaching activities of a nonprofit educational institution, in a classroom or similar place devoted to instruction, unless, in the case of a motion picture or other audiovisual work, the performance, or the display of individual images, is given by means of a copy that was not lawfully made under this title, and that the person responsible for the performance knew or had reason to believe was not lawfully made;

(2) performance of a nondramatic literary or musical work or display of a work, by or in the course of a transmission, if—

(A) the performance or display is a regular part of the systematic instructional activities of a governmental body or a nonprofit educational institution; and

(B) the performance or display is directly related and of material assistance to the teaching content of the transmission; and

(C) the transmission is made primarily for—

(i) reception in classrooms or similar places normally devoted to instruction, or

(ii) reception by persons to whom the transmission is directed because their disabilities or other special circumstances prevent their attendance in classrooms or similar places normally devoted to instruction, or

(iii) reception by officers or employees of governmental bodies as a part of their official duties or employment;

(3) performance of a nondramatic literary or musical work or of a dramatico-musical work of a religious nature, or display of a work, in the course of services at a place of worship or other religious assembly;

(4) performance of a nondramatic literary or musical work otherwise than in a transmission to the public, without any purpose of direct or indirect commercial advantage and without payment of any fee or other compensation for the performance to any of its performers, promoters, or organizers, if—

(A) there is no direct or indirect admission charge; or

Notice of objection to performance.

(B) the proceeds, after deducting the reasonable costs of producing the performance, are used exclusively for educational, religious, or charitable purposes and not for private financial gain, except where the copyright owner has served notice of objection to the performance under the following conditions;

    (i) the notice shall be in writing and signed by the copyright owner or such owner's duly authorized agent; and

    (ii) the notice shall be served on the person responsible for the performance at least seven days before the date of the performance, and shall state the reasons for the objection; and

    (iii) the notice shall comply, in form, content, and manner of service, with requirements that the Register of Copyrights shall prescribe by regulation;   **Regulation.**

(5) communication of a transmission embodying a performance or display of a work by the public reception of the transmission on a single receiving apparatus of a kind commonly used in private homes, unless—

    (A) a direct charge is made to see or hear the transmission; or

    (B) the transmission thus received is further transmitted to the public;

(6) performance of a nondramatic musical work by a governmental body or a nonprofit agricultural or horticultural organization, in the course of an annual agricultural or horticultural fair or exhibition conducted by such body or organization; the exemption provided by this clause shall extend to any liability for copyright infringement that would otherwise be imposed on such body or organization, under doctrines of vicarious liability or related infringement, for a performance by a concessionnaire, business establishment, or other person at such fair or exhibition, but shall not excuse any such person from liability for the performance;

(7) performance of a nondramatic musical work by a vending establishment open to the public at large without any direct or indirect admission charge, where the sole purpose of the performance is to promote the retail sale of copies or phonorecords of the work, and the performance is not transmitted beyond the place where the establishment is located and is within the immediate area where the sale is occurring;

(8) performance of a nondramatic literary work, by or in the course of a transmission specifically designed for and primarily directed to blind or other handicapped persons who are unable to read normal printed material as a result of their handicap, or deaf or other handicapped persons who are unable to hear the aural signals accompanying a transmission of visual signals, if the performance is made without any purpose of direct or indirect commercial advantage and its transmission is made through the facilities of: (i) a governmental body; or (ii) a noncommercial educational broadcast station (as defined in section 397 of title 47); or (iii) a radio subcarrier authorization (as defined in 47

CFR 73.293–73.295 and 73.593–73.595); or (iv) a cable system (as defined in section 111(f)).

(9) performance on a single occasion of a dramatic literary work published at least ten years before the date of the performance, by or in the course of a transmission specifically designed for and primarily directed to blind or other handicapped persons who are unable to read normal printed material as a result of their handicap, if the performance is made without any purpose of direct or indirect commercial advantage and its transmission is made through the facilities of a radio subcarrier authorization referred to in clause (8)(iii), *Provided*, That the provisions of this clause shall not be applicable to more than one performance of the same work by the same performers or under the auspices of the same organization.

17 USC 111. **§ 111. Limitations on exclusive rights: Secondary transmissions**

(a) CERTAIN SECONDARY TRANSMISSIONS EXEMPTED.—The secondary transmission of a primary transmission embodying a performance or display of a work is not an infringement of copyright if—

(1) the secondary transmission is not made by a cable system, and consists entirely of the relaying, by the management of a hotel, apartment house, or similar establishment, of signals transmitted by a broadcast station licensed by the Federal Communications Commission, within the local service area of such station, to the private lodgings of guests or residents of such establishment, and no direct charge is made to see or hear the secondary transmission; or

(2) the secondary transmission is made solely for the purpose and under the conditions specified by clause (2) of section 110; or

(3) the secondary transmission is made by any carrier who has no direct or indirect control over the content or selection of the primary transmission or over the particular recipients of the secondary transmission, and whose activities with respect to the secondary transmission consist solely of providing wires, cables, or other communications channels for the use of others: *Provided*, That the provisions of this clause extend only to the activities of said carrier with respect to secondary transmissions and do not exempt from liability the activities of others with respect to their own primary or secondary transmissions; or

(4) the secondary transmission is not made by a cable system but is made by a governmental body, or other nonprofit organization, without any purpose of direct or indirect commercial advantage, and without charge to the recipients of the secondary transmission other than assessments necessary to defray the actual and reasonable costs of maintaining and operating the secondary transmission service.

(b) SECONDARY TRANSMISSION OF PRIMARY TRANSMISSION TO CON-

TROLLED GROUP.—Notwithstanding the provisions of subsections (a) and (c), the secondary transmission to the public of a primary transmission embodying a performance or display of a work is actionable as an act of infringement under section 501, and is fully subject to the remedies provided by sections 502 through 506 and 509, if the primary transmission is not made for reception by the public at large but is controlled and limited to reception by particular members of the public: *Provided*, however, That such secondary transmission is not actionable as an act of infringement if—

(1) the primary transmission is made by a broadcast station licensed by the Federal Communications Commission; and

(2) the carriage of the signals comprising the secondary transmission is required under the rules, regulations, or authorizations of the Federal Communications Commission; and

(3) the signal of the primary transmitter is not altered or changed in any way by the secondary transmitter.

(c) SECONDARY TRANSMISSIONS BY CABLE SYSTEMS.—

(1) Subject to the provisions of clauses (2), (3), and (4) of this subsection, secondary transmissions to the public by a cable system of a primary transmission made by a broadcast station licensed by the Federal Communications Commission or by an appropriate governmental authority of Canada or Mexico and embodying a performance or display of a work shall be subject to compulsory licensing upon compliance with the requirements of subsection (d) where the carriage of the signals comprising the secondary transmission is permissible under the rules, regulations, or authorizations of the Federal Communications Commission.

(2) Notwithstanding the provisions of clause (1) of this subsection, the willful or repeated secondary transmission to the public by a cable system of a primary transmission made by a broadcast station licensed by the Federal Communications Commission or by an appropriate governmental authority of Canada or Mexico and embodying a performance or display of a work is actionable as an act of infringement under section 501, and is fully subject to the remedies provided by sections 502 through 506 and 509, in the following cases:

(A) where the carriage of the signals comprising the secondary transmission is not permissible under the rules, regulations, or authorizations of the Federal Communications Commission; or

(B) where the cable system has not recorded the notice specified by subsection (d) and deposited the statement of account and royalty fee required by subsection (d).

(3) Notwithstanding the provisions of clause (1) of this subsection and subject to the provisions of subsection (e) of this section, the secondary transmission to the public by a cable system of a primary transmission made by a broadcast station licensed by

Alteration, deletion, or substitution.

the Federal Communications Commission or by an appropriate governmental authority of Canada or Mexico and embodying a performance or display of a work is actionable as an act of infringement under section 501, and is fully subject to the remedies provided by sections 502 through 506 and sections 509 and 510, if the content of the particular program in which the performance or display is embodied, or any commercial advertising or station announcements transmitted by the primary transmitter during, or immediately before or after, the transmission of such program, is in any way willfully altered by the cable system through changes, deletions, or additions, except for the alteration, deletion, or substitution of commercial advertisements performed by those engaged in television commercial advertising market
Prior consent of advertiser
research : *Provided,* That the research company has obtained the prior consent of the advertiser who has purchased the original commercial advertisement, the television station broadcasting that commercial advertisement, and the cable system performing the secondary transmission : *And provided further,* That such commercial alteration, deletion, or substitution is not performed for the purpose of deriving income from the sale of that commercial time.

(4) Notwithstanding the provisions of clause (1) of this subsection, the secondary transmission to the public by a cable system of a primary transmission made by a broadcast station licensed by an appropriate governmental authority of Canada or Mexico and embodying a performance or display of a work is actionable as an act of infringement under section 501, and is fully subject to the remedies provided by sections 502 through 506 and section 509, if (A) with respect to Canadian signals, the community of the cable system is located more than 150 miles from the United States-Canadian border and is also located south of the forty-second parallel of latitude, or (B) with respect to Mexican signals, the secondary transmission is made by a cable system which received the primary transmission by means other than direct interception of a free space radio wave emitted by such broadcast television station, unless prior to April 15, 1976, such cable system was actually carrying, or was specifically authorized to carry, the signal of such foreign station on the system pursuant to the rules, regulations, or authorizations of the Federal Communications Commission.

(d) COMPULSORY LICENSE FOR SECONDARY TRANSMISSIONS BY CABLE SYSTEMS.—

Notice.
(1) For any secondary transmission to be subject to compulsory licensing under subsection (c), the cable system shall, at least one month before the date of the commencement of operations of the cable system or within one hundred and eighty days

after the enactment of this Act, whichever is later, and thereafter within thirty days after each occasion on which the ownership or control or the signal carriage complement of the cable system changes, record in the Copyright Office a notice including a statement of the identity and address of the person who owns or operates the secondary transmission service or has power to exercise primary control over it, together with the name and location of the primary transmitter or primary transmitters whose signals are regularly carried by the cable system, and thereafter, from time to time, such further information as the Register of Copyrights, after consultation with the Copyright Royalty Tribunal (if and when the Tribunal has been constituted), shall prescribe by regulation to carry out the purpose of this clause.

(2) A cable system whose secondary transmissions have been subject to compulsory licensing under subsection (c) shall, on a semiannual basis, deposit with the Register of Copyrights, in accordance with requirements that the Register shall, after consultation with the Copyright Royalty Tribunal (if and when the Tribunal has been constituted), prescribe by regulation—

(A) a statement of account, covering the six months next **Statement of account.** preceding, specifying the number of channels on which the cable system made secondary transmissions to its subscribers, the names and locations of all primary transmitters whose transmissions were further transmitted by the cable system, the total number of subscribers, the gross amounts paid to the cable system for the basic service of providing secondary transmissions of primary broadcast transmitters, and such other data as the Register of Copyrights may, after consultation with the Copyright Royalty Tribunal (if and when the Tribunal has been constituted), from time to time prescribe by regulation. Such statement shall also include a special **Nonnetwork** statement of account covering any nonnetwork television **television** programming that was carried by the cable system in whole **programming.** or in part beyond the local service area of the primary transmitter, under rules, regulations, or authorizations of the Federal Communications Commission permitting the substitution or addition of signals under certain circumstances, together with logs showing the times, dates, stations, and programs involved in such substituted or added carriage; and

(B) except in the case of a cable system whose royalty is **Total royalty** specified in subclause (C) or (D), a total royalty fee for the **fee.** period covered by the statement, computed on the basis of specified percentages of the gross receipts from subscribers to the cable service during said period for the basic service of providing secondary transmissions of primary broadcast transmitters, as follows:

(i) 0.675 of 1 per centum of such gross receipts for the privilege of further transmitting any nonnetwork programing of a primary transmitter in whole or in part beyond the local service area of such primary transmitter, such amount to be applied against the fee, if any, payable pursuant to paragraphs (ii) through (iv);

(ii) 0.675 of 1 per centum of such gross receipts for the first distant signal equivalent;

(iii) 0.425 of 1 per centum of such gross receipts for each of the second, third, and fourth distant signal equivalents;

(iv) 0.2 of 1 per centum of such gross receipts for the fifth distant signal equivalent and each additional distant signal equivalent thereafter; and

in computing the amounts payable under paragraph (ii) through (iv), above, any fraction of a distant signal equivalent shall be computed at its fractional value and, in the case of any cable system located partly within and partly without the local service area of a primary transmitter, gross receipts shall be limited to those gross receipts derived from subscribers located without the local service area of such primary transmitter; and

(C) if the actual gross receipts paid by subscribers to a cable system for the period covered by the statement for the basic service of providing secondary transmissions of primary broadcast transmitters total $80,000 or less, gross receipts of the cable system for the purpose of this subclause shall be computed by subtracting from such actual gross receipts the amount by which $80,000 exceeds such actual gross receipts, except that in no case shall a cable system's gross receipts be reduced to less than $3,000. The royalty fee payable under this subclause shall be 0.5 of 1 per centum, regardless of the number of distant signal equivalents, if any; and

(D) if the actual gross receipts paid by subscribers to a cable system for the period covered by the statement, for the basic service of providing secondary transmissions of primary broadcast transmitters, are more than $80,000 but less than $160,000, the royalty fee payable under this subclause shall be (i) 0.5 of 1 per centum of any gross receipts up to $80,000; and (ii) 1 per centum of any gross receipts in excess of $80,000 but less than $160,000, regardless of the number of distant signal equivalents, if any.

(3) The Register of Copyrights shall receive all fees deposited under this section and, after deducting the reasonable costs incurred by the Copyright Office under this section, shall deposit the balance in the Treasury of the United States, in such manner

as the Secretary of the Treasury directs. All funds held by the Secretary of the Treasury shall be invested in interest-bearing United States securities for later distribution with interest by the Copyright Royalty Tribunal as provided by this title. The Register shall submit to the Copyright Royalty Tribunal, on a semiannual basis, a compilation of all statements of account covering the relevant six-month period provided by clause (2) of this subsection. **Statements of account, submittal to Copyright Royalty Tribunal.**

(4) The royalty fees thus deposited shall, in accordance with the procedures provided by clause (5), be distributed to those among the following copyright owners who claim that their works were the subject of secondary transmissions by cable systems during the relevant semiannual period: **Royalty fees, distribution.**

(A) any such owner whose work was included in a secondary transmission made by a cable system of a nonnetwork television program in whole or in part beyond the local service area of the primary transmitter; and

(B) any such owner whose work was included in a secondary transmission identified in a special statement of account deposited under clause (2)(A); and

(C) any such owner whose work was included in nonnetwork programing consisting exclusively of aural signals carried by a cable system in whole or in part beyond the local service area of the primary transmitter of such programs.

(5) The royalty fees thus deposited shall be distributed in accordance with the following procedures: **Distribution procedures.**

(A) During the month of July in each year, every person claiming to be entitled to compulsory license fees for secondary transmissions shall file a claim with the Copyright Royalty Tribunal, in accordance with requirements that the Tribunal shall prescribe by regulation. Notwithstanding any provisions of the antitrust laws, for purposes of this clause any claimants may agree among themselves as to the proportionate division of compulsory licensing fees among them, may lump their claims together and file them jointly or as a single claim, or may designate a common agent to receive payment on their behalf.

(B) After the first day of August of each year, the Copyright Royalty Tribunal shall determine whether there exists a controversy concerning the distribution of royalty fees. If the Tribunal determines that no such controversy exists, it shall, after deducting its reasonable administrative costs under this section, distribute such fees to the copyright owners entitled, or to their designated agents. If the Tribunal finds the existence of a controversy, it shall, pursuant to chapter 8 of this title, conduct a proceeding to determine the distribution of royalty fees.

(C) During the pendency of any proceeding under this subsection, the Copyright Royalty Tribunal shall withhold from distribution an amount sufficient to satisfy all claims with respect to which a controversy exists, but shall have discretion to proceed to distribute any amounts that are not in controversy.

(e) NONSIMULTANEOUS SECONDARY TRANSMISSIONS BY CABLE SYSTEMS.—

(1) Notwithstanding those provisions of the second paragraph of subsection (f) relating to nonsimultaneous secondary transmissions by a cable system, any such transmissions are actionable as an act of infringement under section 501, and are fully subject to the remedies provided by sections 502 through 506 and sections 509 and 510, unless—

(A) the program on the videotape is transmitted no more than one time to the cable system's subscribers; and

(B) the copyrighted program, episode, or motion picture videotape, including the commercials contained within such program, episode, or picture, is transmitted without deletion or editing; and

(C) an owner or officer of the cable system (i) prevents the duplication of the videotape while in the possession of the system, (ii) prevents unauthorized duplication while in the possession of the facility making the videotape for the system if the system owns or controls the facility, or takes reasonable precautions to prevent such duplication if it does not own or control the facility, (iii) takes adequate precautions to prevent duplication while the tape is being transported, and (iv) subject to clause (2), erases or destroys, or causes the erasure or destruction of, the videotape; and

(D) within forty-five days after the end of each calendar quarter, an owner or officer of the cable system executes an affidavit attesting (i) to the steps and precautions taken to prevent duplication of the videotape, and (ii) subject to clause (2), to the erasure or destruction of all videotapes made or used during such quarter; and

(E) such owner or officer places or causes each such affidavit, and affidavits received pursuant to clause (2)(C), to be placed in a file, open to public inspection, at such system's main office in the community where the transmission is made or in the nearest community where such system maintains an office; and

(F) the nonsimultaneous transmission is one that the cable system would be authorized to transmit under the rules, regulations, and authorizations of the Federal Communications Commission in effect at the time of the nonsimultaneous transmission if the transmission had been made simultaneously, except that this subclause shall not apply to inadvertent or accidental transmissions.

(2) If a cable system transfers to any person a videotape of a program nonsimultaneously transmitted by it, such transfer is actionable as an act of infringement under section 501, and is fully subject to the remedies provided by sections 502 through 506 and 509, except that, pursuant to a written, nonprofit contract providing for the equitable sharing of the costs of such videotape and its transfer, a videotape nonsimultaneously transmitted by it, in accordance with clause (1), may be transferred by one cable system in Alaska to another system in Alaska, by one cable system in Hawaii permitted to make such nonsimultaneous transmissions to another such cable system in Hawaii, or by one cable system in Guam, the Northern Mariana Islands, or the Trust Territory of the Pacific Islands, to another cable system in any of those three territories, if—

(A) each such contract is available for public inspection in the offices of the cable systems involved, and a copy of such contract is filed, within thirty days after such contract is entered into, with the Copyright Office (which Office shall make each such contract available for public inspection) ; and

(B) the cable system to which the videotape is transferred complies with clause (1)(A), (B), (C)(i), (iii), and (iv), and (D) through (F) ; and

(C) such system provides a copy of the affidavit required to be made in accordance with clause (1)(D) to each cable system making a previous nonsimultaneous transmission of the same videotape.

(3) This subsection shall not be construed to supersede the exclusivity protection provisions of any existing agreement, or any such agreement hereafter entered into, between a cable system and a television broadcast station in the area in which the cable system is located, or a network with which such station is affiliated.

(4) As used in this subsection, the term "videotape", and each of its variant forms, means the reproduction of the images and sounds of a program or programs broadcast by a television broadcast station licensed by the Federal Communications Commission, regardless of the nature of the material objects, such as tapes or films, in which the reproduction is embodied.

"Videotape."

(f) DEFINITIONS.—As used in this section, the following terms and their variant forms mean the following:

A "primary transmission" is a transmission made to the public by the transmitting facility whose signals are being received and further transmitted by the secondary transmission service, regardless of where or when the performance or display was first transmitted.

A "secondary transmission" is the further transmitting of a primary transmission simultaneously with the primary transmission, or nonsimultaneously with the primary transmission if by a "cable system" not located in whole or in part within the boundary of the forty-eight contiguous States, Hawaii, or Puerto Rico: *Provided, however*, That a nonsimultaneous further transmission by a cable system located in Hawaii of a primary transmission shall be deemed to be a secondary transmission if the carriage of the television broadcast signal comprising such further transmission is permissible under the rules, regulations, or authorizations of the Federal Communications Commission.

A "cable system" is a facility, located in any State, Territory, Trust Territory, or Possession, that in whole or in part receives signals transmitted or programs broadcast by one or more television broadcast stations licensed by the Federal Communications Commission, and makes secondary transmissions of such signals or programs by wires, cables, or other communications channels to subscribing members of the public who pay for such service. For purposes of determining the royalty fee under subsection (d)(2), two or more cable systems in contiguous communities under common ownership or control or operating from one headend shall be considered as one system.

The "local service area of a primary transmitter", in the case of a television broadcast station, comprises the area in which such station is entitled to insist upon its signal being retransmitted by a cable system pursuant to the rules, regulations, and authorizations of the Federal Communications Commission in effect on April 15, 1976, or in the case of a television broadcast station licensed by an appropriate governmental authority of Canada or Mexico, the area in which it would be entitled to insist upon its signal being retransmitted if it were a television broadcast station subject to such rules, regulations, and authorizations. The "local service area of a primary transmitter", in the case of a radio broadcast station, comprises the primary service area of such station, pursuant to the rules and regulations of the Federal Communications Commission.

A "distant signal equivalent" is the value assigned to the secondary transmission of any nonnetwork television programing carried by a cable system in whole or in part beyond the local service area of the primary transmitter of such programing. It is computed by assigning a value of one to each independent station and a value of one-quarter to each network station and noncommercial educational station for the nonnetwork programing so carried pursuant to the rules, regulations, and authorizations of the Federal Communications Commission. The foregoing values for independent, network, and noncommercial educational stations are subject, however, to the following exceptions and limitations. Where the rules and regulations of the Federal Communications Commission require a cable system to omit the further transmission of a particular program and such rules and regulations also permit the substitution of another program embodying a performance or display of a work in place of the omitted transmission, or where such rules and regulations in effect on the date of enactment of this Act permit a cable system, at its election, to effect such deletion and substitution of a nonlive program or to carry additional programs not transmitted by primary transmitters within whose local service area the cable system is located, no value shall be assigned for the substituted or additional program; where the rules, regulations, or authorizations of the Federal Communications Commission in effect on the date of enactment of this Act permit a cable system, at its election, to omit the further transmission of a particular program and such rules, regulations, or authorizations also permit the substitution of another program embodying a performance or display of a work in place of the omitted transmission, the value assigned for the substituted or additional program shall be, in the case of a live program, the value of one full distant signal equivalent multiplied by a fraction that has as its numerator the number of days in the year in which such substitution occurs and as its denominator the number of days in the year. In the case of a station carried pursuant to the late-night or specialty programing rules of the Federal Communications Commission, or a station carried on a part-time basis where full-time carriage is not possible because the cable system lacks the activated channel capacity to retransmit on a full-time basis all signals which it is authorized to carry, the values for independent, network, and noncommercial educational stations set forth above, as the case may be, shall be multiplied by a fraction which is equal to the ratio of the broadcast hours of such station carried by the cable system to the total broadcast hours of the station.

A "network station" is a television broadcast station that is owned or operated by, or affiliated with, one or more of the television networks in the United States providing nationwide transmissions, and that transmits a substantial part of the programing supplied by such networks for a substantial part of that station's typical broadcast day.

An "independent station" is a commercial television broadcast station other than a network station.

A "noncommercial educational station" is a television station that is a noncommercial educational broadcast station as defined in section 397 of title 47.   47 USC 397.

§ 112. Limitations on exclusive rights: Ephemeral recordings

17 USC 112.

(a) Notwithstanding the provisions of section 106, and except in the case of a motion picture or other audiovisual work, it is not an infringement of copyright for a transmitting organization entitled to transmit to the public a performance or display of a work, under a license or transfer of the copyright or under the limitations on exclusive rights in sound recordings specified by section 114(a), to make no more than one copy or phonorecord of a particular transmission program embodying the performance or display, if—

(1) the copy or phonorecord is retained and used solely by the transmitting organization that made it, and no further copies or phonorecords are reproduced from it; and

(2) the copy or phonorecord is used solely for the transmitting organization's own transmissions within its local service area, or for purposes of archival preservation or security; and

(3) unless preserved exclusively for archival purposes, the copy or phonorecord is destroyed within six months from the date the transmission program was first transmitted to the public.

(b) Notwithstanding the provisions of section 106, it is not an infringement of copyright for a governmental body or other nonprofit organization entitled to transmit a performance or display of a work, under section 110(2) or under the limitations on exclusive rights in sound recordings specified by section 114(a), to make no more than thirty copies or phonorecords of a particular transmission program embodying the performance or display, if—

(1) no further copies or phonorecords are reproduced from the copies or phonorecords made under this clause; and

(2) except for one copy or phonorecord that may be preserved exclusively for archival purposes, the copies or phonorecords are destroyed within seven years from the date the transmission program was first transmitted to the public.

(c) Notwithstanding the provisions of section 106, it is not an infringment of copyright for a governmental body or other nonprofit organization to make for distribution no more than one copy or phonorecord, for each transmitting organization specified in clause (2) of this subsection, of a particular transmission program embodying a performance of a nondramatic musical work of a religious nature, or of a sound recording of such a musical work, if—

(1) there is no direct or indirect charge for making or distributing any such copies or phonorecords; and

(2) none of such copies or phonorecords is used for any performance other than a single transmission to the public by a transmitting organization entitled to transmit to the public a performance of the work under a license or transfer of the copyright; and

(3) except for one copy or phonorecord that may be preserved exclusively for archival purposes, the copies or phonorecords are all destroyed within one year from the date the transmission pro-

gram was first transmitted to the public.

(d) Notwithstanding the provisions of section 106, it is not an infringement of copyright for a governmental body or other nonprofit organization entitled to transmit a performance of a work under section 110(8) to make no more than ten copies or phonorecords embodying the performance, or to permit the use of any such copy or phonorecord by any governmental body or nonprofit organization entitled to transmit a performance of a work under section 110(8), if—

    (1) any such copy or phonorecord is retained and used solely by the organization that made it, or by a governmental body or nonprofit organization entitled to transmit a performance of a work under section 110(8), and no further copies or phonorecords are reproduced from it; and

    (2) any such copy or phonorecord is used solely for transmissions authorized under section 110(8), or for purposes of archival preservation or security; and

    (3) the governmental body or nonprofit organization permitting any use of any such copy or phonorecord by any governmental body or nonprofit organization under this subsection does not make any charge for such use.

(e) The transmission program embodied in a copy or phonorecord made under this section is not subject to protection as a derivative work under this title except with the express consent of the owners of copyright in the preexisting works employed in the program.

§ 113. Scope of exclusive rights in pictorial, graphic, and sculptural works

17 USC 113.

(a) Subject to the provisions of subsections (b) and (c) of this section, the exclusive right to reproduce a copyrighted pictorial, graphic, or sculptural work in copies under section 106 includes the right to reproduce the work in or on any kind of article, whether useful or otherwise.

(b) This title does not afford, to the owner of copyright in a work that portrays a useful article as such, any greater or lesser rights with respect to the making, distribution, or display of the useful article so portrayed than those afforded to such works under the law, whether title 17 or the common law or statutes of a State, in effect on December 31, 1977, as held applicable and construed by a court in an action brought under this title.

17 USC 1 et seq.

(c) In the case of a work lawfully reproduced in useful articles that have been offered for sale or other distribution to the public, copyright does not include any right to prevent the making, distribution, or display of pictures or photographs of such articles in connection with advertisements or commentaries related to the distribution or display of such articles, or in connection with news reports.

§ 114. Scope of exclusive rights in sound recordings

17 USC 114.

(a) The exclusive rights of the owner of copyright in a sound recording are limited to the rights specified by clauses (1), (2), and (3) of section 106, and do not include any right of performance under section 106(4).

(b) The exclusive right of the owner of copyright in a sound recording under clause (1) of section 106 is limited to the right to duplicate the sound recording in the form of phonorecords, or of copies of motion pictures and other audiovisual works, that directly or indirectly recapture the actual sounds fixed in the recording. The exclusive right of the owner of copyright in a sound recording under clause (2) of section 106 is limited to the right to prepare a derivative work in which the actual sounds fixed in the sound recording are rearranged, remixed, or otherwise altered in sequence or quality. The exclusive rights of the owner of copyright in a sound recording under clauses (1) and (2) of section 106 do not extend to the making or duplication of another sound recording that consists entirely of an independent fixation of other sounds, even though such sounds imitate or simulate those in the copyrighted sound recording. The exclusive rights of the owner of copyright in a sound recording under clauses (1), (2), and (3) of section 106 do not apply to sound recordings included in educational **47 USC 397.** television and radio programs (as defined in section 397 of title 47) distributed or transmitted by or through public broadcasting entities (as defined by section 118(g)) : *Provided*, That copies or phonorecords of said programs are not commercially distributed by or through public broadcasting entities to the general public.

(c) This section does not limit or impair the exclusive right to perform publicly, by means of a phonorecord, any of the works specified by section 106(4).

Report to   (d) On January 3, 1978, the Register of Copyrights, after consult-
Congress.   ing with representatives of owners of copyrighted materials, representatives of the broadcasting, recording, motion picture, entertainment industries, and arts organizations, representatives of organized labor and performers of copyrighted materials, shall submit to the Congress a report setting forth recommendations as to whether this section should be amended to provide for performers and copyright owners of copyrighted material any performance rights in such material. The report should describe the status of such rights in foreign countries, the views of major interested parties, and specific legislative or other recommendations, if any.

17 USC 115. § 115. Scope of exclusive rights in nondramatic musical works: Compulsory license for making and distributing phonorecords

In the case of nondramatic musical works, the exclusive rights provided by clauses (1) and (3) of section 106, to make and to distribute phonorecords of such works, are subject to compulsory licensing under the conditions specified by this section.

(a) AVAILABILITY AND SCOPE OF COMPULSORY LICENSE.—
(1) When phonorecords of a nondramatic musical work have

been distributed to the public in the United States under the authority of the copyright owner, any other person may, by complying with the provisions of this section, obtain a compulsory license to make and distribute phonorecords of the work. A person may obtain a compulsory license only if his or her primary purpose in making phonorecords is to distribute them to the public for private use. A person may not obtain a compulsory license for use of the work in the making of phonorecords duplicating a sound recording fixed by another, unless: (i) such sound recording was fixed lawfully; and (ii) the making of the phonorecords was authorized by the owner of copyright in the sound recording or, if the sound recording was fixed before February 15, 1972, by any person who fixed the sound recording pursuant to an express license from the owner of the copyright in the musical work or pursuant to a valid compulsory license for use of such work in a sound recording.

(2) A compulsory license includes the privilege of making a musical arrangement of the work to the extent necessary to conform it to the style or manner of interpretation of the performance involved, but the arrangement shall not change the basic melody or fundamental character of the work, and shall not be subject to protection as a derivative work under this title, except with the express consent of the copyright owner.

(b) NOTICE OF INTENTION TO OBTAIN COMPULSORY LICENSE.—
(1) Any person who wishes to obtain a compulsory license under this section shall, before or within thirty days after making, and before distributing any phonorecords of the work, serve notice of intention to do so on the copyright owner. If the registration or other public records of the Copyright Office do not identify the copyright owner and include an address at which notice can be served, it shall be sufficient to file the notice of intention in the Copyright Office. The notice shall comply, in form, content, and manner of service, with requirements that the Register of Copyrights shall prescribe by regulation.

(2) Failure to serve or file the notice required by clause (1) forecloses the possibility of a compulsory license and, in the absence of a negotiated license, renders the making and distribution of phonorecords actionable as acts of infringement under section 501 and fully subject to the remedies provided by sections 502 through 506 and 509.

Failure to serve or file notice, penalty.

(c) ROYALTY PAYABLE UNDER COMPULSORY LICENSE.—
(1) To be entitled to receive royalties under a compulsory license, the copyright owner must be identified in the registration or other public records of the Copyright Office. The owner is entitled to royalties for phonorecords made and distributed after being so identified, but is not entitled to recover for any phonorecords previously made and distributed.

(2) Except as provided by clause (1), the royalty under a compulsory license shall be payable for every phonorecord made and distributed in accordance with the license. For this purpose, a phonorecord is considered "distributed" if the person exercising the compulsory license has voluntarily and permanently parted with its possession. With respect to each work embodied in the phonorecord, the royalty shall be either two and three-fourths cents, or one-half of one cent per minute of playing time or fraction thereof, whichever amount is larger.

Royalty payments. Regulations.

(3) Royalty payments shall be made on or before the twentieth day of each month and shall include all royalties for the month next preceding. Each monthly payment shall be made under oath and shall comply with requirements that the Register of Copyrights shall prescribe by regulation. The Register shall also prescribe regulations under which detailed cumulative annual statements of account, certified by a certified public accountant, shall be filed for every compulsory license under this section. The regulations covering both the monthly and the annual statements of account shall prescribe the form, content, and manner of certification with respect to the number of records made and the number of records distributed.

(4) If the copyright owner does not receive the monthly payment and the monthly and annual statements of account when due, the owner may give written notice to the licensee that, unless the default is remedied within thirty days from the date of the notice, the compulsory license will be automatically terminated. Such termination renders either the making or the distribution, or both, of all phonorecords for which the royalty has not been paid, actionable as acts of infringement under section 501 and fully subject to the remedies provided by sections 502 through 506 and 509.

17 USC 116. **§ 116. Scope of exclusive rights in nondramatic musical works: Public performances by means of coin-operated phonorecord players**

(a) LIMITATION ON EXCLUSIVE RIGHT.—In the case of a nondramatic musical work embodied in a phonorecord, the exclusive right under clause (4) of section 106 to perform the work publicly by means of a coin-operated phonorecord player is limited as follows:

(1) The proprietor of the establishment in which the public performance takes place is not liable for infringement with respect to such public performance unless—

(A) such proprietor is the operator of the phonorecord player; or

(B) such proprietor refuses or fails, within one month after receipt by registered or certified mail of a request, at a time during which the certificate required by clause (1)(C)

of subsection (b) is not affixed to the phonorecord player, by the copyright owner, to make full disclosure, by registered or certified mail, of the identity of the operator of the phonorecord player.

(2) The operator of the coin-operated phonorecord player may obtain a compulsory license to perform the work publicly on that phonorecord player by filing the application, affixing the certificate, and paying the royalties provided by subsection (b).

(b) RECORDATION OF COIN-OPERATED PHONORECORD PLAYER, AFFIXATION OF CERTIFICATE, AND ROYALTY PAYABLE UNDER COMPULSORY LICENSE.—

(1) Any operator who wishes to obtain a compulsory license for the public performance of works on a coin-operated phonorecord player shall fulfill the following requirements:

(A) Before or within one month after such performances are made available on a particular phonorecord player, and during the month of January in each succeeding year that such performances are made available on that particular phonorecord player, the operator shall file in the Copyright Office, in accordance with requirements that the Register of Copyrights, after consultation with the Copyright Royalty Tribunal (if and when the Tribunal has been constituted), shall prescribe by regulation, an application containing the name and address of the operator of the phonorecord player and the manufacturer and serial number or other explicit identification of the phonorecord player, and deposit with the Register of Copyrights a royalty fee for the current calendar year of $8 for that particular phonorecord player. If such performances are made available on a particular phonorecord player for the first time after July 1 of any year, the royalty fee to be deposited for the remainder of that year shall be $4.

(B) Within twenty days of receipt of an application and a royalty fee pursuant to subclause (A), the Register of Copyrights shall issue to the applicant a certificate for the phonorecord player.

(C) On or before March 1 of the year in which the certificate prescribed by subclause (B) of this clause is issued, or within ten days after the date of issue of the certificate, the operator shall affix to the particular phonorecord player, in a position where it can be readily examined by the public, the certificate, issued by the Register of Copyrights under subclause (B), of the latest application made by such operator under subclause (A) of this clause with respect to that phonorecord player.

(2) Failure to file the application, to affix the certificate, or to pay the royalty required by clause (1) of this subsection renders

the public performance actionable as an act of infringement under section 501 and fully subject to the remedies provided by sections 502 through 506 and 509.

(c) Distribution of Royalties.—

(1) The Register of Copyrights shall receive all fees deposited under this section and, after deducting the reasonable costs incurred by the Copyright Office under this section, shall deposit the balance in the Treasury of the United States, in such manner as the Secretary of the Treasury directs. All funds held by the Secretary of the Treasury shall be invested in interest-bearing United States securities for later distribution with interest by the Copyright Royalty Tribunal as provided by this title. The Register shall submit to the Copyright Royalty Tribunal, on an annual basis, a detailed statement of account covering all fees received for the relevant period provided by subsection (b).

Statements of account, submittal to Copyright Royalty Tribunal. Claims.

(2) During the month of January in each year, every person claiming to be entitled to compulsory license fees under this section for performances during the preceding twelve-month period shall file a claim with the Copyright Royalty Tribunal, in accordance with requirements that the Tribunal shall prescribe by regulation. Such claim shall include an agreement to accept as final, except as provided in section 810 of this title, the determination of the Copyright Royalty Tribunal in any controversy concerning the distribution of royalty fees deposited under subclause (A) of subsection (b)(1) of this section to which the claimant is a party. Notwithstanding any provisions of the antitrust laws, for purposes of this subsection any claimants may agree among themselves as to the proportionate division of compulsory licensing fees among them, may lump their claims together and file them jointly or as a single claim, or may designate a common agent to receive payment on their behalf.

(3) After the first day of October of each year, the Copyright Royalty Tribunal shall determine whether there exists a controversy concerning the distribution of royalty fees deposited under subclause (A) of subsection (b)(1). If the Tribunal determines that no such controversy exists, it shall, after deducting its reasonable administrative costs under this section, distribute such fees to the copyright owners entitled, or to their designated agents. If it finds that such a controversy exists, it shall, pursuant to chapter 8 of this title, conduct a proceeding to determine the distribution of royalty fees.

Distribution procedures.

(4) The fees to be distributed shall be divided as follows:

(A) to every copyright owner not affiliated with a performing rights society, the pro rata share of the fees to be distributed to which such copyright owner proves entitlement.

(B) to the performing rights societies, the remainder of the fees to be distributed in such pro rata shares as they shall by agreement stipulate among themselves, or, if they fail to agree, the pro rata share to which such performing rights societies prove entitlement.

(C) during the pendency of any proceeding under this section, the Copyright Royalty Tribunal shall withhold from distribution an amount sufficient to satisfy all claims with respect to which a controversy exists, but shall have discretion to proceed to distribute any amounts that are not in controversy.

(5) The Copyright Royalty Tribunal shall promulgate regulations under which persons who can reasonably be expected to have claims may, during the year in which performances take place, without expense to or harassment of operators or proprietors of establishments in which phonorecord players are located, have such access to such establishments and to the phonorecord players located therein and such opportunity to obtain information with respect thereto as may be reasonably necessary to determine, by sampling procedures or otherwise, the proportion of contribution of the musical works of each such person to the earnings of the phonorecord players for which fees shall have been deposited. Any person who alleges that he or she has been denied the access permitted under the regulations prescribed by the Copyright Royalty Tribunal may bring an action in the United States District Court for the District of Columbia for the cancellation of the compulsory license of the phonorecord player to which such access has been denied, and the court shall have the power to declare the compulsory license thereof invalid from the date of issue thereof. *(Regulations.)* *(Civil action.)*

(d) CRIMINAL PENALTIES.—Any person who knowingly makes a false representation of a material fact in an application filed under clause (1)(A) of subsection (b), or who knowingly alters a certificate issued under clause (1)(B) of subsection (b) or knowingly affixes such a certificate to a phonorecord player other than the one it covers, shall be fined not more than $2,500.

(e) DEFINITIONS.—As used in this section, the following terms and their variant forms mean the following:

(1) A "coin-operated phonorecord player" is a machine or device that—

(A) is employed solely for the performance of non-dramatic musical works by means of phonorecords upon being activated by insertion of coins, currency, tokens, or other monetary units or their equivalent;

(B) is located in an establishment making no direct or indirect charge for admission;

(C) is accompanied by a list of the titles of all the musical works available for performance on it, which list is affixed to the phonorecord player or posted in the establishment in a prominent position where it can be readily examined by the public; and

(D) affords a choice of works available for performance and permits the choice to be made by the patrons of the establishment in which it is located.

(2) An "operator" is any person who, alone or jointly with others:

(A) owns a coin-operated phonorecord player; or

(B) has the power to make a coin-operated phonorecord player available for placement in an establishment for purposes of public performance; or

(C) has the power to exercise primary control over the selection of the musical works made available for public performance on a coin-operated phonorecord player.

(3) A "performing rights society" is an association or corporation that licenses the public performance of nondramatic musical works on behalf of the copyright owners, such as the American Society of Composers, Authors and Publishers, Broadcast Music, Inc., and SESAC, Inc.

17 USC 117. § 117. Scope of exclusive rights: Use in conjunction with computers and similar information systems

Notwithstanding the provisions of sections 106 through 116 and 118, this title does not afford to the owner of copyright in a work any greater or lesser rights with respect to the use of the work in conjunction with automatic systems capable of storing, processing, retrieving, or transferring information, or in conjunction with any similar device, machine, or process, than those afforded to works under the law, whether title 17 or the common law or statutes of a State, in effect on December 31, 1977, as held applicable and construed by a court in an action brought under this title.

17 USC 118. § 118. Scope of exclusive rights: Use of certain works in connection with noncommercial broadcasting

(a) The exclusive rights provided by section 106 shall, with respect to the works specified by subsection (b) and the activities specified by subsection (d), be subject to the conditions and limitations prescribed by this section.

Notice, publication in Federal Register. (b) Not later than thirty days after the Copyright Royalty Tribunal has been constituted in accordance with section 802, the Chairman of the Tribunal shall cause notice to be published in the Federal Register of the initiation of proceedings for the purpose of determining reasonable terms and rates of royalty payments for the activities specified by subsection (d) with respect to published nondramatic musical works and published pictorial, graphic, and sculptural works during a period beginning as provided in clause (3) of this subsection and ending on December 31, 1982. Copyright owners and public broadcasting entities shall negotiate in good faith and cooperate fully with the Tribunal in an effort to reach reasonable and expeditious results. Notwithstanding any provision of the antitrust laws, any owners of copyright in works specified by this subsection and any public broadcasting entities, respectively, may negotiate and agree upon the terms and rates of royalty payments and the proportionate division of fees paid among various copyright owners, and may designate common agents to negotiate, agree to, pay, or receive payments.

(1) Any owner of copyright in a work specified in this subsection or any public broadcasting entity may, within one hundred and twenty days after publication of the notice specified in this subsection, submit to the Copyright Royalty Tribunal proposed licenses covering such activities with respect to such works. The Copyright Royalty Tribunal shall proceed on the basis of the proposals submitted to it as well as any other relevant information. The Copyright Royalty Tribunal shall permit any interested party to submit information relevant to such proceedings.

(2) License agreements voluntarily negotiated at any time between one or more copyright owners and one or more public broadcasting entities shall be given effect in lieu of any determination by the Tribunal: *Provided*, That copies of such agreements are filed in the Copyright Office within thirty days of execution in accordance with regulations that the Register of Copyrights shall prescribe.

(3) Within six months, but not earlier than one hundred and twenty days, from the date of publication of the notice specified in this subsection the Copyright Royalty Tribunal shall make a determination and publish in the Federal Register a schedule of rates and terms which, subject to clause (2) of this subsection, shall be binding on all owners of copyright in works specified by this subsection and public broadcasting entities, regardless of whether or not such copyright owners and public broadcasting entities have submitted proposals to the Tribunal. In establishing such rates and terms the Copyright Royalty Tribunal may consider the rates for comparable circumstances under voluntary license agreements negotiated as provided in clause (2) of this subsection. The Copyright Royalty Tribunal shall also establish requirements by which copyright owners may receive reasonable notice of the use of their works under this section, and under which records of such use shall be kept by public broadcasting entities.

Rates
and terms,
publication
in Federal
Register.

(4) With respect to the period beginning on the effective date of this title and ending on the date of publication of such rates and terms, this title shall not afford to owners of copyright or public broadcasting entities any greater or lesser rights with respect to the activities specified in subsection (d) as applied to works specified in this subsection than those afforded under the law in effect on December 31, 1977, as held applicable and con-

strued by a court in an action brought under this title.

(c) The initial procedure specified in subsection (b) shall be repeated and concluded between June 30 and December 31, 1982, and at five-year intervals thereafter, in accordance with regulations that the Copyright Royalty Tribunal shall prescribe.

(d) Subject to the transitional provisions of subsection (b) (4), and to the terms of any voluntary license agreements that have been negotiated as provided by subsection (b) (2), a public broadcasting entity may, upon compliance with the provisions of this section, including the rates and terms established by the Copyright Royalty Tribunal under subsection (b) (3), engage in the following activities with respect to published nondramatic musical works and published pictorial, graphic, and sculptural works:

(1) performance or display of a work by or in the course of a transmission made by a noncommercial educational broadcast station referred to in subsection (g) ; and

(2) production of a transmission program, reproduction of copies or phonorecords of such a transmission program, and distribution of such copies or phonorecords, where such production, reproduction, or distribution is made by a nonprofit institution or organization solely for the purpose of transmissions specified in clause (1) ; and

(3) the making of reproductions by a governmental body or a nonprofit institution of a transmission program simultaneously with its transmission as specified in clause (1), and the performance or display of the contents of such program under the conditions specified by clause (1) of section 110, but only if the reproductions are used for performances or displays for a period of no more than seven days from the date of the transmission specified in clause (1), and are destroyed before or at the end of such period. No person supplying, in accordance with clause (2), a reproduction of a transmission program to governmental bodies or nonprofit institutions under this clause shall have any liability as a result of failure of such body or institution to destroy such reproduction: *Provided,* That it shall have notified such body or institution of the requirement for such destruction pursuant to this clause: *And provided further,* That if such body or institution itself fails to destroy such reproduction it shall be deemed to have infringed.

(e) Except as expressly provided in this subsection, this section shall have no applicability to works other than those specified in subsection (b).

(1) Owners of copyright in nondramatic literary works and public broadcasting entities may, during the course of voluntary negotiations, agree among themselves, respectively, as to the terms and rates of royalty payments without liability under the antitrust laws. Any such terms and rates of royalty payments shall be

effective upon filing in the Copyright Office, in accordance with regulations that the Register of Copyrights shall prescribe.

(2) On January 3, 1980, the Register of Copyrights, after consulting with authors and other owners of copyright in nondramatic literary works and their representatives, and with public broadcasting entities and their representatives, shall submit to the Congress a report setting forth the extent to which voluntary licensing arrangements have been reached with respect to the use of nondramatic literary works by such broadcast stations. The report should also describe any problems that may have arisen, and present legislative or other recommendations, if warranted.

Report to Congress.

(f) Nothing in this section shall be construed to permit, beyond the limits of fair use as provided by section 107, the unauthorized dramatization of a nondramatic musical work, the production of a transmission program drawn to any substantial extent from a published compilation of pictorial, graphic, or sculptural works, or the unauthorized use of any portion of an audiovisual work.

(g) As used in this section, the term "public broadcasting entity" means a noncommercial educational broadcast station as defined in section 397 of title 47 and any nonprofit institution or organization engaged in the activities described in clause (2) of subsection (d).

"Public broadcasting entity." 47 USC 397.

Chapter 2.—COPYRIGHT OWNERSHIP AND TRANSFER

Sec.
201. Ownership of copyright.
202. Ownership of copyright as distinct from ownership of material object.
203. Termination of transfers and licenses granted by the author.
204. Execution of transfers of copyright ownership.
205. Recordation of transfers and other documents.

17 USC 201.

§ 201. Ownership of copyright

(a) INITIAL OWNERSHIP.—Copyright in a work protected under this title vests initially in the author or authors of the work. The authors of a joint work are coowners of copyright in the work.

(b) WORKS MADE FOR HIRE.—In the case of a work made for hire, the employer or other person for whom the work was prepared is considered the author for purposes of this title, and, unless the parties have expressly agreed otherwise in a written instrument signed by them, owns all of the rights comprised in the copyright.

(c) CONTRIBUTIONS TO COLLECTIVE WORKS.—Copyright in each separate contribution to a collective work is distinct from copyright in the collective work as a whole, and vests initially in the author of the contribution. In the absence of an express transfer of the copyright or of any rights under it, the owner of copyright in the collective work is presumed to have acquired only the privilege of reproducing and distributing the contribution as part of that particular collective work, any revision of that collective work, and any later collective work in the same series.

(d) Transfer of Ownership.—

(1) The ownership of a copyright may be transferred in whole or in part by any means of conveyance or by operation of law, and may be bequeathed by will or pass as personal property by the applicable laws of intestate succession.

(2) Any of the exclusive rights comprised in a copyright, including any subdivision of any of the rights specified by section 106, may be transferred as provided by clause (1) and owned separately. The owner of any particular exclusive right is entitled, to the extent of that right, to all of the protection and remedies accorded to the copyright owner by this title.

(e) Involuntary Transfer.—When an individual author's ownership of a copyright, or of any of the exclusive rights under a copyright, has not previously been transferred voluntarily by that individual author, no action by any governmental body or other official or organization purporting to seize, expropriate, transfer, or exercise rights of ownership with respect to the copyright, or any of the exclusive rights under a copyright, shall be given effect under this title.

17 USC 202. **§ 202. Ownership of copyright as distinct from ownership of material object**

Ownership of a copyright, or of any of the exclusive rights under a copyright, is distinct from ownership of any material object in which the work is embodied. Transfer of ownership of any material object, including the copy or phonorecord in which the work is first fixed, does not of itself convey any rights in the copyrighted work embodied in the object; nor, in the absence of an agreement, does transfer of ownership of a copyright or of any exclusive rights under a copyright convey property rights in any material object.

17 USC 203. **§ 203. Termination of transfers and licenses granted by the author**

(a) Conditions for Termination.—In the case of any work other than a work made for hire, the exclusive or nonexclusive grant of a transfer or license of copyright or of any right under a copyright, executed by the author on or after January 1, 1978, otherwise than by will, is subject to termination under the following conditions:

(1) In the case of a grant executed by one author, termination of the grant may be effected by that author or, if the author is dead, by the person or persons who, under clause (2) of this subsection, own and are entitled to exercise a total of more than one-half of that author's termination interest. In the case of a grant executed by two or more authors of a joint work, termination of the grant may be effected by a majority of the authors who executed it; if any of such authors is dead, the termination interest of any such author may be exercised as a unit by the person or persons who, under clause (2) of this subsection, own

and are entitled to exercise a total of more than one-half of that author's interest.

(2) Where an author is dead, his or her termination interest is owned, and may be exercised, by his widow or her widower and his or her children or grandchildren as follows:

(A) the widow or widower owns the author's entire termination interest unless there are any surviving children or grandchildren of the author, in which case the widow or widower owns one-half of the author's interest;

(B) the author's surviving children, and the surviving children of any dead child of the author, own the author's entire termination interest unless there is a widow or widower, in which case the ownership of one-half of the author's interest is divided among them;

(C) the rights of the author's children and grandchildren are in all cases divided among them and exercised on a per stirpes basis according to the number of such author's children represented; the share of the children of a dead child in a termination interest can be exercised only by the action of a majority of them.

(3) Termination of the grant may be effected at any time during a period of five years beginning at the end of thirty-five years from the date of execution of the grant; or, if the grant covers the right of publication of the work, the period begins at the end of thirty-five years from the date of publication of the work under the grant or at the end of forty years from the date of execution of the grant, whichever term ends earlier.

(4) The termination shall be effected by serving an advance **Notice.** notice in writing, signed by the number and proportion of owners of termination interests required under clauses (1) and (2) of this subsection, or by their duly authorized agents, upon the grantee or the grantee's successor in title.

(A) The notice shall state the effective date of the termination, which shall fall within the five-year period specified by clause (3) of this subsection, and the notice shall be served not less than two or more than ten years before that date. A copy of the notice shall be recorded in the Copyright Office before the effective date of termination, as a condition to its taking effect.

(B) The notice shall comply, in form, content, and manner of service, with requirements that the Register of Copyrights shall prescribe by regulation.

(5) Termination of the grant may be effected notwithstanding any agreement to the contrary, including an agreement to make a will or to make any future grant.

(b) EFFECT OF TERMINATION.—Upon the effective date of termination, all rights under this title that were covered by the terminated

grants revert to the author, authors, and other persons owning termination interests under clauses (1) and (2) of subsection (a), including
those owners who did not join in signing the notice of termination
Limitations. under clause (4) of subsection (a), but with the following limitations:

(1) A derivative work prepared under authority of the grant
before its termination may continue to be utilized under the terms
of the grant after its termination, but this privilege does not
extend to the preparation after the termination of other derivative works based upon the copyrighted work covered by the terminated grant.

(2) The future rights that will revert upon termination of the
grant become vested on the date the notice of termination has
been served as provided by clause (4) of subsection (a). The
rights vest in the author, authors, and other persons named in,
and in the proportionate shares provided by, clauses (1) and (2)
of subsection (a).

(3) Subject to the provisions of clause (4) of this subsection,
a further grant, or agreement to make a further grant, of any
right covered by a terminated grant is valid only if it is signed
by the same number and proportion of the owners, in whom the
right has vested under clause (2) of this subsection, as are
required to terminate the grant under clauses (1) and (2) of
subsection (a). Such further grant or agreement is effective with
respect to all of the persons in whom the right it covers has
vested under clause (2) of this subsection, including those who
did not join in signing it. If any person dies after rights under
a terminated grant have vested in him or her, that person's legal
representatives, legatees, or heirs at law represent him or her for
purposes of this clause.

(4) A further grant, or agreement to make a further grant, of
any right covered by a terminated grant is valid only if it is
made after the effective date of the termination. As an exception,
however, an agreement for such a further grant may be made
between the persons provided by clause (3) of this subsection
and the original grantee or such grantee's successor in title, after
the notice of termination has been served as provided by clause
(4) of subsection (a).

(5) Termination of a grant under this section affects only
those rights covered by the grants that arise under this title, and
in no way affects rights arising under any other Federal, State,
or foreign laws.

(6) Unless and until termination is effected under this section,
the grant, if it does not provide otherwise, continues in effect for
the term of copyright provided by this title.

17 USC 204. **§ 204. Execution of transfers of copyright ownership**

(a) A transfer of copyright ownership, other than by operation of law, is not valid unless an instrument of conveyance, or a note or memorandum of the transfer, is in writing and signed by the owner of the rights conveyed or such owner's duly authorized agent.

(b) A certificate of acknowledgement is not required for the validity of a transfer, but is prima facie evidence of the execution of the transfer if—

(1) in the case of a transfer executed in the United States, the certificate is issued by a person authorized to administer oaths within the United States; or

(2) in the case of a transfer executed in a foreign country, the certificate is issued by a diplomatic or consular officer of the United States, or by a person authorized to administer oaths whose authority is proved by a certificate of such an officer.

§ 205. Recordation of transfers and other documents

17 USC 205.

(a) CONDITIONS FOR RECORDATION.—Any transfer of copyright ownership or other document pertaining to a copyright may be recorded in the Copyright Office if the document filed for recordation bears the actual signature of the person who executed it, or if it is accompanied by a sworn or official certification that it is a true copy of the original, signed document.

(b) CERTIFICATE OF RECORDATION.—The Register of Copyrights shall, upon receipt of a document as provided by subsection (a) and of the fee provided by section 708, record the document and return it with a certificate of recordation.

(c) RECORDATION AS CONSTRUCTIVE NOTICE.—Recordation of a document in the Copyright Office gives all persons constructive notice of the facts stated in the recorded document, but only if—

(1) the document, or material attached to it, specifically identifies the work to which it pertains so that, after the document is indexed by the Register of Copyrights, it would be revealed by a reasonable search under the title or registration number of the work; and

(2) registration has been made for the work.

(d) RECORDATION AS PREREQUISITE TO INFRINGEMENT SUIT.—No person claiming by virtue of a transfer to be the owner of copyright or of any exclusive right under a copyright is entitled to institute an infringement action under this title until the instrument of transfer under which such person claims has been recorded in the Copyright Office, but suit may be instituted after such recordation on a cause of action that arose before recordation.

(e) PRIORITY BETWEEN CONFLICTING TRANSFERS.—As between two conflicting transfers, the one executed first prevails if it is recorded, in the manner required to give constructive notice under subsection (c), within one month after its execution in the United States or within two months after its execution outside the United States, or at any time before recordation in such manner of the later transfer.

Otherwise the later transfer prevails if recorded first in such manner, and if taken in good faith, for valuable consideration or on the basis of a binding promise to pay royalties, and without notice of the earlier transfer.

(f) PRIORITY BETWEEN CONFLICTING TRANSFER OF OWNERSHIP AND NONEXCLUSIVE LICENSE.—A nonexclusive license, whether recorded or not, prevails over a conflicting transfer of copyright ownership if the license is evidenced by a written instrument signed by the owner of the rights licensed or such owner's duly authorized agent, and if—

(1) the license was taken before execution of the transfer; or

(2) the license was taken in good faith before recordation of the transfer and without notice of it.

Chapter 3.—DURATION OF COPYRIGHT

Sec.
301. Preemption with respect to other laws.
302. Duration of copyright: Works created on or after January 1, 1978.
303. Duration of copyright: Works created but not published or copyrighted before January 1, 1978.
304. Duration of copyright: Subsisting copyrights.
305. Duration of copyright: Terminal date.

17 USC 301. **§ 301. Preemption with respect to other laws**

(a) On and after January 1, 1978, all legal or equitable rights that are equivalent to any of the exclusive rights within the general scope of copyright as specified by section 106 in works of authorship that are fixed in a tangible medium of expression and come within the subject matter of copyright as specified by sections 102 and 103, whether created before or after that date and whether published or unpublished, are governed exclusively by this title. Thereafter, no person is entitled to any such right or equivalent right in any such work under the common law or statutes of any State.

(b) Nothing in this title annuls or limits any rights or remedies under the common law or statutes of any State with respect to—

(1) subject matter that does not come within the subject matter of copyright as specified by sections 102 and 103, including works of authorship not fixed in any tangible medium of expression; or

(2) any cause of action arising from undertakings commenced before January 1, 1978; or

(3) activities violating legal or equitable rights that are not equivalent to any of the exclusive rights within the general scope of copyright as specified by section 106.

(c) With respect to sound recordings fixed before February 15, 1972, any rights or remedies under the common law or statutes of any State shall not be annulled or limited by this title until February 15, 2047. The preemptive provisions of subsection (a) shall apply to any such rights and remedies pertaining to any cause of action arising from undertakings commenced on and after February 15. 2047. Notwithstanding the provisions of section 303, no sound recording fixed before February 15, 1972, shall be subject to copyright under this title before, on, or after February 15, 2047.

(d) Nothing in this title annuls or limits any rights or remedies under any other Federal statute.

§ 302. **Duration of copyright: Works created on or after January 1, 1978**

    (a) IN GENERAL.—Copyright in a work created on or after January 1, 1978, subsists from its creation and, except as provided by the following subsections, endures for a term consisting of the life of the author and fifty years after the author's death.

    (b) JOINT WORKS.—In the case of a joint work prepared by two or more authors who did not work for hire, the copyright endures for a term consisting of the life of the last surviving author and fifty years after such last surviving author's death.

    (c) ANONYMOUS WORKS, PSEUDONYMOUS WORKS, AND WORKS MADE FOR HIRE.—In the case of an anonymous work, a pseudonymous work, or a work made for hire, the copyright endures for a term of seventy-five years from the year of its first publication, or a term of one hundred years from the year of its creation, whichever expires first. If, before the end of such term, the identity of one or more of the authors of an anonymous or pseudonymous work is revealed in the records of a registration made for that work under subsections (a) or (d) of section 408, or in the records provided by this subsection, the copyright in the work endures for the term specified by subsection (a) or (b), based on the life of the author or authors whose identity has been revealed. Any person having an interest in the copyright in an anonymous or pseudonymous work may at any time record, in records to be maintained by the Copyright Office for that purpose, a statement identifying one or more authors of the work; the statement shall also identify the person filing it, the nature of that person's interest, the source of the information recorded, and the particular work affected, and shall comply in form and content with requirements that the Register of Copyrights shall prescribe by regulation.

    (d) RECORDS RELATING TO DEATH OF AUTHORS.—Any person having an interest in a copyright may at any time record in the Copyright Office a statement of the date of death of the author of the copyrighted work, or a statement that the author is still living on a particular date. The statement shall identify the person filing it, the nature of that person's interest, and the source of the information recorded, and shall comply in form and content with requirements that the Register of Copyrights shall prescribe by regulation. The Register shall maintain current records of information relating to the death of authors of copyrighted works, based on such recorded statements and, to the extent the Register considers practicable, on data contained in any of the records of the Copyright Office or in other reference sources.

17 USC 302.

Recordkeeping.

(e) PRESUMPTION AS TO AUTHOR'S DEATH.—After a period of seventy-five years from the year of first publication of a work, or a period of one hundred years from the year of its creation, whichever expires first, any person who obtains from the Copyright Office a certified report that the records provided by subsection (d) disclose nothing to indicate that the author of the work is living, or died less than fifty years before, is entitled to the benefit of a presumption that the author has been dead for at least fifty years. Reliance in good faith upon this presumption shall be a complete defense to any action for infringement under this title.

17 USC 303. ## § 303. Duration of copyright: Works created but not published or copyrighted before January 1, 1978

Copyright in a work created before January 1, 1978, but not theretofore in the public domain or copyrighted, subsists from January 1, 1978, and endures for the term provided by section 302. In no case, however, shall the term of copyright in such a work expire before December 31, 2002; and, if the work is published on or before December 31, 2002, the term of copyright shall not expire before December 31, 2027.

17 USC 304. ## § 304. Duration of copyright: Subsisting copyrights

(a) COPYRIGHTS IN THEIR FIRST TERM ON JANUARY 1, 1978.—Any copyright, the first term of which is subsisting on January 1, 1978, shall endure for twenty-eight years from the date it was originally secured: *Provided*, That in the case of any posthumous work or of any periodical, cyclopedic, or other composite work upon which the copyright was originally secured by the proprietor thereof, or of any work copyrighted by a corporate body (otherwise than as assignee or licensee of the individual author) or by an employer for whom such work is made for hire, the proprietor of such copyright shall be entitled to a renewal and extension of the copyright in such work for the further term of forty-seven years when application for such renewal and extension shall have been made to the Copyright Office and duly registered therein within one year prior to the expiration of the original term of copyright: *And provided further*, That in the case of any other copyrighted work, including a contribution by an individual author to a periodical or to a cyclopedic or other composite work, the author of such work, if still living, or the widow, widower, or children of the author, if the author be not living, or if such author, widow, widower, or children be not living, then the author's executors, or in the absence of a will, his or her next of kin shall be entitled to a renewal and extension of the copyright in such work for a further term of forty-seven years when application for such renewal and extension shall have been made to the Copyright Office and duly registered therein within one year prior to the expiration of the original term of copyright: *And provided further*, That in default of the registration of such application for renewal and extension, the copyright in any work shall terminate at the expiration of twenty-eight years from the date copyright was originally secured.

(b) COPYRIGHTS IN THEIR RENEWAL TERM OR REGISTERED FOR RENEWAL BEFORE JANUARY 1, 1978.—The duration of any copyright, the renewal term of which is subsisting at any time between December 31, 1976, and December 31, 1977, inclusive, or for which renewal registration is made between December 31, 1976, and December 31, 1977, inclusive, is extended to endure for a term of seventy-five years from the date copyright was originally secured.

(c) TERMINATION OF TRANSFERS AND LICENSES COVERING EXTENDED RENEWAL TERM.—In the case of any copyright subsisting in either its first or renewal term on January 1, 1978, other than a copyright in a work made for hire, the exclusive or nonexclusive grant of a transfer or license of the renewal copyright or any right under it, executed before January 1, 1978, by any of the persons designated by the second proviso of subsection (a) of this section, otherwise than by will, is subject to termination under the following conditions:

(1) In the case of a grant executed by a person or persons other than the author, termination of the grant may be effected by the surviving person or persons who executed it. In the case of a grant executed by one or more of the authors of the work, termination of the grant may be effected, to the extent of a particular author's share in the ownership of the renewal copyright, by the author who executed it or, if such author is dead, by the person or persons who, under clause (2) of this subsection, own and are entitled to exercise a total of more than one-half of that author's termination interest.

(2) Where an author is dead, his or her termination interest is owned, and may be exercised, by his widow or her widower and his or her children or grandchildren as follows:

(A) the widow or widower owns the author's entire termination interest unless there are any surviving children or grandchildren of the author, in which case the widow or widower owns one-half of the author's interest;

(B) the author's surviving children, and the surviving children of any dead child of the author, own the author's entire termination interest unless there is a widow or widower, in which case the ownership of one-half of the author's interest is divided among them;

(C) the rights of the author's children and grandchildren are in all cases divided among them and exercised on a per stirpes basis according to the number of such author's children represented; the share of the children of a dead child in a termination interest can be exercised only by the action of a majority of them.

(3) Termination of the grant may be effected at any time during a period of five years beginning at the end of fifty-six years from

the date copyright was originally secured, or beginning on January 1, 1978, whichever is later.

Advance notice.   (4) The termination shall be effected by serving an advance notice in writing upon the grantee or the grantee's successor in title. In the case of a grant executed by a person or persons other than the author, the notice shall be signed by all of those entitled to terminate the grant under clause (1) of this subsection, or by their duly authorized agents. In the case of a grant executed by one or more of the authors of the work, the notice as to any one author's share shall be signed by that author or his or her duly authorized agent or, if that author is dead, by the number and proportion of the owners of his or her termination interest required under clauses (1) and (2) of this subsection, or by their duly authorized agents.

(A) The notice shall state the effective date of the termination, which shall fall within the five-year period specified by clause (3) of this subsection, and the notice shall be served not less than two or more than ten years before that date. A copy of the notice shall be recorded in the Copyright Office before the effective date of termination, as a condition to its taking effect.

(B) The notice shall comply, in form, content, and manner of service, with requirements that the Register of Copyrights shall prescribe by regulation.

(5) Termination of the grant may be effected notwithstanding any agreement to the contrary, including an agreement to make a will or to make any future grant.

Reversion.   (6) In the case of a grant executed by a person or persons other than the author, all rights under this title that were covered by the terminated grant revert, upon the effective date of termination, to all of those entitled to terminate the grant under clause (1) of this subsection. In the case of a grant executed by one or more of the authors of the work, all of a particular author's rights under this title that were covered by the terminated grant revert, upon the effective date of termination, to that author or, if that author is dead, to the persons owning his or her termination interest under clause (2) of this subsection, including those owners who did not join in signing the notice of termination under clause (4) of this subsection. In all cases the reversion of rights is subject

Limitations.   to the following limitations:

(A) A derivative work prepared under authority of the grant before its termination may continue to be utilized under the terms of the grant after its termination, but this privilege does not extend to the preparation after the termination of other derivative works based upon the copyrighted work covered by the terminated grant.

(B) The future rights that will revert upon termination

of the grant become vested on the date the notice of termination has been served as provided by clause (4) of this subsection.

(C) Where the author's rights revert to two or more persons under clause (2) of this subsection, they shall vest in those persons in the proportionate shares provided by that clause. In such a case, and subject to the provisions of subclause (D) of this clause, a further grant, or agreement to make a further grant, of a particular author's share with respect to any right covered by a terminated grant is valid only if it is signed by the same number and proportion of the owners, in whom the right has vested under this clause, as are required to terminate the grant under clause (2) of this subsection. Such further grant or agreement is effective with respect to all of the persons in whom the right it covers has vested under this subclause, including those who did not join in signing it. If any person dies after rights under a terminated grant have vested in him or her, that person's legal representatives, legatees, or heirs at law represent him or her for purposes of this subclause.

(D) A further grant, or agreement to make a further grant, of any right covered by a terminated grant is valid only if it is made after the effective date of the termination. As an exception, however, an agreement for such a further grant may be made between the author or any of the persons provided by the first sentence of clause (6) of this subsection, or between the persons provided by subclause (C) of this clause, and the original grantee or such grantee's successor in title, after the notice of termination has been served as provided by clause (4) of this subsection.

(E) Termination of a grant under this subsection affects only those rights covered by the grant that arise under this title, and in no way affects rights arising under any other Federal, State, or foreign laws.

(F) Unless and until termination is effected under this subsection, the grant, if it does not provide otherwise, continues in effect for the remainder of the extended renewal term.

§ 305. Duration of copyright: Terminal date

17 USC 305.

All terms of copyright provided by sections 302 through 304 run to the end of the calendar year in which they would otherwise expire.

Chapter 4.—COPYRIGHT NOTICE, DEPOSIT, AND REGISTRATION

403. Notice of copyright: Publications incorporating United States Government works.
404. Notice of copyright: Contributions to collective works.
405. Notice of copyright: Omission of notice.
406. Notice of copyright: Error in name or date.
407. Deposit of copies or phonorecords for Library of Congress.
408. Copyright registration in general.
409. Application for copyright registration.
410. Registration of claim and issuance of certificate.
411. Registration as prerequisite to infringement suit.
412. Registration as prerequisite to certain remedies for infringement.

17 USC 401. § 401. Notice of copyright: Visually perceptible copies

(a) GENERAL REQUIREMENT.—Whenever a work protected under this title is published in the United States or elsewhere by authority of the copyright owner, a notice of copyright as provided by this section shall be placed on all publicly distributed copies from which the work can be visually perceived, either directly or with the aid of a machine or device.

(b) FORM OF NOTICE.—The notice appearing on the copies shall consist of the following three elements:

(1) the symbol © (the letter C in a circle), or the word "Copyright", or the abbreviation "Copr."; and

(2) the year of first publication of the work; in the case of compilations or derivative works incorporating previously published material, the year date of first publication of the compilation or derivative work is sufficient. The year date may be omitted where a pictorial, graphic, or sculptural work, with accompanying text matter, if any, is reproduced in or on greeting cards, postcards, stationery, jewelry, dolls, toys, or any useful articles; and

(3) the name of the owner of copyright in the work, or an abbreviation by which the name can be recognized, or a generally known alternative designation of the owner.

(c) POSITION OF NOTICE.—The notice shall be affixed to the copies in such manner and location as to give reasonable notice of the claim of copyright. The Register of Copyrights shall prescribe by regulation, as examples, specific methods of affixation and positions of the notice on various types of works that will satisfy this requirement, but these specifications shall not be considered exhaustive.

17 USC 402. § 402. Notice of copyright: Phonorecords of sound recordings

(a) GENERAL REQUIREMENT.—Whenever a sound recording protected under this title is published in the United States or elsewhere by authority of the copyright owner, a notice of copyright as provided by this section shall be placed on all publicly distributed phonorecords of the sound recording.

(b) FORM OF NOTICE.—The notice appearing on the phonorecords shall consist of the following three elements:

(1) the symbol ℗ (the letter P in a circle); and

(2) the year of first publication of the sound recording; and

(3) the name of the owner of copyright in the sound recording, or an abbreviation by which the name can be recognized, or a generally known alternative designation of the owner; if the producer of the sound recording is named on the phonorecord labels or containers, and if no other name appears in conjunction with the notice, the producer's name shall be considered a part of the notice.

(c) POSITION OF NOTICE.—The notice shall be placed on the surface of the phonorecord, or on the phonorecord label or container, in such manner and location as to give reasonable notice of the claim of copyright.

§ 403. Notice of copyright: Publications incorporating United States Government works

17 USC 403.

Whenever a work is published in copies or phonorecords consisting preponderantly of one or more works of the United States Government, the notice of copyright provided by sections 401 or 402 shall also include a statement identifying, either affirmatively or negatively, those portions of the copies or phonorecords embodying any work or works protected under this title.

§ 404. Notice of copyright: Contributions to collective works

17 USC 404.

(a) A separate contribution to a collective work may bear its own notice of copyright, as provided by sections 401 through 403. However, a single notice applicable to the collective work as a whole is sufficient to satisfy the requirements of sections 401 through 403 with respect to the separate contributions it contains (not including advertisements inserted on behalf of persons other than the owner of copyright in the collective work), regardless of the ownership of copyright in the contributions and whether or not they have been previously published.

(b) Where the person named in a single notice applicable to a collective work as a whole is not the owner of copyright in a separate contribution that does not bear its own notice, the case is governed by the provisions of section 406(a).

§ 405. Notice of copyright: Omission of notice

17 USC 405.

(a) EFFECT OF OMISSION ON COPYRIGHT.—The omission of the copyright notice prescribed by sections 401 through 403 from copies or phonorecords publicly distributed by authority of the copyright owner does not invalidate the copyright in a work if—

(1) the notice has been omitted from no more than a relatively small number of copies or phonorecords distributed to the public; or

(2) registration for the work has been made before or is made within five years after the publication without notice, and a reasonable effort is made to add notice to all copies or phonorecords that are distributed to the public in the United States after the omission has been discovered; or

(3) the notice has been omitted in violation of an express requirement in writing that, as a condition of the copyright owner's authorization of the public distribution of copies or phonorecords, they bear the prescribed notice.

(b) EFFECT OF OMISSION ON INNOCENT INFRINGERS.—Any person who innocently infringes a copyright, in reliance upon an authorized copy or phonorecord from which the copyright notice has been omitted, incurs no liability for actual or statutory damages under section 504 for any infringing acts committed before receiving actual notice that registration for the work has been made under section 408, if such person proves that he or she was misled by the omission of notice. In a suit for infringement in such a case the court may allow or disallow recovery of any of the infringer's profits attributable to the infringement, and may enjoin the continuation of the infringing undertaking or may require, as a condition or permitting the continuation of the infringing undertaking, that the infringer pay the copyright owner a reasonable license fee in an amount and on terms fixed by the court.

(c) REMOVAL OF NOTICE.—Protection under this title is not affected by the removal, destruction, or obliteration of the notice, without the authorization of the copyright owner, from any publicly distributed copies or phonorecords.

17 USC 406. **§ 406. Notice of copyright: Error in name or date**

(a) ERROR IN NAME.—Where the person named in the copyright notice on copies or phonorecords publicly distributed by authority of the copyright owner is not the owner of copyright, the validity and ownership of the copyright are not affected. In such a case, however, any person who innocently begins an undertaking that infringes the copyright has a complete defense to any action for such infringement if such person proves that he or she was misled by the notice and began the undertaking in good faith under a purported transfer or license from the person named therein, unless before the undertaking was begun—

(1) registration for the work had been made in the name of the owner of copyright; or

(2) a document executed by the person named in the notice and showing the ownership of the copyright had been recorded.

The person named in the notice is liable to account to the copyright owner for all receipts from transfers or licenses purportedly made under the copyright by the person named in the notice.

(b) ERROR IN DATE.—When the year date in the notice on copies or phonorecords distributed by authority of the copyright owner is earlier than the year in which publication first occurred, any period computed from the year of first publication under section 302 is to be computed from the year in the notice. Where the year date is more than one year later than the year in which publication first occurred, the work is considered to have been published without any notice and is governed by the provisions of section 405.

(c) OMISSION OF NAME OR DATE.—Where copies or phonorecords publicly distributed by authority of the copyright owner contain no name or no date that could reasonably be considered a part of the notice, the work is considered to have been published without any notice and is governed by the provisions of section 405.

§ 407. Deposit of copies or phonorecords for Library of Congress   17 USC 407.

(a) Except as provided by subsection (c), and subject to the provisions of subsection (e), the owner of copyright or of the exclusive right of publication in a work published with notice of copyright in the United States shall deposit, within three months after the date of such publication—

(1) two complete copies of the best edition; or

(2) if the work is a sound recording, two complete phonorecords of the best edition, together with any printed or other visually perceptible material published with such phonorecords.

Neither the deposit requirements of this subsection nor the acquisition provisions of subsection (e) are conditions of copyright protection.

(b) The required copies or phonorecords shall be deposited in the Copyright Office for the use or disposition of the Library of Congress. The Register of Copyrights shall, when requested by the depositor and upon payment of the fee prescribed by section 708, issue a receipt for the deposit.

(c) The Register of Copyrights may by regulation exempt any **Exemption.** categories of material from the deposit requirements of this section, or require deposit of only one copy or phonorecord with respect to any categories. Such regulations shall provide either for complete exemption from the deposit requirements of this section, or for alternative forms of deposit aimed at providing a satisfactory archival record of a work without imposing practical or financial hardships on the depositor, where the individual author is the owner of copyright in a pictorial, graphic, or sculptural work and (i) less than five copies of the work have been published, or (ii) the work has been published in a limited edition consisting of numbered copies, the monetary value of which would make the mandatory deposit of two copies of the best edition of the work burdensome, unfair, or unreasonable.

(d) At any time after publication of a work as provided by subsection (a), the Register of Copyrights may make written demand for the required deposit on any of the persons obligated to make the deposit under subsection (a). Unless deposit is made within three **Penalties.** months after the demand is received, the person or persons on whom the demand was made are liable—

(1) to a fine of not more than $250 for each work; and

(2) to pay into a specially designated fund in the Library of Congress the total retail price of the copies or phonorecords demanded, or, if no retail price has been fixed, the reasonable cost of the Library of Congress of acquiring them; and

(3) to pay a fine of $2,500, in addition to any fine or liability

imposed under clauses (1) and (2), if such person willfully or
repeatedly fails or refuses to comply with such a demand.

Regulations.   (e) With respect to transmission programs that have been fixed and
transmitted to the public in the United States but have not been published, the Register of Copyrights shall, after consulting with the
Librarian of Congress and other interested organizations and officials,
establish regulations governing the acquisition, through deposit or
otherwise, of copies or phonorecords of such programs for the collections of the Library of Congress.

(1) The Librarian of Congress shall be permitted, under the
standards and conditions set forth in such regulations, to make
a fixation of a transmission program directly from a transmission
to the public, and to reproduce one copy or phonorecord from such
fixation for archival purposes.

(2) Such regulations shall also provide standards and procedures by which the Register of Copyrights may make written
demand, upon the owner of the right of transmission in the United
States, for the deposit of a copy or phonorecord of a specific transmission program. Such deposit may, at the option of the owner
of the right of transmission in the United States, be accomplished
by gift, by loan for purposes of reproduction, or by sale at a price
not to exceed the cost of reproducing and supplying the copy or
phonorecord. The regulations established under this clause shall
provide reasonable periods of not less than three months for compliance with a demand, and shall allow for extensions of such
periods and adjustments in the scope of the demand or the methods for fulfilling it, as reasonably warranted by the circumstances.
Willful failure or refusal to comply with the conditions prescribed by such regulations shall subject the owner of the right
of transmission in the United States to liability for an amount,
not to exceed the cost of reproducing and supplying the copy or
phonorecord in question, to be paid into a specially designated
fund in the Library of Congress.

(3) Nothing in this subsection shall be construed to require
the making or retention, for purposes of deposit, of any copy or
phonorecord of an unpublished transmission program, the transmission of which occurs before the receipt of a specific written
demand as provided by clause (2).

(4) No activity undertaken in compliance with regulations
prescribed under clauses (1) or (2) of this subsection shall result
in liability if intended solely to assist in the acquisition of copies
or phonorecords under this subsection.

17 USC 408.   § 408. Copyright registration in general

(a) REGISTRATION PERMISSIVE.—At any time during the subsistence
of copyright in any published or unpublished work, the owner of copyright or of any exclusive right in the work may obtain registra-

tion of the copyright claim by delivering to the Copyright Office the deposit specified by this section, together with the application and fee specified by sections 409 and 708. Subject to the provisions of section 405(a), such registration is not a condition of copyright protection.

(b) DEPOSIT FOR COPYRIGHT REGISTRATION.—Except as provided by subsection (c), the material deposited for registration shall include—

(1) in the case of an unpublished work, one complete copy or phonorecord;

(2) in the case of a published work, two complete copies or phonorecords of the best edition;

(3) in the case of a work first published outside the United States, one complete copy or phonorecord as so published;

(4) in the case of a contribution to a collective work, one complete copy or phonorecord of the best edition of the collective work.

Copies or phonorecords deposited for the Library of Congress under section 407 may be used to satisfy the deposit provisions of this section, if they are accompanied by the prescribed application and fee, and by any additional identifying material that the Register may, by regulation, require. The Register shall also prescribe regulations establishing requirements under which copies or phonorecords acquired for the Library of Congress under subsection (e) of section 407, otherwise than by deposit, may be used to satisfy the deposit provisions of this section. **Regulations.**

(c) ADMINISTRATIVE CLASSIFICATION AND OPTIONAL DEPOSIT.—

(1) The Register of Copyrights is authorized to specify by regulation the administrative classes into which works are to be placed for purposes of deposit and registration, and the nature of the copies or phonorecords to be deposited in the various classes specified. The regulations may require or permit, for particular classes, the deposit of identifying material instead of copies or phonorecords, the deposit of only one copy or phonorecord where two would normally be required, or a single registration for a group of related works. This administrative classification of works has no significance with respect to the subject matter of copyright or the exclusive rights provided by this title.

(2) Without prejudice to the general authority provided under clause (1), the Register of Copyrights shall establish regulations specifically permitting a single registration for a group of works by the same individual author, all first published as contributions to periodicals, including newspapers, within a twelve-month period, on the basis of a single deposit, application, and registration fee, under all of the following conditions— **Regulations.**

(A) if each of the works as first published bore a separate copyright notice, and the name of the owner of copyright in the work, or an abbreviation by which the name can be recognized, or a generally known alternative designation of the owner was the same in each notice; and

(B) if the deposit consists of one copy of the entire issue of the periodical, or of the entire section in the case of a newspaper, in which each contribution was first published; and

(C) if the application identifies each work separately, including the periodical containing it and its date of first publication.

(3) As an alternative to separate renewal registrations under subsection (a) of section 304, a single renewal registration may be made for a group of works by the same individual author, all first published as contributions to periodicals, including newspapers, upon the filing of a single application and fee, under all of the following conditions:

(A) the renewal claimant or claimants, and the basis of claim or claims under section 304(a), is the same for each of the works; and

(B) the works were all copyrighted upon their first publication, either through separate copyright notice and registration or by virtue of a general copyright notice in the periodical issue as a whole; and

(C) the renewal application and fee are received not more than twenty-eight or less than twenty-seven years after the thirty-first day of December of the calendar year in which all of the works were first published; and

(D) the renewal application identifies each work separately, including the periodical containing it and its date of first publication.

(d) CORRECTIONS AND AMPLIFICATIONS.—The Register may also establish, by regulation, formal procedures for the filing of an application for supplementary registration, to correct an error in a copyright registration or to amplify the information given in a registration. Such application shall be accompanied by the fee provided by section 708, and shall clearly identify the registration to be corrected or amplified. The information contained in a supplementary registration augments but does not supersede that contained in the earlier registration.

(e) PUBLISHED EDITION OF PREVIOUSLY REGISTERED WORK.—Registration for the first published edition of a work previously registered in unpublished form may be made even though the work as published is substantially the same as the unpublished version.

17 USC 409.   § 409. Application for copyright registration

The application for copyright registration shall be made on a form prescribed by the Register of Copyrights and shall include—

(1) the name and address of the copyright claimant;

(2) in the case of a work other than an anonymous or pseudon-

ymous work, the name and nationality or domicile of the author
or authors, and, if one or more of the authors is dead, the dates
of their deaths;

(3) if the work is anonymous or pseudonymous, the nationality
or domicile of the author or authors;

(4) in the case of a work made for hire, a statement to this
effect;

(5) if the copyright claimant is not the author, a brief statement of how the claimant obtained ownership of the copyright;

(6) the title of the work, together with any previous or alternative titles under which the work can be identified;

(7) the year in which creation of the work was completed;

(8) if the work has been published, the date and nation of its
first publication;

(9) in the case of a compilation or derivative work, an identification of any preexisting work or works that it is based on or
incorporates, and a brief, general statement of the additional
material covered by the copyright claim being registered;

(10) in the case of a published work containing material of
which copies are required by section 601 to be manufactured in
the United States, the names of the persons or organizations who
performed the processes specified by subsection (c) of section 601
with respect to that material, and the places where those processes
were performed; and

(11) any other information regarded by the Register of Copyrights as bearing upon the preparation or identification of the
work or the existence, ownership, or duration of the copyright.

17 USC 410.

§ 410. Registration of claim and issuance of certificate

(a) When, after examination, the Register of Copyrights determines that, in accordance with the provisions of this title, the material
deposited constitutes copyrightable subject matter and that the other
legal and formal requirements of this title have been met, the Register
shall register the claim and issue to the applicant a certificate of registration under the seal of the Copyright Office. The certificate shall
contain the information given in the application, together with the
number and effective date of the registration.

(b) In any case in which the Register of Copyrights determines
that, in accordance with the provisions of this title, the material
deposited does not constitute copyrightable subject matter or that
the claim is invalid for any other reason, the Register shall refuse
registration and shall notify the applicant in writing of the reasons
for such refusal.

(c) In any judicial proceedings the certificate of a registration
made before or within five years after first publication of the work
shall constitute prima facie evidence of the validity of the copyright
and of the facts stated in the certificate. The evidentiary weight to

Prima facie evidence.

be accorded the certificate of a registration made thereafter shall be within the discretion of the court.

Effective date.   (d) The effective date of a copyright registration is the day on which an application, deposit, and fee, which are later determined by the Register of Copyrights or by a court of competent jurisdiction to be acceptable for registration, have all been received in the Copyright Office.

17 USC 411.   **§ 411. Registration as prerequisite to infringement suit**

(a) Subject to the provisions of subsection (b), no action for infringement of the copyright in any work shall be instituted until registration of the copyright claim has been made in accordance with this title. In any case, however, where the deposit, application, and fee required for registration have been delivered to the Copyright Office in proper form and registration has been refused, the applicant is entitled to institute an action for infringement if notice thereof, with a copy of the complaint, is served on the Register of Copyrights. The Register may, at his or her option, become a party to the action with respect to the issue of registrability of the copyright claim by entering an appearance within sixty days after such service, but the Register's failure to become a party shall not deprive the court of jurisdiction to determine that issue.

(b) In the case of a work consisting of sounds, images, or both, the first fixation of which is made simultaneously with its transmission, the copyright owner may, either before or after such fixation takes place, institute an action for infringement under section 501, fully subject to the remedies provided by sections 502 through 506 and sections 509 and 510, if, in accordance with requirements that the Register of Copyrights shall prescribe by regulation, the copyright owner—

(1) serves notice upon the infringer, not less than ten or more than thirty days before such fixation, identifying the work and the specific time and source of its first transmission, and declaring an intention to secure copyright in the work; and

(2) makes registration for the work within three months after its first transmission.

17 USC 412.   **§ 412. Registration as prerequisite to certain remedies for infringement**

In any action under this title, other than an action instituted under section 411(b), no award of statutory damages or of attorney's fees, as provided by sections 504 and 505, shall be made for—

(1) any infringement of copyright in an unpublished work commenced before the effective date of its registration; or

(2) any infringement of copyright commenced after first publication of the work and before the effective date of its registration, unless such registration is made within three months after the first publication of the work.

Chapter 5.—COPYRIGHT INFRINGEMENT AND REMEDIES

§ 501. Infringement of copyright

17 USC 501.

(a) Anyone who violates any of the exclusive rights of the copyright owner as provided by sections 106 through 118, or who imports copies or phonorecords into the United States in violation of section 602, is an infringer of the copyright.

(b) The legal or beneficial owner of an exclusive right under a copyright is entitled, subject to the requirements of sections 205(d) and 411, to institute an action for any infringement of that particular right committed while he or she is the owner of it. The court may require such owner to serve written notice of the action with a copy of the complaint upon any person shown, by the records of the Copyright Office or otherwise, to have or claim an interest in the copyright, and shall require that such notice be served upon any person whose interest is likely to be affected by a decision in the case. The court may require the joinder, and shall permit the intervention, of any person having or claiming an interest in the copyright.

(c) For any secondary transmission by a cable system that embodies a performance or a display of a work which is actionable as an act of infringement under subsection (c) of section 111, a television broadcast station holding a copyright or other license to transmit or perform the same version of that work shall, for purposes of subsection (b) of this section, be treated as a legal or beneficial owner if such secondary transmission occurs within the local service area of that television station.

(d) For any secondary transmission by a cable system that is actionable as an act of infringement pursuant to section 111(c)(3), the following shall also have standing to sue: (i) the primary transmitter whose transmission has been altered by the cable system; and (ii) any broadcast station within whose local service area the secondary transmission occurs.

§ 502. Remedies for infringement: Injunctions

17 USC 502.

(a) Any court having jurisdiction of a civil action arising under this title may, subject to the provisions of section 1498 of title 28, grant temporary and final injunctions on such terms as it may deem reasonable to prevent or restrain infringement of a copyright.

(b) Any such injunction may be served anywhere in the United States on the person enjoined; it shall be operative throughout the United States and shall be enforceable, by proceedings in contempt or otherwise, by any United States court having jurisdiction of that person. The clerk of the court granting the injunction shall, when requested by any other court in which enforcement of the injunction is sought, transmit promptly to the other court a certified copy of all the papers in the case on file in such clerk's office.

17 USC 503. **§ 503. Remedies for infringement: Impounding and disposition of infringing articles**

(a) At any time while an action under this title is pending, the court may order the impounding, on such terms as it may deem reasonable, of all copies or phonorecords claimed to have been made or used in violation of the copyright owner's exclusive rights, and of all plates, molds, matrices, masters, tapes, film negatives, or other articles by means of which such copies or phonorecords may be reproduced.

(b) As part of a final judgment or decree, the court may order the destruction or other reasonable disposition of all copies or phonorecords found to have been made or used in violation of the copyright owner's exclusive rights, and of all plates, molds, matrices, masters, tapes, film negatives, or other articles by means of which such copies or phonorecords may be reproduced.

17 USC 504. **§ 504. Remedies for infringement: Damages and profits**

(a) IN GENERAL.—Except as otherwise provided by this title, an infringer of copyright is liable for either—

    (1) the copyright owner's actual damages and any additional profits of the infringer, as provided by subsection (b); or

    (2) statutory damages, as provided by subsection (c).

(b) ACTUAL DAMAGES AND PROFITS.—The copyright owner is entitled to recover the actual damages suffered by him or her as a result of the infringement, and any profits of the infringer that are attributable to the infringement and are not taken into account in computing the actual damages. In establishing the infringer's profits, the copyright owner is required to present proof only of the infringer's gross revenue, and the infringer is required to prove his or her deductible expenses and the elements of profit attributable to factors other than the copyrighted work.

(c) STATUTORY DAMAGES.—

    (1) Except as provided by clause (2) of this subsection, the copyright owner may elect, at any time before final judgment is rendered, to recover, instead of actual damages and profits, an award of statutory damages for all infringements involved in the action, with respect to any one work, for which any one infringer is liable individually, or for which any two or more infringers are liable jointly and severally, in a sum of not less than $250 or more than $10,000 as the court considers just. For the purposes of this

subsection, all the parts of a compilation or derivative work constitute one work.

(2) In a case where the copyright owner sustains the burden of proving, and the court finds, that infringement was committed willfully, the court in its discretion may increase the award of statutory damages to a sum of not more than $50,000. In a case where the infringer sustains the burden of proving, and the court finds, that such infringer was not aware and had no reason to believe that his or her acts constituted an infringement of copyright, the court it its discretion may reduce the award of statutory damages to a sum of not less than $100. The court shall remit statutory damages in any case where an infringer believed and had reasonable grounds for believing that his or her use of the copyrighted work was a fair use under section 107, if the infringer was: (i) an employee or agent of a nonprofit educational institution, library, or archives acting within the scope of his or her employment who, or such institution, library, or archives itself, which infringed by reproducing the work in copies or phonorecords; or (ii) a public broadcasting entity which or a person who, as a regular part of the nonprofit activities of a public broadcasting entity (as defined in subsection (g) of section 118) infringed by performing a published nondramatic literary work or by reproducing a transmission program embodying a performance of such a work.

§ 505. Remedies for infringement: Costs and attorney's fees

17 USC 505.

In any civil action under this title, the court in its discretion may allow the recovery of full costs by or against any party other than the United States or an officer thereof. Except as otherwise provided by this title, the court may also award a reasonable attorney's fee to the prevailing party as part of the costs.

§ 506. Criminal offenses

17 USC 506.

(a) CRIMINAL INFRINGEMENT.—Any person who infringes a copyright willfully and for purposes of commercial advantage or private financial gain shall be fined not more than $10,000 or imprisoned for not more than one year, or both: *Provided, however,* That any person who infringes willfully and for purposes of commercial advantage or private financial gain the copyright in a sound recording afforded by subsections (1), (2), or (3) of section 106 or the copyright in a motion picture afforded by subsections (1), (3), or (4) of section 106 shall be fined not more than $25,000 or imprisoned for not more than one year, or both, for the first such offense and shall be fined not more than $50,000 or imprisoned for not more than two years, or both, for any subsequent offense.

(b) FORFEITURE AND DESTRUCTION.—When any person is convicted of any violation of subsection (a), the court in its judgment of conviction shall, in addition to the penalty therein prescribed. order the forfeiture and destruction or other disposition of all infringing copies or phonorecords and all implements, devices, or equipment used in the manufacture of such infringing copies or phonorecords.

(c) FRAUDULENT COPYRIGHT NOTICE.—Any person who, with fraudulent intent, places on any article a notice of copyright or words of the same purport that such person knows to be false, or who, with fraudulent intent, publicly distributes or imports for public distribution any article bearing such notice or words that such person knows to be false, shall be fined not more than $2,500.

(d) FRAUDULENT REMOVAL OF COPYRIGHT NOTICE.—Any person who, with fraudulent intent, removes or alters any notice of copyright appearing on a copy of a copyrighted work shall be fined not more than $2.500.

(e) FALSE REPRESENTATION.—Any person who knowingly makes a false representation of a material fact in the application for copyright registration provided for by section 409, or in any written statement filed in connection with the application, shall be fined not more than $2,500.

17 USC 507. § 507. Limitations on actions

(a) CRIMINAL PROCEEDINGS.—No criminal proceeding shall be maintained under the provisions of this title unless it is commenced within three years after the cause of action arose.

(b) CIVIL ACTIONS.—No civil action shall be maintained under the provisions of this title unless it is commenced within three years after the claim accrued.

17 USC 508. § 508. Notification of filing and determination of actions

(a) Within one month after the filing of any action under this title, the clerks of the courts of the United States shall send written notification to the Register of Copyrights setting forth, as far as is shown by the papers filed in the court, the names and addresses of the parties and the title, author, and registration number of each work involved in the action. If any other copyrighted work is later included in the action by amendment, answer, or other pleading, the clerk shall also send a notification concerning it to the Register within one month after the pleading is filed.

(b) Within one month after any final order or judgment is issued in the case, the clerk of the court shall notify the Register of it, sending with the notification a copy of the order or judgment together with the written opinion, if any, of the court.

(c) Upon receiving the notifications specified in this section, the Register shall make them a part of the public records of the Copyright Office.

17 USC 509. § 509. Seizure and forfeiture

(a) All copies or phonorecords manufactured, reproduced, distributed, sold, or otherwise used, intended for use, or possessed with intent to use in violation of section 506(a), and all plates, molds, matrices, masters, tapes, film negatives, or other articles by means of which such copies or phonorecords may be reproduced, and all electronic, mechanical, or other devices for manufacturing, reproducing, or assembling such copies or phonorecords may be seized and forfeited to the United States.

(b) The applicable procedures relating to (i) the seizure, summary and judicial forfeiture, and condemnation of vessels, vehicles, merchandise, and baggage for violations of the customs laws contained in title 19, (ii) the disposition of such vessels, vehicles, merchandise, **19 USC 1** and baggage or the proceeds from the sale thereof, (iii) the remission **et seq.** or mitigation of such forfeiture, (iv) the compromise of claims, and (v) the award of compensation to informers in respect of such forfeitures, shall apply to seizures and forfeitures incurred, or alleged to have been incurred, under the provisions of this section, insofar as applicable and not inconsistent with the provisions of this section; except that such duties as are imposed upon any officer or employee of the Treasury Department or any other person with respect to the seizure and forfeiture of vessels, vehicles, merchandise; and baggage under the provisions of the customs laws contained in title 19 shall be performed with respect to seizure and forfeiture of all articles described in subsection (a) by such officers, agents, or other persons as may be authorized or designated for that purpose by the Attorney General.

§ 510. Remedies for alteration of programing by cable systems   17 USC 510.

(a) In any action filed pursuant to section 111(c)(3), the following remedies shall be available:

(1) Where an action is brought by a party identified in subsections (b) or (c) of section 501, the remedies provided by sections 502 through 505, and the remedy provided by subsection (b) of this section; and

(2) When an action is brought by a party identified in subsection (d) of section 501, the remedies provided by sections 502 and 505, together with any actual damages suffered by such party as a result of the infringement, and the remedy provided by subsection (b) of this section.

(b) In any action filed pursuant to section 111(c)(3), the court may decree that, for a period not to exceed thirty days, the cable system shall be deprived of the benefit of a compulsory license for one or more distant signals carried by such cable system.

Chapter 6.—MANUFACTURING REQUIREMENTS AND IMPORTATION

Sec.
601. Manufacture, importation, and public distribution of certain copies.
602. Infringing importation of copies or phonorecords.
603. Importation prohibitions: Enforcement and disposition of excluded articles.

17 USC 601. § 601. **Manufacture, importation, and public distribution of certain copies**

(a) Prior to July 1, 1982, and except as provided by subsection (b), the importation into or public distribution in the United States of copies of a work consisting preponderantly of nondramtic literary material that is in the English language and is protected under this title is prohibited unless the portions consisting of such material have been manufactured in the United States or Canada.

(b) The provisions of subsection (a) do not apply—

(1) where, on the date when importation is sought or public distribution in the United States is made, the author of any substantial part of such material is neither a national nor a domiciliary of the United States or, if such author is a national of the United States, he or she has been domiciled outside the United States for a continuous period of at least one year immediately preceding that date; in the case of a work made for hire, the exemption provided by this clause does not apply unless a subsustantial part of the work was prepared for an employer or other person who is not a national or domiciliary of the United States or a domestic corporation or enterprise;

(2) where the United States Customs Service is presented with an import statement issued under the seal of the Copyright Office, in which case a total of no more than two thousand copies of any one such work shall be allowed entry; the import statement shall be issued upon request to the copyright owner or to a person designated by such owner at the time of registration for the work under section 408 or at any time thereafter;

(3) where importation is sought under the authority or for the use, other than in schools, of the Government of the United States or of any State or political subdivision of a State;

(4) where importation, for use and not for sale, is sought—

(A) by any person with respect to no more than one copy of any work at any one time;

(B) by any person arriving from outside the United States, with respect to copies forming part of such person's personal baggage; or

(C) by an organization operated for scholarly, educational, or religious purposes and not for private gain, with respect to copies intended to form a part of its library;

(5) where the copies are reproduced in raised characters for the use of the blind; or

(6) where, in addition to copies imported under clauses (3) and (4) of this subsection, no more than two thousand copies of any one such work, which have not been manufactured in the United States or Canada, are publicly distributed in the United States; or

(7) where, on the date when importation is sought or public distribution in the United States is made—

(A) the author of any substantial part of such material is an individual and receives compensation for the transfer or license of che right to distribute the work in the United States; and

(B) the first publication of the work has previously taken place outside the United States under a transfer or license granted by such author to a transferee or licensee who was not a national or domiciliary of the United States or a domestic corporation or enterprise; and

(C) there has been no publication of an authorized edition of the work of which the copies were manufactured in the United States; and

(D) the copies were reproduced under a transfer or license granted by such author or by the transferee or licensee of the right of first publication as mentioned in subclause (B), and the transferee or the licensee of the right of reproduction was not a national or domiciliary of the United States or a domestic corporation or enterprise.

(c) The requirement of this section that copies be manufactured in the United States or Canada is satisfied if—

(1) in the case where the copies are printed directly from type that has been set, or directly from plates made from such type, the setting of the type and the making of the plates have been performed in the United States or Canada; or

(2) in the case where the making of plates by a lithographic or photoengraving process is a final or intermediate step preceding the printing of the copies, the making of the plates has been performed in the United States or Canada; and

(3) in any case, the printing or other final process of producing multiple copies and any binding of the copies have been performed in the United States or Canada.

(d) Importation or public distribution of copies in violation of this section does not invalidate protection for a work under this title. However, in any civil action or criminal proceeding for infringement of the exclusive rights to reproduce and distribute copies of the work, the infringer has a complete defense with respect to all of the non-dramatic literary material comprised in the work and any other parts of the work in which the exclusive rights to reproduce and distribute copies are owned by the same person who owns such exclusive rights in the nondramatic literary material, if the infringer proves—

(1) that copies of the work have been imported into or publicly distributed in the United States in violation of this section by or with the authority of the owner of such exclusive rights; and

(2) that the infringing copies were manufactured in the United

States or Canada in accordance with the provisions of subsection (c) ; and

(3) that the infringement was commenced before the effective date of registration for an authorized edition of the work, the copies of which have been manufactured in the United States or Canada in accordance with the provisions of subsection (c).

(e) In any action for infringement of the exclusive rights to reproduce and distribute copies of a work containing material required by this section to be manufactured in the United States or Canada, the copyright owner shall set forth in the complaint the names of the persons or organizations who performed the processes specified by subsection (c) with respect to that material, and the places where those processes were performed.

§ 602. Infringing importation of copies or phonorecords

17 USC 602.

(a) Importation into the United States, without the authority of the owner of copyright under this title, of copies or phonorecords of a work that have been acquired outside the United States is an infringement of the exclusive right to distribute copies or phonorecords under section 106, actionable under section 501. This subsection does not apply to—

(1) importation of copies or phonorecords under the authority or for the use of the Government of the United States or of any State or political subdivision of a State, but not including copies or phonorecords for use in schools, or copies of any audiovisual work imported for purposes other than archival use ;

(2) importation, for the private use of the importer and not for distribution, by any person with respect to no more than one copy or phonorecord of any one work at any one time, or by any person arriving from outside the United States with respect to copies or phonorecords forming part of such person's personal baggage; or

(3) importation by or for an organization operated for scholarly, educational, or religious purposes and not for private gain, with respect to no more than one copy of an audiovisual work solely for its archival purposes, and no more than five copies or phonorecords of any other work for its library lending or archival purposes, unless the importation of such copies or phonorecords is part of an activity consisting of systematic reproduction or distribution, engaged in by such organization in violation of the provisions of section 108(g)(2).

(b) In a case where the making of the copies or phonorecords would have constituted an infringement of copyright if this title had been applicable, their importation is prohibited. In a case where the copies or phonorecords were lawfully made, the United States Customs Service has no authority to prevent their importation unless the provisions of section 601 are applicable. In either case, the Secretary of the

Regulations.

Treasury is authorized to prescribe, by regulation, a procedure under which any person claiming an interest in the copyright in a particular work may, upon payment of a specified fee, be entitled to notification by the Customs Service of the importation of articles that appear to be copies or phonorecords of the work.

17 USC 603.

§ 603. Importation prohibitions: Enforcement and disposition of excluded articles

Regulations.

(a) The Secretary of the Treasury and the United States Postal Service shall separately or jointly make regulations for the enforcement of the provisions of this title prohibiting importation.

(b) These regulations may require, as a condition for the exclusion of articles under section 602—

(1) that the person seeking exclusion obtain a court order enjoining importation of the articles; or

Surety bond.

(2) that the person seeking exclusion furnish proof, of a specified nature and in accordance with prescribed procedures, that the copyright in which such person claims an interest is valid and that the importation would violate the prohibition in section 602; the person seeking exclusion may also be required to post a surety bond for any injury that may result if the detention or exclusion of the articles proves to be unjustified.

(c) Articles imported in violation of the importation prohibitions of this title are subject to seizure and forfeiture in the same manner as property imported in violation of the customs revenue laws. Forfeited articles shall be destroyed as directed by the Secretary of the Treasury or the court, as the case may be; however, the articles may be returned to the country of export whenever it is shown to the satisfaction of the Secretary of the Treasury that the importer had no reasonable grounds for believing that his or her acts constituted a violation of law.

Chapter 7.—COPYRIGHT OFFICE

§ 701. The Copyright Office: General responsibilities and organization

17 USC 701.

(a) All administrative functions and duties under this title, except as otherwise specified, are the responsibility of the Register of Copyrights as director of the Copyright Office of the Library of Congress. The Register of Copyrights, together with the subordinate officers and employees of the Copyright Office, shall be appointed by the Librarian of Congress, and shall act under the Librarian's general direction and supervision.

(b) The Register of Copyrights shall adopt a seal to be used on and after January 1, 1978, to authenticate all certified documents issued by the Copyright Office.

(c) The Register of Copyrights shall make an annual report to the Librarian of Congress of the work and accomplishments of the Copyright Office during the previous fiscal year. The annual report of the Register of Copyrights shall be published separately and as a part of the annual report of the Librarian of Congress.

(d) Except as provided by section 706(b) and the regulations issued thereunder, all actions taken by the Register of Copyrights under this title are subject to the provisions of the Administrative Procedure Act of June 11, 1946, as amended (c. 324, 60 Stat. 237, title 5, United States Code, Chapter 5, Subchapter II and Chapter 7).

§ 702. Copyright Office regulations

The Register of Copyrights is authorized to establish regulations not inconsistent with law for the administration of the functions and duties made the responsibility of the Register under this title. All regulations established by the Register under this title are subject to the approval of the Librarian of Congress.

§ 703. Effective date of actions in Copyright Office

In any case in which time limits are prescribed under this title for the performance of an action in the Copyright Office, and in which the last day of the prescribed period falls on a Saturday, Sunday, holiday, or other nonbusiness day within the District of Columbia or the Federal Government, the action may be taken on the next succeeding business day, and is effective as of the date when the period expired.

§ 704. Retention and disposition of articles deposited in Copyright Office

(a) Upon their deposit in the Copyright Office under sections 407 and 408, all copies, phonorecords, and identifying material, including those deposited in connection with claims that have been refused registration, are the property of the United States Government.

(b) In the case of published works, all copies, phonorecords, and identifying material deposited are available to the Library of Congress for its collections, or for exchange or transfer to any other library. In the case of unpublished works, the Library is entitled, under regulations that the Register of Copyrights shall prescribe, to select any deposits for its collections or for transfer to the National Archives of the United States or to a Federal records center, as defined in section 2901 of title 44.

(c) The Register of Copyrights is authorized, for specific or general categories of works, to make a facsimile reproduction of all or any part of the material deposited under section 408, and to make such reproduction a part of the Copyright Office records of the registration, before transferring such material to the Library of Congress as provided by subsection (b), or before destroying or otherwise disposing of such material as provided by subsection (d).

(d) Deposits not selected by the Library under subsection (b), or identifying portions or reproductions of them, shall be retained under the control of the Copyright Office, including retention in Government storage facilities, for the longest period considered practicable and desirable by the Register of Copyrights and the Librarian of Congress. After that period it is within the joint discretion of the Register and the Librarian to order their destruction or other disposition; but, in the case of unpublished works, no deposit shall be knowingly or intentionally destroyed or otherwise disposed of during its term of copyright unless a facsimile reproduction of the entire deposit has been made a part of the Copyright Office records as provided by subsection (c).

(e) The depositor of copies, phonorecords, or identifying material under section 408, or the copyright owner of record, may request retention, under the control of the Copyright Office, of one or more of such articles for the full term of copyright in the work. The Register of Copyrights shall prescribe, by regulation, the conditions under which such requests are to be made and granted, and shall fix the fee to be charged under section 708(a)(11) if the request is granted.

§ 705. Copyright Office records: Preparation, maintenance, public inspection, and searching

17 USC 705.

(a) The Register of Copyrights shall provide and keep in the Copyright Office records of all deposits, registrations, recordations, and other actions taken under this title, and shall prepare indexes of all such records.

(b) Such records and indexes, as well as the articles deposited in connection with completed copyright registrations and retained under the control of the Copyright Office, shall be open to public inspection.

(c) Upon request and payment of the fee specified by section 708, the Copyright Office shall make a search of its public records, indexes, and deposits, and shall furnish a report of the information they disclose with respect to any particular deposits, registrations, or recorded documents.

Report.

§ 706. Copies of Copyright Office records

17 USC 706.

(a) Copies may be made of any public records or indexes of the Copyright Office; additional certificates of copyright registration and copies of any public records or indexes may be furnished upon request and payment of the fees specified by section 708.

(b) Copies or reproductions of deposited articles retained under the control of the Copyright Office shall be authorized or furnished only under the conditions specified by the Copyright Office regulations.

17 USC 707. **§ 707. Copyright Office forms and publications**

(a) CATALOG OF COPYRIGHT ENTRIES.—The Register of Copyrights shall compile and publish at periodic intervals catalogs of all copyright registrations. These catalogs shall be divided into parts in accordance with the various classes of works, and the Register has discretion to determine, on the basis of practicability and usefulness, the form and frequency of publication of each particular part.

(b) OTHER PUBLICATIONS.—The Register shall furnish, free of charge upon request, application forms for copyright registration and general informational material in connection with the functions of the Copyright Office. The Register also has the authority to publish compilations of information, bibliographies, and other material he or she considers to be of value to the public.

(c) DISTRIBUTION OF PUBLICATIONS.—All publications of the Copyright Office shall be furnished to depository libraries as specified under section 1905 of title 44, and, aside from those furnished free of charge, shall be offered for sale to the public at prices based on the cost of reproduction and distribution.

17 USC 708. **§ 708. Copyright Office fees**

(a) The following fees shall be paid to the Register of Copyrights:

(1) for the registration of a copyright claim or a supplementary registration under section 408, including the issuance of a certificate of registration, $10;

(2) for the registration of a claim to renewal of a subsisting copyright in its first term under section 304(a), including the issuance of a certificate of registration, $6;

(3) for the issuance of a receipt for a deposit under section 407, $2;

(4) for the recordation, as provided by section 205, of a transfer of copyright ownership or other document of six pages or less, covering no more than one title, $10; for each page over six and each title over one, 50 cents additional;

(5) for the filing, under section 115(b), of a notice of intention to make phonorecords, $6;

(6) for the recordation, under section 302(c), of a statement revealing the identity of an author of an anonymous or pseudonymous work, or for the recordation, under section 302(d), of a statement relating to the death of an author, $10 for a document of six pages or less, covering no more than one title; for each page over six and for each title over one, $1 additional;

(7) for the issuance, under section 601, of an import statement, $3;

(8) for the issuance, under section 706, of an additional certifiicate of registration, $4;

(9) for the issuance of any other certification, $4; the Register of Copyrights has discretion, on the basis of their cost, to fix the fees for preparing copies of Copyright Office records, whether they are to be certified or not;

(10) for the making and reporting of a search as provided by section 705, and for any related services, $10 for each hour or fraction of an hour consumed;

(11) for any other special services requiring a substantial amount of time or expense, such fees as the Register of Copyrights may fix on the basis of the cost of providing the service.

(b) The fees prescribed by or under this section are applicable to **Waiver** the United States Government and any of its agencies, employees, or officers, but the Register of Copyrights has discretion to waive the requirement of this subsection in occasional or isolated cases involving relatively small amounts.

(c) The Register of Copyrights shall deposit all fees in the Treasury of the United States in such manner as the Secretary of the Treasury directs. The Register may, in accordance with regulations that **Regulations** he or she shall prescribe, refund any sum paid by mistake or in excess of the fee required by this section; however, before making a refund in any case involving a refusal to register a claim under section 410(b), the Register may deduct all or any part of the prescribed registration fee to cover the reasonable administrative costs of processing the claim.

§ 709. Delay in delivery caused by disruption of postal or other services   17 USC 709.

In any case in which the Register of Copyrights determines, on the basis of such evidence as the Register may by regulation require, that a deposit, application, fee, or any other material to be delivered to the Copyright Office by a particular date, would have been received in the Copyright Office in due time except for a general disruption or suspension of postal or other transportation or communications services, the actual receipt of such material in the Copyright Office within one month after the date on which the Register determines that the disruption or suspension of such services has terminated, shall be considered timely.

§ 710. Reproduction for use of the blind and physically handicapped: Voluntary licensing forms and procedures   17 USC 710.

The Register of Copyrights shall, after consultation with the Chief **Regulation.** of the Division for the Blind and Physically Handicapped and other appropriate officials of the Library of Congress, establish by regulation standardized forms and procedures by which, at the time applications covering certain specified categories of nondramatic literary works are submitted for registration under section 408 of this title, the copyright owner may voluntarily grant to the Library of Congress a license to reproduce the copyrighted work by means of Braille or similar tactile symbols, or by fixation of a reading of the work in a phonorecord, or both, and to distribute the resulting copies or phonorecords solely for the use of the blind and physically handicapped and under limited conditions to be specified in the standardized forms.

Chapter 8.—COPYRIGHT ROYALTY TRIBUNAL

17 USC 801. ** § 801. Copyright Royalty Tribunal: Establishment and purpose**

(a) There is hereby created an independent Copyright Royalty Tribunal in the legislative branch.

(b) Subject to the provisions of this chapter, the purposes of the Tribunal shall be—

(1) to make determinations concerning the adjustment of reasonable copyright royalty rates as provided in sections 115 and 116, and to make determinations as to reasonable terms and rates of royalty payments as provided in section 118. The rates applicable under sections 115 and 116 shall be calculated to achieve the following objectives:

(A) To maximize the availability of creative works to the public;

(B) To afford the copyright owner a fair return for his creative work and the copyright user a fair income under existing economic conditions;

(C) To reflect the relative roles of the copyright owner and the copyright user in the product made available to the public with respect to relative creative contribution, technological contribution, capital investment, cost, risk, and contribution to the opening of new markets for creative expression and media for their communication;

(D) To minimize any disruptive impact on the structure of the industries involved and on generally prevailing industry practices.

(2) to make determinations concerning the adjustment of the copyright royalty rates in section 111 solely in accordance with the following provisions:

(A) The rates established by section 111(d)(2)(B) may be adjusted to reflect (i) national monetary inflation or deflation or (ii) changes in the average rates charged cable subscribers for the basic service of providing secondary transmissions to maintain the real constant dollar level of the royalty fee per subscriber which existed as of the date of enactment of this Act: *Provided*, That if the average rates charged cable system subscribers for the basic service of providing secondary transmissions are changed so that the average rates exceed national monetary inflation, no change in the rates established by section 111(d)(2)(B) shall be permitted: *And provided further*, That no increase in the royalty fee shall be permitted based on any reduction in the average number of distant signal equivalents per subscriber. The Commission may consider all factors relating to the maintenance of such level of payments including, as an extenuating factor, whether the cable industry has been restrained by subscriber rate regulating authorities from increasing the rates for the basic service of providing secondary transmissions.

(B) In the event that the rules and regulations of the Federal Communications Commission are amended at any time after April 15, 1976, to permit the carriage by cable systems of additional television broadcast signals beyond the local service area of the primary transmitters of such signals, the royalty rates established by section 111(d)(2)(B) may be adjusted to insure that the rates for the additional distant signal equivalents resulting from such carriage are reasonable in the light of the changes effected by the amendment to such rules and regulations. In determining the reasonableness of rates proposed following an amendment of Federal Communications Commission rules and regulations, the Copyright Royalty Tribunal shall consider, among other factors, the economic impact on copyright owners and users: *Provided*, That no adjustment in royalty rates shall be made under this subclause with respect to any distant signal equivalent or fraction thereof represented by (i) carriage of any signal permitted under the rules and regulations of the Federal Communications Commission in effect on April 15, 1976, or the carriage of a signal of the same type (that is, independent, network, or noncommercial educational) substituted for such permitted signal, or (ii) a television broadcast signal first carried after April 15, 1976, pursuant to an individual waiver of the rules and regulations of the Federal Communications Commission, as such rules and regulations were in effect on April 15, 1976.

(C) In the event of any change in the rules and regulations

of the Federal Communications Commission with respect to syndicated and sports program exclusivity after April 15, 1976, the rates established by section 111(d)(2)(B) may be adjusted to assure that such rates are reasonable in light of the changes to such rules and regulations, but any such adjustment shall apply only to the affected television broadcast signals carried on those systems affected by the change.

(D) The gross receipts limitations established by section 111(d)(2) (C) and (D) shall be adjusted to reflect national monetary inflation or deflation or changes in the average rates charged cable system subscribers for the basic service of providing secondary transmissions to maintain the real constant dollar value of the exemption provided by such section; and the royalty rate specified therein shall not be subject to adjustment; and

(3) to distribute royalty fees deposited with the Register of Copyrights under sections 111 and 116, and to determine, in cases where controversy exists, the distribution of such fees.

Notice.   (c) As soon as possible after the date of enactment of this Act, and no later than six months following such date, the President shall publish a notice announcing the initial appointments provided in section 802, and shall designate an order of seniority among the initially-appointed commissioners for purposes of section 802(b).

17 USC 802. **§ 802. Membership of the Tribunal**

(a) The Tribunal shall be composed of five commissioners appointed by the President with the advice and consent of the Senate for a term of seven years each; of the first five members appointed, three shall be designated to serve for seven years from the date of the notice specified in section 801(c), and two shall be designated to serve for five years from such date, respectively. Commissioners shall be compensated at the highest rate now or hereafter prescribe for grade 18 of the General Schedule pay rates (5 U.S.C. 5332).

(b) Upon convening the commissioners shall elect a chairman from among the commissioners appointed for a full seven-year term. Such chairman shall serve for a term of one year. Thereafter, the most senior commissioner who has not previously served as chairman shall serve as chairman for a period of one year, except that, if all commissioners have served a full term as chairman, the most senior commissioner who has served the least number of terms as chairman shall be designated as chairman.

(c) Any vacancy in the Tribunal shall not affect its powers and shall be filled, for the unexpired term of the appointment, in the same manner as the original appointment was made.

17 USC 803. **§ 803. Procedures of the Tribunal**

(a) The Tribunal shall adopt regulations, not inconsistent with law, governing its procedure and methods of operation. Except as otherwise

provided in this chapter, the Tribunal shall be subject to the provisions
of the Administrative Procedure Act of June 11, 1946, as amended (c.
324, 60 Stat. 237, title 5, United States Code, chapter 5, subchapter II
and chapter 7).

    (b) Every final determination of the Tribunal shall be published in
the Federal Register. It shall state in detail the criteria that the Tribunal determined to be applicable to the particular proceeding, the
various facts that it found relevant to its determination in that proceeding, and the specific reasons for its determination.

5 USC 551, 701.

Publication
in Federal
Register.

§ 804. Institution and conclusion of proceedings

17 USC 804.

    (a) With respect to proceedings under section 801(b)(1) concern-
ing the adjustment of royalty rates as provided in sections 115 and
116, and with respect to proceedings under section 801(b)(2)(A) and
(D)—

        (1) on January 1, 1980, the Chairman of the Tribunal shall
cause to be published in the Federal Register notice of commencement of proceedings under this chapter; and

        (2) during the calendar years specified in the following schedule,
any owner or user of a copyrighted work whose royalty rates
are specified by this title, or by a rate established by the Tribunal,
may file a petition with the Tribunal declaring that the petitioner
requests an adjustment of the rate. The Tribunal shall make a
determination as to whether the applicant has a significant interest in the royalty rate in which an adjustment is requested. If the
Tribunal determines that the petitioner has a significant interest,
the Chairman shall cause notice of this determination, with the
reasons therefor, to be published in the Federal Register, together
with notice of commencement of proceedings under this chapter.

        (A) In proceedings under section 801(b)(2) (A) and (D),
such petition may be filed during 1985 and in each subsequent
fifth calendar year.

        (B) In proceedings under section 801(b)(1) concerning
the adjustment of royalty rates as provided in section 115,
such petition may be filed in 1987 and in each subsequent tenth
calendar year.

        (C) In proceedings under section 801(b)(1) concerning
the adjustment of royalty rates under section 116, such petition may be filed in 1990 and in each subsequent tenth calendar
year.

    (b) With respect to proceedings under subclause (B) or (C) of
section 801(b)(2), following an event described in either of those subsections, any owner or user of a copyrighted work whose royalty rates
are specified by section 111, or by a rate established by the Tribunal,
may, within twelve months, file a petition with the Tribunal declaring
that the petitioner requests an adjustment of the rate. In this event the
Tribunal shall proceed as in subsection (a)(2), above. Any change in

royalty rates made by the Tribunal pursuant to this subsection may be reconsidered in 1980, 1985, and each fifth calendar year thereafter, in accordance with the provisions in section 801(b)(2) (B) or (C), as the case may be.

(c) With respect to proceedings under section 801(b)(1), concerning the determination of reasonable terms and rates of royalty payments as provided in section 118, the Tribunal shall proceed when and as provided by that section.

(d) With respect to proceedings under section 801(b)(3), concerning the distribution of royalty fees in certain circumstances under sections 111 or 116, the Chairman of the Tribunal shall, upon determination by the Tribunal that a controversy exists concerning such distribution, cause to be published in the Federal Register notice of commencement of proceedings under this chapter.

(e) All proceedings under this chapter shall be initiated without delay following publication of the notice specified in this section, and the Tribunal shall render its final decision in any such proceeding within one year from the date of such publication.

17 USC 805.

§ 805. Staff of the Tribunal

(a) The Tribunal is authorized to appoint and fix the compensation of such employees as may be necessary to carry out the provisions of this chapter, and to prescribe their functions and duties.

5 USC 3109.

(b) The Tribunal may procure temporary and intermittent services to the same extent as is authorized by section 3109 of title 5.

17 USC 806.

§ 806. Administrative support of the Tribunal

(a) The Library of Congress shall provide the Tribunal with necessary administrative services, including those related to budgeting, accounting, financial reporting, travel, personnel, and procurement. The Tribunal shall pay the Library for such services, either in advance or by reimbursement from the funds of the Tribunal, at amounts to be agreed upon between the Librarian and the Tribunal.

(b) The Library of Congress is authorized to disburse funds for the Tribunal, under regulations prescribed jointly by the Librarian of Congress and the Tribunal and approved by the Comptroller General. Such regulations shall establish requirements and procedures under which every voucher certified for payment by the Library of Congress under this chapter shall be supported with a certification by a duly authorized officer or employee of the Tribunal, and shall prescribe the responsibilities and accountability of said officers and employees of the Tribunal with respect to such certifications.

17 USC 807.

§ 807. Deduction of costs of proceedings

Before any funds are distributed pursuant to a final decision in a proceeding involving distribution of royalty fees, the Tribunal shall assess the reasonable costs of such proceeding.

§ 808. Reports

17 USC 808.

In addition to its publication of the reports of all final determinations as provided in section 803(b), the Tribunal shall make an annual report to the President and the Congress concerning the Tribunal's work during the preceding fiscal year, including a detailed fiscal statement of account.

§ 809. Effective date of final determinations

17 USC 809.

Any final determination by the Tribunal under this chapter shall become effective thirty days following its publication in the Federal Register as provided in section 803(b), unless prior to that time an appeal has been filed pursuant to section 810, to vacate, modify, or correct such determination, and notice of such appeal has been served on all parties who appeared before the Tribunal in the proceeding in question. Where the proceeding involves the distribution of royalty fees under sections 111 or 116, the Tribunal shall, upon the expiration of such thirty-day period, distribute any royalty fees not subject to an appeal filed pursuant to section 810.

§ 810. Judicial review

17 USC 810.

Any final decision of the Tribunal in a proceeding under section 801(b) may be appealed to the United States Court of Appeals, within thirty days after its publication in the Federal Register by an aggrieved party. The judicial review of the decision shall be had, in accordance with chapter 7 of title 5, on the basis of the record before the Tribunal. No court shall have jurisdiction to review a final decision of the Tribunal except as provided in this section.

5 USC 701.

TRANSITIONAL AND SUPPLEMENTARY PROVISIONS

SEC. 102. This Act becomes effective on January 1, 1978, except as otherwise expressly provided by this Act, including provisions of the first section of this Act. The provisions of sections 118, 304(b), and chapter 8 of title 17, as amended by the first section of this Act, take effect upon enactment of this Act.

17 USC note prec. 101.

SEC. 103. This Act does not provide copyright protection for any work that goes into the public domain before January 1, 1978. The exclusive rights, as provided by section 106 of title 17 as amended by the first section of this Act, to reproduce a work in phonorecords and to distribute phonorecords of the work, do not extend to any nondramatic musical work copyrighted before July 1, 1909.

17 USC note prec. 101.

SEC. 104. All proclamations issued by the President under section 1(e) or 9(b) of title 17 as it existed on December 31, 1977, or under previous copyright statutes of the United States, shall continue in force until terminated, suspended, or revised by the President.

17 USC note prec. 101.

SEC. 105. (a) (1) Section 505 of title 44 is amended to read as follows:

"§ 505. Sale of duplicate plates

44 USC 505.

"The Public Printer shall sell, under regulations of the Joint Committee on Printing to persons who may apply, additional or duplicate stereotype or electrotype plates from which a Government publication is printed, at a price not to exceed the cost of composition, the metal, and making to the Government, plus 10 per centum, and the full amount of the price shall be paid when the order is filed.".

(2) The item relating to section 505 in the sectional analysis at the beginning of chapter 5 of title 44, is amended to read as follows:

"505. Sale of duplicate plates.".

(b) Section 2113 of title 44 is amended to read as follows:

44 USC 2113. **"§ 2113. Limitation on liability**

"When letters and other intellectual productions (exclusive of patented material, published works under copyright protection, and unpublished works for which copyright registration has been made) come into the custody or possession of the Administrator of General Services, the United States or its agents are not liable for infringement of copyright or analogous rights arising out of use of the materials for display, inspection, research, reproduction, or other purposes.".

28 USC 1498.   (c) In section 1498(b) of title 28, the phrase "section 101(b) of title 17" is amended to read "section 504(c) of title 17".

26 USC 543.   (d) Section 543(a)(4) of the Internal Revenue Code of 1954, as amended, is amended by striking out "(other than by reason of section 2 or 6 thereof)".

39 USC 3202, 3206.   (e) Section 3202(a) of title 39 is amended by striking out clause (5). Section 3206 of title 39 is amended by deleting the words "subsections (b) and (c)" and inserting "subsection (b)" in subsection (a), and by deleting subsection (c). Section 3206(d) is renumbered (c).

15 USC 290e.   (f) Subsection (a) of section 290(e) of title 15 is amended by deleting the phrase "section 8" and inserting in lieu thereof the phrase "section 105".

2 USC 131.   (g) Section 131 of title 2 is amended by deleting the phrase "deposit to secure copyright," and inserting in lieu thereof the phrase "acquisition of material under the copyright law,".

17 USC 115 note.   Sec. 106. In any case where, before January 1, 1978, a person has lawfully made parts of instruments serving to reproduce mechanically a copyrighted work under the compulsory license provisions of section 1(e) of title 17 as it existed on December 31, 1977, such person may continue to make and distribute such parts embodying the same mechanical reproduction without obtaining a new compulsory license under the terms of section 115 of title 17 as amended by the first section of this Act. However, such parts made on or after January 1, 1978, constitute phonorecords and are otherwise subject to the provisions of said section 115.

17 USC 304 note.   Sec. 107. In the case of any work in which an ad interim copyright is subsisting or is capable of being secured on December 31, 1977, under section 22 of title 17 as it existed on that date, copyright protection is hereby extended to endure for the term or terms provided by section 304 of title 17 as amended by the first section of this Act.

Sec. 108. The notice provisions of sections 401 through 403 of title 17 as amended by the first section of this Act apply to all copies or phonorecords publicly distributed on or after January 1, 1978. However, in the case of a work published before January 1, 1978, compliance with the notice provisions of title 17 either as it existed on December 31, 1977, or as amended by the first section of this Act, is adequate with respect to copies publicly distributed after December 31, 1977. — *17 USC 401 note.*

Sec. 109. The registration of claims to copyright for which the required deposit, application, and fee were received in the Copyright Office before January 1, 1978, and the recordation of assignments of copyright or other instruments received in the Copyright Office before January 1, 1978, shall be made in accordance with title 17 as it existed on December 31, 1977. — *17 USC 410 note.*

Sec. 110. The demand and penalty provisions of section 14 of title 17 as it existed on December 31, 1977, apply to any work in which copyright has been secured by publication with notice of copyright on or before that date, but any deposit and registration made after that date in response to a demand under that section shall be made in accordance with the provisions of title 17 as amended by the first section of this Act. — *17 USC 407 note.*

Sec. 111. Section 2318 of title 18 of the United States Code is amended to read as follows:

"§ 2318. Transportation, sale or receipt of phonograph records bearing forged or counterfeit labels — *18 USC 2318.*

"(a) Whoever knowingly and with fraudulent intent transports, causes to be transported, receives, sells, or offers for sale in interstate or foreign commerce any phonograph record, disk, wire, tape, film, or other article on which sounds are recorded, to which or upon which is stamped, pasted, or affixed any forged or counterfeited label, knowing the label to have been falsely made, forged, or counterfeited shall be fined not more than $10,000 or imprisoned for not more than one year, or both, for the first such offense and shall be fined not more than $25,000 or imprisoned for not more than two years, or both, for any subsequent offense.

"(b) When any person is convicted of any violation of subsection (a), the court in its judgment of conviction shall, in addition to the penalty therein prescribed, order the forfeiture and destruction or other disposition of all counterfeit labels and all articles to which counterfeit labels have been affixed or which were intended to have had such labels affixed.".

"(c) Except to the extent they are inconsistent with the provisions of this title, all provisions of section 509, title 17, United States Code,

214　　*Law and The Writer*

17 USC
501 note.

are applicable to violations of subsection (a).".

Sec. 112. All causes of action that arose under title 17 before January 1, 1978, shall be governed by title 17 as it existed when the cause of action arose.

American
Television
and Radio
Archives Act.
2 USC 170.

Sec. 113. (a) The Librarian of Congress (hereinafter referred to as the "Librarian") shall establish and maintain in the Library of Congress a library to be known as the American Television and Radio Archives (hereinafter referred to as the "Archives"). The purpose of the Archives shall be to preserve a permanent record of the television and radio programs which are the heritage of the people of the United States and to provide access to such programs to historians and scholars without encouraging or causing copyright infringement.

(1) The Librarian, after consultation with interested organizations and individuals, shall determine and place in the Archives such copies and phonorecords of television and radio programs transmitted to the public in the United States and in other countries which are of present or potential public or cultural interest, historical significance, cognitive value, or otherwise worthy of preservation, including copies and phonorecords of published and unpublished transmission programs—

(A) acquired in accordance with sections 407 and 408 of title 17 as amended by the first section of this Act; and

(B) transferred from the existing collections of the Library of Congress; and

(C) given to or exchanged with the Archives by other libraries, archives, organizations, and individuals; and

(D) purchased from the owner thereof.

(2) The Librarian shall maintain and publish appropriate catalogs and indexes of the collections of the Archives, and shall make such collections available for study and research under the conditions prescribed under this section.

(b) Notwithstanding the provisions of section 106 of title 17 as amended by the first section of this Act, the Librarian is authorized with respect to a transmission program which consists of a regularly scheduled newscast or on-the-spot coverage of news events and, under standards and conditions that the Librarian shall prescribe by regulation—

(1) to reproduce a fixation of such a program, in the same or another tangible form, for the purposes of preservation or security or for distribution under the conditions of clause (3) of this subsection; and

(2) to compile, without abridgment or any other editing, portions of such fixations according to subject matter, and to reproduce such compilations for the purpose of clause (1) of this subsection; and

(3) to distribute a reproduction made under clause (1) or (2) of this subsection—

(A) by loan to a person engaged in research; and

(B) for deposit in a library or archives which meets the requirements of section 108(a) of title 17 as amended by the first section of this Act,

in either case for use only in research and not for further reproduction or performance.

(c) The Librarian or any employee of the Library who is acting under the authority of this section shall not be liable in any action for copyright infringement committed by any other person unless the Librarian or such employee knowingly participated in the act of infringement committed by such person. Nothing in this section shall be construed to excuse or limit liability under title 17 as amended by the first section of this Act for any act not authorized by that title or this section, or for any act performed by a person not authorized to act under that title or this section.

(d) This section may be cited as the "American Television and Radio Archives Act". Citation of section.

SEC. 114. There are hereby authorized to be appropriated such funds as may be necessary to carry out the purposes of this Act. Appropriation authorization. 17 USC note prec. 101.

SEC. 115. If any provision of title 17, as amended by the first section of this Act, is declared unconstitutional, the validity of the remainder of this title is not affected. Severability. 17 USC note prec. 101.

Approved October 19, 1976.

LEGISLATIVE HISTORY:

HOUSE REPORTS: No. 94–1476 (Comm. on the Judiciary) and No. 94–1733 (Comm. of Conference).
SENATE REPORT No. 94–473 (Comm. on the Judiciary).
CONGRESSIONAL RECORD, Vol. 122 (1976):
    Feb. 6, 16–19, considered and passed Senate.
    Sept. 22, considered and passed Senate, amended.
    Sept. 30, Senate and House agreed to conference report.

A GLOSSARY OF LEGAL TERMS

(Condensed from *The Newsman's Guide to Legalese,*
courtesy, Theodore Stellwag, Pennsylvania Bar
Association.)

A

abstract of title—A chronological history, in abbreviated form, of the ownership of a parcel of land.

action in personam—An action against the person, founded on a personal liability.

action in rem—An action for the recovery of a specific object, usually an item of personal property such as an automobile.

adjective law—law regulating procedure.

adjudication—Giving or pronouncing a judgment or decree; also the judgment given.

adversary system—The system of trial practice in the United States and some other countries in which each of the opposing, or adversary, parties has full opportunity to present and establish opposing contentions before the court.

allegation—The assertion, declaration, or statement of a party to an action, made in a pleading, setting out what he expects to prove.

amicus curiae—A friend of the court; one who interposes, with the permission of the court, and volunteers information upon some matter of law.

answer—A pleading by which the defendant endeavors to resist the plaintiff's allegation of facts.

appearance—The formal proceeding by which a party submits himself to the jurisdiction of the court.

appellant—The party appealing a decision or judgment — which he considers incorrect — to a higher court.

appellate court—A court having jurisdiction of appeal and review; not a "trial court."

appellee—The party against whom an appeal is taken.

arraignment—In criminal practice, to bring a prisoner to court to answer to a criminal charge.

at issue—Whenever the parties to a suit come to a point in the pleadings which is affirmed on one side and denied on the other, they are said to be "at issue" and ready for trial.

attachment—A remedy by which plaintiff is enabled to acquire a lien upon property or effects of the defendant for satisfaction of judgment.

B

bail—Security given for the release of an arrested person to assure his appearance in court.

bail bond—An obligation signed by the accused, with sureties, to secure his presence in court.

bailiff—A court attendant whose duties are to keep order in the courtroom and to have custody of the jury.

bench warrant—Process issued by the court itself, or "from the bench" for the attachment or arrest of a person.

best evidence—Primary evidence, as distinguished from secondary; the best and highest evidence of which the nature of the case is susceptible.

brief—A written or printed document prepared by counsel to file in court, usually setting forth both facts and law in support of his case.

burden of proof—In the law of evidence, the necessity or duty of affirmatively proving a fact or facts in dispute.

C

case law—see common law.

change of venue—The removal of a suit begun in one county or district to another, for trial, or from one court to another in the same county or district.

circumstantial evidence—All evidence of indirect nature: the process of decision by which court or jury may reason from circumstances known or proved to establish by inference the principal fact.

code—A collection, compendium or revision of laws systematically arranged into chapters, table of contents and index and promulgated by legislative authority.

codicil—A supplement or an addition to a will.

common law—Law which derives its authority solely from usages and customs of immemorial antiquity, or from the judgments and decrees of courts. Also called "case law."

commutation—The change of a punishment from a greater degree to a lesser degree, as from death to life imprisonment.

comparative negligence—The doctrine by which acts of opposing parties are compared in the degrees of "slight," "ordinary" and "gross" negligence, frequently on a percentage basis.

complainant—Synonymous with "plaintiff."

condemnation—The legal process by which real estate of a private owner is taken for public use without his consent, but upon the award and payment of just compensation.

contempt of court—Any act calculated to embarrass, hinder or obstruct a court in the administration of justice, or calculated to lessen its authority or dignity. Contempts are of two kinds: direct and indirect. Direct contempts are those committed in the immediate presence of the court; indirect is the term chiefly used with reference to the failure or refusal to obey a lawful order.

contract—An oral or written agreement between two or more parties which is enforceable by law.

corpus delicti—The body (material substance) upon which a crime has been committed, e.g., the corpse of a murdered man, the charred remains of a burned house.

costs—An allowance for expenses in prosecuting or defending a suit. Ordinarily this does not include attorney's fees.

counterclaim—A claim presented by a defendant in opposition to the claim of a plaintiff.

courts of record—Those whose proceedings are permanently recorded, and which have the power to fine or imprison for contempt. Courts not of record are those of lesser authority whose proceedings are not permanently recorded.

D

damages—Pecuniary compensation which may be recovered in the courts by any person who has suffered loss, detriment, or injury to his person, property or rights, through the unlawful act or negligence of another.

declaratory judgment—One which declares the rights of the parties or expresses the opinion of the court on a question of law, without ordering anything to be done.

decree—A decision or order of the court. A final decree is one which fully and finally disposes of the litigation; an interlocutory is a provisional or preliminary decree which is not final.

defamation—An attack on the good name of another through either libel or slander.

default—A "default" in an action at law occurs when a party omits to plead within the time allowed or fails to appear at the trial.

demur—To file a pleading (called "a demurrer"), admitting the truth of the facts in the complaint, or answer, but contending they are legally insufficient.

deposition—The testimony of a witness not taken in open court, but in pursuance of authority given by statute or rule of court to take testimony elsewhere.

direct evidence—Proof of facts by witnesses who saw acts done or heard words spoken as distinguished from circumstantial evidence, which is called indirect.

direct examination—The first interrogation of a witness by the attorney for the party on whose behalf he is called.

directed verdict—An instruction by the judge to the jury to return a specific verdict.

discovery—A proceeding whereby one party to an action may be informed as to facts known by other parties or witnesses.

domicile—That place where a person has his true and permanent home. A person may have several residences, but only one domicile.

double jeopardy—Common-law and constitutional prohibition against more than one prosecution for the same crime.

due process—Law in its regular course of administration through the courts of justice. The guarantee of due process requires that every man have the protection of a fair trail.

E

embezzlement—The fraudulent appropriation by a person to his own use or benefit of property or money entrusted to him by another.

eminent domain—The power to take private property for public use by condemnation.

enjoin—To require a person, by writ of injunction from a court of equity, to perform or to abstain or desist from some act.

entrapment—The act of officers or agents of a government in inducing a person to commit a crime not contemplated by him, for the purpose of instituting a criminal prosecution against him.

escheat—In American law, the right of the state to property to which no one is able to make a valid claim.

escrow—An arrangement under which something is delivered to a third person to be held until the happening of a contingency or performance of a condition.

estoppel—A person's own act, or acceptance of facts, which preclude his later making claims to the contrary.

ex parte—By or for one party; done for, in behalf of or on the application of one party only.

ex post facto—After the fact; an act or fact occurring after some previous act or fact, and relating thereto.

executor—A person named by the decedent in his will to carry out the provisions of that will.

extradition—The surrender by one state to another of an individual accused or convicted of an offense outside its own territory, and within the territorial jurisdiction of the other.

F

fair comment—A term used in the law of libel, applying to statements made by a writer in an honest belief of their truth, even though the statements are not true in fact.

felony—a crime of a graver nature than a misdemeanor. Generally, an offense punishable by death or imprisonment in a penitentiary.

fiduciary—A term derived from the Roman law, meaning a person holding the character of a trustee, with obligations of trust, confidence, scrupulous good faith and candor.

forgery—The false making or material altering, with intent to defraud, of any writing which, if genuine, might be the foundation of a legal liability.

fraud—An intentional perversion of truth; deceitful practice or device resorted to with intent to deprive another of property or other right, or in some manner to do him injury.

G

garnishment—A proceeding whereby property, money or credits of a debtor in the possession of another (the garnishee) are applied to the debts of the debtor.

garnishee—The person upon whom a garnishment is served, usually a person holding assets of a debtor.

guardian ad litem—A person appointed by a court to look after the interests of an infant whose property is involved in litigation.

H

habeas corpus—"You have the body." The name given a variety of writs whose object is to bring a person before a court or judge. In most common usage, it is directed to the official or person detaining another, commanding him to produce the body of the prisoner or person detained so the court may determine if such person has been denied his liberty without due process of law.

harmless error—In appellate practice, an error committed by a lower court during a trial, but not prejudicial to the rights of the losing party and for which the court will not reverse the judgment.

hearsay—Evidence not proceeding from the personal knowledge of the witness.

holographic will—A testamentary instrument entirely written, dated and signed by the testator in his own handwriting, not valid in every state.

hostile witness—A witness who is subject to cross-examination by the party who called him to testify, because of his evident antagonism toward that party as exhibited in his direct examination.

hypothetical question—A combination of facts and circumstances, assumed or proved, stated in such a form as to constitute a coherent state of facts upon which the opinion of an expert can be asked by way of evidence in a trial.

I

impeachment of witness—An attack on the credibility of a witness by the testimony of other witnesses.

implied contract—A contract in which the promise made by the obligor is not expressed, but inferred by his conduct or implied in law.

imputed negligence—Negligence which is not directly attributable to the person himself, but which is the negligence of a person with whose fault he is chargeable. An example of this might be when the negligence of an employee is chargeable (imputed) to the employer.

inadmissible—That which, under the established rules of evidence, cannot be admitted or received.

in banc—On the bench; all judges of the court sitting together to hear a cause.

incompetent evidence—Evidence which is not admissible under the established rules of evidence.

indeterminate sentence—An indefinite sentence of "not less than" and "not more than" so many years, the exact term to be served being afterwards determined by parole authorities within the minimum and maximum limits set by the court or by statute.

indictment—An accusation in writing by a grand jury, charging that a person has done some act, or been guilty of some omission, which, by law, is a crime.

inferior court—Any court subordinate to the chief appellate tribunal in a particular judicial system.

information—An accusation for some criminal offense, in the nature of an indictment, from which it differs only in being presented by a competent public officer instead of a grand jury.

injunction—A mandatory or prohibitive writ issued by a court.

instruction—A direction given by the judge to the jury.

interlocutory—Provisional; temporary; not final. Refers to orders and decrees of a court.

interrogatories—Written questions propounded by one party and served on adversary, who must provide written answers under oath.

intervention—A proceeding in a suit or action by which a third person is permitted by the court to make himself a party.

intestate—One who dies without leaving a will.

irrelevant—Evidence not relating or applicable to the matter in issue; not supporting the issue.

J

jurisprudence—The philosophy of law, or the science which treats of the principles of positive law and legal relations.

jury—A certain number of people, selected according to law, and sworn to inquire of certain matters of fact, and declare the truth upon evidence laid before them.

grand jury—A jury whose duty is to receive complaints and accusations in criminal cases, hear the evidence and find bills of indictment in cases where they are satisfied a trial ought to be had.

petit jury—The ordinary jury of 12 (or fewer) persons for the trial of a civil or criminal case. So called to distinguish it from the grand jury.

jury commissioner—An officer charged with the duty of selecting the names to be put into a jury wheel, or of drawing the panel of jurors for a particular term of court.

L

leading question—One which instructs a witness how to answer or puts into his mouth words to be echoed back; one which suggests to the witness the answer desired. Prohibited on direct examination.

levy—A seizure; the obtaining of money by legal process through seizure and sale of property. The raising of the money for which an execution has been issued.

libel—A method of defamation expressed by print, writing, pictures or signs. In its most general sense any publication that is untruthfully injurious to the reputation of another.

lis pendens—A pending suit.

locus delicti—The place of the offense.

M

malfeasance—Evil doing; ill conduct; the commission of some act which is positively prohibited by law.

malicious prosecution—An action instituted with intention of injuring a defendant without probable cause, and which terminates in favor of the person prosecuted.

mandamus—The name of a writ which issues from a court of superior jurisdiction, directed to an inferior court, commanding the performance of a particular act.

mandate—A judicial command or precept proceeding from a court or judicial officer, directing the proper officer to enforce a judgment, sentence, or decree.

manslaughter—The unlawful killing of another without malice; may be either voluntary, upon a sudden impulse, or involuntary, in the commission of some unlawful act.

master—An officer of the court, usually an attorney, appointed for the purpose of taking testimony and making a report to the court.

material evidence—Such as is relevant and goes to the substantial issues in dispute.

misdemeanor—Offenses less than felonies; generally those punishable by fine or imprisonment other than in penitentiaries.

misfeasance—A misdeed or trespass. The improper performance of some act which a person may lawfully do, such as misconduct by a public official in performance of an official discretionary act, with an improper motive, e.g. for personal gain.

mistrial—An erroneous or invalid trial; a trial which cannot stand in law because of lack of jurisdiction, wrong drawing of jurors or disregard of some other fundamental requisite.

mitigating circumstance—One which does not constitute a justification or excuse of an offense, but which may be considered as reducing the degree of liability.

moot—Unsettled; undecided. A moot point is one not settled by judicial decision.

moral turpitude—An act of baseness or depravity which contravenes the accepted, customary social and private rights and duties of humankind.

municipal courts—In the judicial organization of some states, courts whose territorial authority is confined to the city or community.

murder—The unlawful killing of a human being by another with malice aforethought, either express or implied.

N

ne exeat—A writ which forbids the person to whom it is addressed to leave the country, the state or the jurisdiction of the court.

negligence—The omission to do something which a reasonable man, guided by ordinary considerations, would do; or the doing of something which a reasonable and prudent man would not do.

next friend—One acting for the benefit of an infant or other person without being regularly appointed as guardian.

no bill—This phrase, indorsed by a grand jury on an indictment, is equivalent to "not found" or "not a true bill." It means that, in the opinion of the jury, evidence was insufficient to warrant the return of a formal charge.

nolle prosequi—A formal entry upon the record by the prosecuting officer in a criminal case, by which he declares that he "will no further prosecute" the case.

nolo contendere—A pleading usually used by defendants in criminal cases, which literally means "I will not contest it."

nominal party—One who is joined as a party or defendant merely because the technical rules of pleading require his presence in the record.

non obstante veredicto—Notwithstanding the verdict. A judgment entered by order of court for one party, although there has been a jury verdict against him.

notice to produce—A notice in writing requiring the opposite party to produce a certain described paper or object at the trial.

O

objection—The act of taking exception to some statement or procedure in trial. Used to call the court's attention to improper evidence or procedure.

of counsel—A phrase commonly applied to counsel employed to assist in the preparation or management of the case, or its presentation on appeal, but who is not the principal attorney of record.

opinion evidence—Evidence of what the witness thinks, believes or infers in regard to fact in dispute, as distinguished from his personal knowledge of the facts; not admissible except (under certain limitations) in the case of experts.

out of court—One who has no legal status in court is said to be "out of court," i.e., he is not before the court. For example, when a plaintiff, by some act of omission or commission, shows that he is unable to maintain his action he is frequently said to have put himself "out of court."

P

panel—A list of jurors to serve in a particular court, or for the trial of a particular action; denotes either the whole body of persons summoned as jurors for a particular term of court or those selected by the clerk by lot.

parties—The persons who are actively concerned in the prosecution or defense of any legal proceeding.

peremptory challenge—The challenge which the prosecution or defense may use to reject a certain number of prospective jurors without assigning any cause.

plaintiff—A person who brings an action; the party who complains or sues in a legal action and is so named on the record.

plaintiff in error—The party who obtains a writ of error to have a judgment or other proceeding at law reviewed by an appellate court.

pleading—The process by which the parties in a suit or action alternately present written statements of their contentions, each responsive to that which precedes and each serving to narrow the field of controversy, until there evolves one or more points, affirmed on one side and denied on the other, called the "issue" or "issues" upon which they then go to trial.

polling the jury—A practice whereby the jurors are asked individually whether they assented, and still assent, to the verdict.

power of attorney—An instrument authorizing another to act as one's agent or attorney.

praecipe—An original writ commanding the defendant to do the thing required; also, an order addressed to the clerk of a court, requesting him to issue a particular writ.

prejudicial error—Synonymous with "reversible error"; an error which warrants the appellate court in reversing the judgment before it.

preliminary hearing—Synonymous with "preliminary examination"; the hearing given a person charged with crime by a magistrate or judge to determine whether he should be held for trial.

preponderance of evidence—Greater weight of evidence, or evidence which is more credible and convincing to the mind, not necessarily the greater number of witnesses.

presentment—An informal statement in writing by a grand jury to the court that a crime has been committed, from their own knowledge or observation, without any bill of indictment laid before them.

presumption of facts—An inference as to the truth or falsity of any proposition or fact, drawn by a process of reasoning in the absence of actual certainty of its truth or falsity, or until such certainty can be ascertained.

presumption of law—A rule of law that courts and judges shall draw a particular inference from a particular fact, or from particular evidence.

probate—The act or process of proving a will. In some states, probate includes proceedings relating to mental incompetence.

probation—In modern criminal administration, allowing a convicted person (particularly juvenile offenders) to go at large, under a suspension of sentence, during good behavior, and generally under the supervision or guardianship of a probation office.

prosecutor—One who instigates the prosecution upon which an accused is arrested or who prefers an accusation against the party whom he suspects to be guilty; also one who takes charge of a case and performs function of trial lawyer for the people.

Q

quaere—A query; question; doubt.

quash—To overthrow; vacate; to annul or void a summons or indictment.

quasi judicial—Authority or discretion vested in an officer wherein his acts partake of a judicial character.

quid pro quo—"What for what," a fair return or consideration.

quo warranto—A writ issuable by the state, through which it demands an individual to show by what right he exercises an authority which can only be exercised through grant or franchise emanating from the state.

R

reasonable doubt—An accused person is entitled to acquittal if, in the minds of the jury, his guilt has not been proved beyond a "reasonable doubt"; that state of the minds of jurors in which they cannot say they feel an abiding conviction as to the truth of the charge.

rebuttal—The introduction of rebutting evidence; the showing that statements of witnesses as to what occurred is not true; the stage of a trial at which such evidence may be introduced.

redirect examination—Follows cross-examination, and is had by the party who first examined the witness.

referee—A person to whom a cause pending in a court is referred by the court to take testimony, hear the parties and report thereon to the court. He is an officer exercising judicial powers and is an arm of the court for a specific purpose.

removal, order of—An order by a court directing the transfer of a cause to another court.

reply—When a case is tried or argued in court, the argument of the plaintiff in answer to that of the defendant. A pleading in response to an answer.

rest—A party is said to "rest" or "rest his case" when he has presented all the evidence he intends to offer.

retainer—Act of the client in employing his attorney or counsel; also denotes the fee which the client pays when he retains the attorney to act for him.

robbery—The taking or stealing of property from another with force or the threat of force.

rule nisi, or rule to show cause—A court order obtained on motion by either party to show cause why the particular relief sought should not be granted.

S

search and seizure, unreasonable—In general, an examination without authority of law of one's premises or person with a view to discovering evidence to be used in prosecuting a crime.

search warrant—An order in writing, issued by a justice or magistrate in the name of the state, directing an officer to search a specified house or other premises for evidence. Usually required as a condition precedent to a legal search and seizure.

self-defense—The protection of one's person or property against some injury attempted by another. The law of "self defense" justifies an act done in the reasonable belief of immediate danger. When acting in justifiable self-defense, a person may not be punished criminally nor held responsible for civil damages.

separate maintenance—Allowance granted to a wife for support of herself and children while she is living apart from her husband but not divorced from him.

separation of witnesses—An order of the court requiring all witnesses to remain outside the courtroom until each is called to testify, except the plaintiff and defendant.

sheriff—An officer of a county, usually chosen by popular election, whose principal duties are to aid the criminal and civil court; chief preserver of the peace. He serves processes, summons juries, executes judgments and holds judicial sales.

sine qua non—An indispensable requisite.

slander—Base and defamatory spoken words tending to prejudice another in his reputation, business or means of livelihood. "Libel" and "slander" both are methods of defamation, the former being expressed by print, writings, pictures or signs; the latter orally.

specific performance—Where money damages would be inadequate compensation for the breach of an obligation, the defaulting party will be compelled to perform specifically what he has agreed to do.

stare decisis—The doctrine that, when a court has once laid down a principle of law as applicable to a certain set of facts, it will adhere to that principle and apply it to future cases where the facts are substantially the same.

state's evidence—Testimony given by an accomplice or participant in a crime tending to convict others.

statute—The written or legislatively enacted law as distinguished from the common law.

stay—A stopping or arresting of a judicial proceeding by order of the court.

stipulation—An agreement by attorneys on opposite sides of a case as to any matter pertaining to the proceedings or trial. It is not binding unless assented to by the parties, and most stipulations must be in writing.

subpoena—A process to cause a witness to appear and give testimony before a court or magistrate.

subpoena duces tecum—A process by which the court commands a witness to produce certain documents or records in a trial.

substantive law—The law dealing with rights, duties and liabilities, as distinguished from procedural law.

summons—A writ directing the sheriff or other officer to notify the named person that an action has been commenced against him in court and that he is required to appear, on the day named, and answer the complaint in such action.

supersedeas—A writ containing a command to stay proceedings at law, such as the enforcement of a judgment pending an appeal.

T

talesman—A person summoned to act as a juror from among the bystanders in a court.

testimony—Evidence given by a witness, under oath; as distinguished from evidence derived from writings and other sources.

tort—An injury or wrong committed, either with or without force, to the person or property of another.

transcript—The official record of proceedings in a trial or hearing.

trial de novo—A new trial or retrial in an appellate court in which the whole case is gone into as if no trial had been had in a lower court.

true bill—In criminal practice, the endorsement made in a grand jury upon a bill of indictment when they find it sufficient to warrant a criminal charge.

U

undue influence—Whatever destroys free will and causes a person to do something he would not do if left to himself.

unlawful detainer—A detention of real estate without the consent of the owner or other person entitled to its possession.

usury—The taking of more interest for the use of money than the law allows.

V

venire—Technically, a writ summoning persons to court to act as jurors; popularly used as meaning the body of names thus summoned.

veniremen—Members of a panel of jurors.

venue—The particular county, city or geographical area in which a court with jurisdiction may hear and determine a case.

verdict—The formal decision or finding made by a jury, reported to the court and accepted by it.

voir dire—To speak the truth. The phrase denotes the preliminary examination which the court may make of one presented as a witness or juror, as to his qualifications.

W

waiver of immunity—A means authorized by statutes by which a witness, in advance of giving testimony or producing evidence, may renounce the fundamental right guaranteed by the constitution that no person shall be compelled to be a witness against himself.

warrant of arrest—A writ issued by a magistrate, justice or other competent authority, to a sheriff or other officer, requiring him to arrest the person therein named and bring him before the magistrate or court to answer to a specified charge.

weight of evidence—The balance or preponderance of evidence; the inclination of the greater amount of credible evidence, offered in a trial, to support one side of the issue rather than the other.

willful—A "willful" act is one done intentionally, as distinguished from an act done negligently or inadvertently.

with prejudice—The term, as applied to judgment of dismissal, is a final disposition of a case.

without prejudice—A dismissal "without prejudice" allows a new suit to be brought on the same claim.

witness—One who testifies to what he has seen, heard or knows.

writ—An order issuing from a court requiring the performance of a specified act, or giving authority and commission to have it done.

Bibliography

Books & Library Reference Volumes

Advertising Law Anthology, Volume 4, 1976, International Library, Arlington, Virginia.

American Digest, West Publishing Company, St. Paul, Minnesota.

American Jurisprudence 2d, Lawyer's Co-operative Publishing, Rochester, New York.

Ballentine's Law Dictionary with Pronunciations, Lawyer's Co-operative Publishing, Rochester, New York.

Communications Law, Practicing Law Institute of America, New York City.

Contracts In Plain English, by Richard Wincor, McGraw Hill, 1976.

Copyright Law, Cases and Materials, West Publishing Co.

Corpus Juris Secundum, West Publishing Co.

Current Developments in Copyright Law, 1977, Practicing Law Institute, New York City.

Elements of Photo Reporting, Amphoto, New York City.

Entertainment, Publishing and the Arts, Clark Boardman Co., Ltd., New York City.

Law and the Student Press, Iowa State University Press, Ames, Iowa.

Law of Advertising, The, Matthew Bender & Company, New York City.

Legal Guide for the Visual Artist, 1977, Hawthorn, New York City.

Martindale-Hubbell Legal Directory, Summit, New Jersey.

Mass Media Law and Regulation, 1976, Grid Books, Columbus, Ohio.

Nimmer on Copyright, Matthew Bender & Company, New York City.

Patents, Copyrights, Trademarks and Literary Property, 1974, Practicing Law Institute, New York City.

Performing Arts Management & Law, 6 Vols., Law-Arts Publishers, Inc., New York City.

Photography and the Law, Amphoto, New York City.

Photography: What's the Law, 1976, Crown Publishers, New York City.

Rights of Reporters, The, 1976, E. P. Dutton, New York City.

Say It Safely, Legal Limits in Publishing, Radio and Television, 1976, U. of Washington Press, Seattle.

Shopper's Guidebook to . . . (The), Lawyers, Consumer News, Inc., Washington D.C.

Sue the Bastards, 1975, Dell Books, New York City.

Summary of American Law, Lawyers Co-Operative Publishing, Rochester, New York.

United States Code Service, Lawyers Co-operative Publishing, Rochester, New York.

What Everyone Needs to Know About Law, 1975, U.S. News and World Report, Washington, D.C.

Writer's Legal Guide, Hawthorn Books, New York City.

Periodicals & Looseleaf Services

Bulletin of the Copyright Society, New York City.

Dateline 77: The Press and the Law, Overseas Press Club, New York City.

Federal Communications Bar Journal, Washington, D.C.

Legal Briefs for Editors, Publishers and Writers, New York City.

Librarian's Guide to the New Copyright Law, American Library Assn., Chicago.

Media Law Reporter, Bureau of National Affairs, Inc., Washington, D.C.

Patent, Trademark and Copyright Journal, Bureau of National Affairs, Washington, D.C.

Performing Arts Review, Law Arts Publishers, New York City.

Practical Lawyer, The, Philadelphia.

Publishing, Entertainment, Advertising and Allied Fields Law Quarterly, Pittsburgh.

You and the Law, Research Institute of America, New York City.

For additional new books as they are published, see, in your local public library a directory called *Subject Guide to Books in Print.* Titles of interest will be found under the subject categories of:

Advertising Laws

Journalism, Legal

Journalistic Ethics

Law — Bibliography

Law — Popular Works

Contributors to This Book

Louise Boggess's work on her book *Your Social Security Benefits,* (Funk and Wagnalls), provided the background for her chapter on the same subject in this book. Other books include *Journey to Citizenship* about the immigration laws, three books in the writing field *(Writing Articles That Sell, Fiction Techniques That Sell* and *Writing Fillers That Sell);* and her most recent, *American Brilliant Cut Glass,* (Crown). Mrs. Boggess is also a successful writing teacher for the University of California, Writer's Digest School, and via TV for the College of San Mateo.

Georges Borchardt is the president and founder of Georges Borchardt, Inc., a New York literary agency. He has taught at New York University, is a panel member of the American Arbitration Association, has written articles on publishing for *Publishers Weekly* and has lectured on publishing at UCLA, Johns Hopkins and Columbia.

William Donaldson earned his law degree from the University of Minnesota Law School. He was admitted to the State Bar of Michigan in 1937, and was a veteran of World War II. For over 20 years he wrote the "You Be The Judge" legal features for the *Saturday Evening Post.* He was an attorney with the United States Government's Anti-Trust Division and subsequently with the Veterans Administration in Detroit, until he took an early retirement in 1974.

Herald Price Fahringer is a practicing lawyer in New York City who has defended obscenity prosecutions throughout the United States. He defended *Hustler Magazine* in Cincinnati, and Al Goldstein, the publisher of *Screw,* in Wichita, Kansas. He is general counsel to the First Amendment Lawyers Association.

Lipman G. Feld is a graduate of Harvard and the University of Missouri Law School. He's published over 350 articles for consumer professional and trade magazines. His recent book on credit, *Harassment and Other Collection Taboos,* was a study for the National Association of Credit Management.

Patricia Ann Fox has been a copywriter and continuity director for radio stations in New Jersey and Pennsylvania. She's published articles in American and Canadian magazines and won awards for her fiction at writers conferences and in the WRITER'S DIGEST Creative Writing Contest.

William E. Francois is a professor of journalism at Drake University, Des Moines, Iowa, where he has taught communication law for eight years. He is the author of four books, including *Mass Media Law & Regulation* which is widely used as a college textbook. He also has written several hundred magazine articles and, for three years, wrote a monthly column for WRITER'S DIGEST entitled "Law & the Writer," which won two American Bar Association certificates of merit for outstanding service in connection with making the law more understandable. Prof. Francois has been a college journalism teacher for 18 years. Prior to that he was a newspaper reporter/editor for ten years.

Harry M. Johnston III is a graduate of Columbia College of Columbia University and the New York University law school. From 1968 to 1970 he served as a Vista volunteer attorney and then joined Time, Inc. He is presently editorial counsel for that firm.

Perry Knowlton has been president of the New York literary agency, Curtis Brown, Ltd., since 1968. Prior to that, he served as vice president and head of the book division for that agency, coming to the position from Charles Scribner's Sons where he was an editor in the trade division. Mr. Knowlton is also president of the Society of Authors' Representatives.

Michael S. Lasky has written for dozens of top national magazines including, *Playboy, Esquire, Gentlemen's Quarterly, Family Health,* WRITER'S DIGEST and *The New York Times.* He is author of *The Complete Junk Food Book* (McGraw-Hill) and *The Films Of Alfred*

Hitchcock (Citadel Press). Currently a freelance writer, he was formerly associate editor of *Folio: The Magazine For Magazine Management* for which his article on libel was originally prepared.

Richard H. Logan III is Professor of Journalism at Mississippi University for Women and for the past 17 years has taught photography and journalism in colleges and universities in Florida, Texas and Mississippi. He formerly worked as a photographer and reporter for daily newspapers and operated his own advertising and industrial photography agency. He received his Ph.D. degree from the University of Southern Mississippi and has received professional honors for his work both as an educator and as a photographer.

Leonard S. Meranus is a senior partner in the law firm of Paxton and Seasongood in Cincinnati. He is in charge of the Corporate and Business Law Department of the firm, and has been associated with the firm for 23 years. In addition to his cum laude law degree from Harvard Law School, he is a Phi Beta Kappa graduate of Rutgers with a major in journalism. Before entering the legal field, he was a reporter for the *Newark Evening News* and assistant director of public relations at the University of Cincinnati.

Forrest M. Mims was graduated from Texas A & M University in 1966 with a degree in government. He served four years in the Air Force as an intelligence officer in Vietnam and as a laser development engineer. Mims has been freelancing fulltime since 1970.

Waldo H. Moore, assistant register of copyrights for registration, has been an employee of the Copyright Office of The Library of Congress for over 25 years. He is a member of The American Bar Association; the Federal Bar Association (past president, Capitol Hill Chapter); Government Patent Lawyers Association; the Copyright Society of the US (former trustee); and the Bibliographical Society of America. His bar memberships include those of the District of Columbia and the State of Virginia. Moore is also a professorial lecturer in Copyright Law at George Washington University Law School.

Kirk Polking is Director of Writer's Digest School, a national correspondence school in writing for freelancers; and a former editor of WRITER'S DIGEST. As a freelance writer, she has published magazine articles and a number of books, the latest of which is *The Private Pilot's Dictionary and Handbook* (Arco). She published four juvenile books with G.P. Putnam's in their "Let's Go" series and edited for *Writer's Digest, The Beginning Writer's Answer Book* and *Artist's Market,* and for Cornerstone Library, *How To Make Money In Your Spare Time By Writing.*

John C. Runka and **Steven Weller** are Director and Associate Director of the Small Claims Project in Denver for the National Center for State Courts. Both are 1967 graduates of Yale Law School. The National Center for State Courts is an information clearinghouse on judicial administration in the state courts.

Richard Sherry is president and editor of Field Newspaper Syndicate. He joined the syndicate in 1965 as promotion manager and associate editor after a 15-year newspaper career in editorial, reporting and promotion capacities. A graduate of Richmond, Virginia Professional Institute of the College of William and Mary, Sherry is a member of the Society of Professional Journalists (Sigma Delta Chi) and the Chicago Press Club; is past president of the South Florida Industrial Editors Assn.; and has received various journalism awards.

Theodore Stellwag is assistant director for public information of the Pennsylvania Bar Association. His "Newsman's Guide to Legalese" from which the Glossary in this book was excerpted was created for those persons assigned to cover courts in Pennsylvania and for editors and station managers. He is a former newspaper columnist and court reporter for newspapers in New Jersey and Pennsylvania.

Robert Trager is an associate professor and head of graduate studies in the School of Journalism, Southern Illinois University at Carbondale. He has also taught high school and community college journalism and has worked for a daily newspaper. He has published law review articles concerning the legal rights and responsibilities of student journalists. Among his books are *Student Press Rights, College Student Press Law* (with Donna L. Dickerson) and *The Mass Media* *and the Law in Illinois* (with Harry W. Stonecipher). He earned his Ph.D. at the University of Minnesota.

Grace W. Weinstein is a freelance writer whose numerous articles, many of them on money management, have appeared in *Money Magazine, Redbook* and *House Beautiful.* Her column, "You and Retirement," appears monthly in *The Elks Magazine.* Ms. Weinstein's books include *Children & Money: A Guide for Parents, Retire Tomorrow-Plan Today,* and *Money Of Your Own.* A graduate of Cornell University and a resident of New Jersey, she is a member of the American Society of Journalists & Authors, the Authors Guild, and National Press Women.

Index

Books of Interest From Writer's Digest

Art & Crafts Market, edited by Lynne Lapin and Betsy Wones. Lists 4,498 places where you can show and sell your crafts and artwork. Galleries, competitions and exhibitions, craft dealers, record companies, fashion-related firms, magazines that buy illustrations and cartoons, book publishers and advertising agencies — they're all there, complete with names, addresses, submission requirements, phone numbers and payment rates. 672 pp. $10.95.

The Beginning Writer's Answer Book, edited by Kirk Polking, Jean Chimsky, and Rose Adkins. "What is a query letter?" "If I use a pen name, how can I cash the check?" These are among 567 questions most frequently asked by beginning writers — and expertly answered in this down-to-earth handbook. Cross-indexed. 270 pp. $7.95.

The Cartoonist's and Gag Writer's Handbook, by Jack Markow. Longtime cartoonist with thousands of sales reveals the secrets of successful cartooning — step by step. Richly illustrated. 157 pp. $7.95.

A Complete Guide to Marketing Magazine Articles, by Duane Newcomb. "Anyone who can write a clear sentence can learn to write and sell articles on a consistent basis," says Newcomb (who has published well over 3,000 articles). Here's how. 248 pp. $6.95.

The Confession Writer's Handbook, by Florence K. Palmer. A stylish and informative guide to getting started and getting ahead in the confessions. How to start a confession and carry it through. How to take an insignificant event and make it significant. 171 pp. $6.95.

The Craft of Interviewing, by John Brady. Everything you always wanted to know about asking questions, but were afraid to ask — from an experienced interviewer and editor of *Writer's Digest.* The most comprehensive guide to interviewing on the market. 256 pp. $9.95.

The Creative Writer, edited by Aron Mathieu. This book opens the door to the real world of publishing. Inspiration, techniques, and ideas, plus inside tips from Maugham, Caldwell, Purdy, others. 416 pp. $6.95.

The Greeting Card Writer's Handbook, by H. Joseph Chadwick. A former greeting card editor tells you what editors look for in inspirational verse . . . how to write humor . . . what to write about for conventional, studio and juvenile cards. Extra: a renewable list of greeting card markets. Will be greeted by any freelancer. 268 pp. $6.95.

A Guide to Writing History, by Doris Ricker Marston. How to track down Big Foot — or your family Civil War letters, or your hometown's last century — for publication and profit. A timely handbook for history buffs and writers. 258 pp. $8.50.

Handbook of Short Story Writing, edited by Frank A. Dickson and Sandra Smythe. You provide the pencil, paper, and sweat — and this book will provide the expert guidance. Features include James Hilton on creating a lovable character; R.V. Cassill on plotting a short story. 238 pp. $6.95.

Law and The Writer, edited by Kirk Polking and Attorney Leonard S. Meranus. Don't let legal hassles slow down your progress as a writer. Now you can find good counsel on libel, invasion of privacy, fair use, plagiarism, taxes, contracts, social security, and more — all in one volume. 265 pp. $9.95.

Magazine Writing Today, by Jerome E. Kelley. If you sometimes feel like a mouse in a maze of magazines, with a fat manuscript check at the end of the line, don't fret. Kelley tells you how to get a piece of the action. Covers ideas, research, interviewing, organization, the writing process, and ways to get photos. Plus advice on getting started. 300 pp. $9.95.

The Mystery Writer's Handbook, by the Mystery Writers of America. A howtheydunit to the whodunit, newly written and revised by members of the Mystery Writers of America. Includes the four elements essential to the classic mystery. A clear and comprehensive handbook that takes the mystery out of mystery writing. 275 pp. $8.95.

One Way to Write Your Novel, by Dick Perry. For Perry, a novel is 200 pages. Or, two pages a day for 100 days. You can start — and finish — *your* novel, with the help of this step-by-step guide taking you from the blank sheet to the polished page. 138 pp. $6.95.

Photographer's Market, edited by Melissa Milar and Bill Brohaugh. Contains what you need to know to be a successful freelance photographer. Names, addresses, photo requirements, and payment rates for 1,616 markets. Plus, information on preparing a portfolio, basic equipment needed, the business side of photography, and packaging and shipping your work. 408 pp. $9.95.

The Poet and the Poem, by Judson Jerome. A rare journey into the night of the poem — the mechanics, the mystery, the craft and sullen art. Written by the most widely read authority on poetry in America, and a major contemporary poet in his own right. 482 pp. $7.95 ($4.95 paperback).

Stalking the Feature Story, by William Ruehlmann. Besides a nose for news, the newspaper feature writer needs an ear for dialog and an eye for detail. He must also be adept at handling off-the-record remarks, organization, grammar, and the investigative story. Here's the "scoop" on newspaper feature writing. 314 pp. $9.95.

A Treasury of Tips for Writers, edited by Marvin Weisbord. Everything from Vance Packard's system of organizing notes to tips on how to get research done free, by 86 magazine writers. 174 pp. $5.95.

Writer's Digest. The world's leading magazine for writers. Monthly issues include timely articles, interviews, columns, tips to keep writers informed on where and how to sell their work. One year subscription, $12.

Writer's Market, edited by Jane Koester and Bruce Joel Hillman. The freelancer's Bible, containing 4,454 places to sell what you write. Includes the name, address and phone number of the buyer, a description of material wanted and how much the payment is. 912 pp. $13.95.

Writer's Yearbook, edited by John Brady. This large annual magazine contains how-to articles, interviews and special features, along with analysis of 500 major markets for writers. $2.75 (includes 80¢ for postage and handling).

Writing and Selling Non-Fiction, by Hayes B. Jacobs. Explores with style and know-how the book market, organization and research, finding new markets, interviewing, humor, agents, writer's fatigue and more. 317 pp. $7.95.

Writing and Selling Science Fiction, compiled by the Science Fiction Writers of America. A comprehensive handbook to an exciting but oft-misunderstood genre. Eleven articles by top-flight sf writers on markets, characters, dialog, "crazy" ideas, world-building, alien-building, money and more. 191 pp. $7.95.

Writing for Children and Teen-agers, by Lee Wyndham. Author of over 50 children's books shares her secrets for selling to this large, lucrative market. Features: the 12-point recipe for plotting, and the Ten Commandments for writers. 253 pp. $8.95.

Writing Popular Fiction, by Dean R. Koontz. How to write mysteries, suspense thrillers, science fiction. Gothic romances, adult fantasy, Westerns and erotica. Here's an inside guide to lively fiction, by a lively novelist. 232 pp. $7.95.

(Add 50¢ for postage and handling.
Prices subject to change without notice.)
Writer's Digest Books, Dept. B, 9933 Alliance Road, Cincinnati, Ohio 45242